'Was Caligula really mad, bad and dangerous to know? Discover whether he deserves his infamy—or not—in this engrossing character study of the famous emperor.'

—**MARGARET GEORGE**, *New York Times* bestselling author of *The Confessions of the Young Nero* and *The Splendor Before the Dark*

'*Caligula, The Mad Emperor of Rome* is a compelling page-turner. It reads like a political thriller. Which it is. It reads like a work of investigative journalism. Which it is. It reads like a myth-busting period history. Which it is. The author, clearly familiar with the primary sources, dispels many old libels masquerading for centuries as fake news. Meanwhile he provides us with an abundance of documented stories so lurid as to dwarf the overhyped misdemeanors of today. Long ago I was tipped off to an open secret. Colleen McCullough's pulp masterpieces in *Masters of Rome* were so accurate as to be held in awe as a kind of quasi-history by the 'Secret Fraternity of Latin Teachers.' If you enjoy historical fiction you will love this historical fact of Caligula (the book, not the emperor!) *Caligula* may herald the perfection of a new literary genre: 'forensic history.' It takes narrative history to a virtuosic level with a timeless story extremely well told.'

—**RALPH BENKO**, US columnist

'A marvelous book. Stephen Dando-Collins offers a fresh scholarly perspective on the notorious emperor that succeeds admirably in being of interest to professional scholars of the early Roman Empire and to the general reader. This is a lively, engaging volume that is a true pleasure to read. Anyone interested in ancient Rome will want to acquire and enjoy this great new addition to the bibliography.'

—**DR. LEE FRATANTUONO**, Professor of Classics, Ohio Wesleyan University, author of *Caligula: An Unexpected General*

'Since ancient Roman times Caligula has ranked alongside Nero as one of the "mad emperors of Rome." In this new biography, Stephen Dando-Collins has used a wide range of ancient sources to construct a far more three-dimensional portrait of this important ruler. By linking his adult actions and behaviors to early childhood experiences, all well attested in the ancient sources, the author is able to evoke the turbulent world of early imperial Rome, and clearly delineate Caligula's important role in its development.'

—**PROFESSOR JOHN R. HALE**, University of Louisville, author of *Lords of the Sea*

'The short, sordid and violent life of the notorious Roman emperor some have compared to Donald Trump. Dando-Collins (*The Big Break*), who has published often about the ancient world, begins when Caligula (12-41 CE) was two and marches resolutely and straightforwardly to his assassination in 41, a group stabbing that, as the author points out, reminds us of the Ides of March. Dando-Collins aims at general readers, often employing contemporary allusions, diction and comparisons (chariot drivers were "the rock stars of their day"), and he pauses occasionally to explain such things as the Roman handshake and wax writing tablets. He also informs us about shipbuilding, the types of legions, and slavery—one of Caligula's villas had some 250 slaves. Carefully identifying his sources as he proceeds, Dando-Collins tries to come to some resolutions about the questions and controversies about Caligula: Was he mad? Did he enjoy wild orgies? The author believes that he was mostly competent at first (he became emperor at 24), a period of "wise and lauded rule"—but then there was a change, perhaps occasioned by an epidemic? From around page 75 onward, we learn details about the man that are shocking but not surprising: multiple murders, self-aggrandizement (he ordered a statue of himself be installed in Jerusalem, outraging Jews), paranoia, profound insecurity, and jealousy. The author also discusses Caligula's travels, his wars (his legions refused to invade Britain), and the lives and deaths of some prominent New Testament figures, including Pontius Pilate and Herod Antipas. Dando-Collins argues that Caligula was probably bi-polar, and he does see parallels to Trump. A sturdy account of blood, sexual perversion, beheadings, war, intrigue, betrayal and assassination.

—*KIRKUS REVIEW*

'There have been many biographies of Caligula, but none that have such spark and vivacity: this reads more like a thriller than a biography, and the balance of good and bad in the terrified young man who gained too much power is deftly done. If you want to read a fast-flowing well-crafted book, you can't do better than this. And the final chapter making the comparison with Trump us excellent. We can only hope that when Trump is finally deposed there isn't a Claudius hiding behind a curtain, ready to be dragged into power.'

—**MANDA SCOTT**, bestselling author of the *Boudica* and *Rome* series
and *A Treachery of Spies,* and former president of the
Historical Writers Association of the UK

# CALIGULA

## THE MAD EMPEROR OF ROME

### STEPHEN DANDO-COLLINS

TURNER PUBLISHING COMPANY

Turner Publishing Company
Nashville, Tennessee
www.turnerpublishing.com

Cover design: Jeremy Child, The Artifex Forge Limited

Library of Congress Cataloging-in-Publication Data
Names: Dando-Collins, Stephen, author.
Title: Caligula : the mad Emperor of Rome / Stephen Dando-Collins.
Other titles: Caligula, the mad Emperor of Rome
Description: Nashvile, TN : Turner Publishing Company, [2019] | Includes
  bibliographical references and index. |
Identifiers: LCCN 2018049261 (print) | LCCN 2018049772 (ebook) | ISBN
  9781684422876 (ebook) | ISBN 9781684422852 (pbk.) | ISBN 9781684422869
  (hardcover)
Subjects: LCSH: Caligula, Emperor of Rome, 12-41. |
  Emperors--Rome--Biography. | Rome--Kings and rulers--Biography. |
  Rome--History--Caligula, 37-41. | Political corruption--Rome--History. |
  Power (Social sciences)--Rome--History.
Classification: LCC DG283 (ebook) | LCC DG283 .D36 2019 (print) | DDC
  937/.07092 [B] --dc23
LC record available at https://lccn.loc.gov/2018049261

Printed in the United States of America
17 18 19 20 10 9 8 7 6 5 4 3 2 1

"Beware of the snake lurking in the grass."
—Virgil, *Ecologues*

With thanks to
my New York literary agent, Richard Curtis, for his perseverance;
my publisher, Stephanie Beard, for her enthusiasm;
and my empress, Louise, the power behind my throne.

# TABLE OF CONTENTS

# MAPS

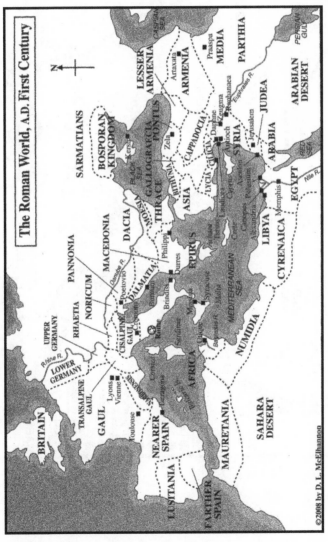

The Roman World, AD First Century. (From *Blood of the Caesars,* Wiley, 2008)

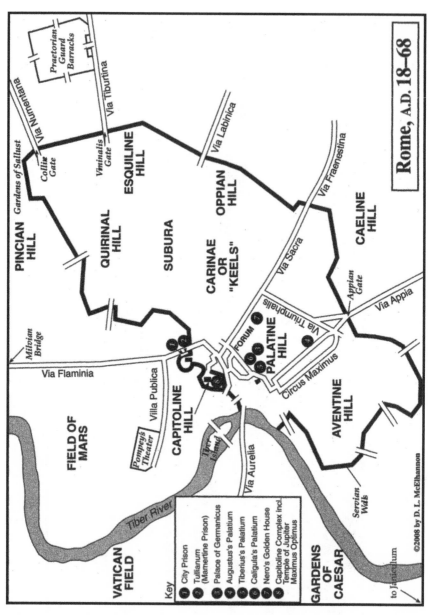

Rome, AD 18–68. (As above.)

# PHOTOGRAPHS

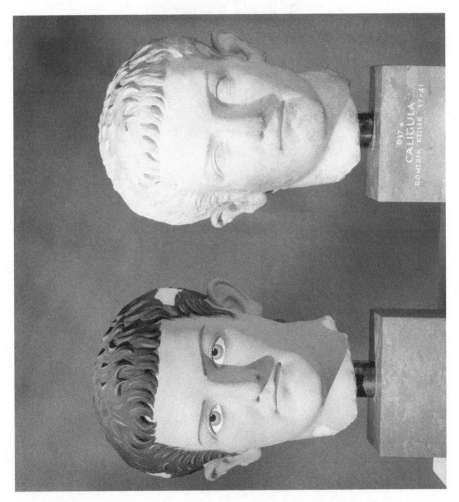

#1. A bust of the young emperor Caligula, made during his reign, beside a lifelike modern colored reconstruction using traces of paint found on the original—classical statues were painted using life like colors. NY Carlsberg Glyptotek, Copenhagen. Photo: Ole Haupt.

#2. Black marble bust of Caligula's ambitious sister Agrippina the Younger, mother of the emperor Nero. NY Carlsberg Glyptotek, Copenhagen. Photo: Ole Haupt.

#3. Shield emblem of the 22nd Primigenia Legion, a unit raised by Caligula in AD 39/40 for his German and British campaigns. From Stephen Dando-Collins' *Legions of Rome*, © Copyright Quercus Publishing, UK.

#4. Arch of Germanicus, Orange, France, celebrating Caligula's father. It's highly likely that Caligula visited the arch on his way through Gaul in AD 39. © Copyright Louise Dando-Collins.

#5. Detail, Arch of Germanicus at Orange, showing trophies of German military equipment captured during the German campaigns of Caligula's father. © Copyright Louise Dando-Collins.

#6. The Roman Theater at Lyon, France, is still in use today for concerts and plays. In AD 39, Caligula held shows here, including an unusual oratory contest. © Copyright Louise Dando-Collins.

#7. Caligula's Egyptian obelisk, which stood on the spine of the Gaianum, his private hippodrome at Rome, is now in St. Peter's Square, Rome, close to its original location. © Copyright Louise Dando-Collins.

#8. The author at the Pont du Gard Roman aqueduct, near Nimes, France. Commenced in AD 40 during Caligula's reign, it was probably inspired by Caligula during his AD 39–40 visit to Gaul after he commenced two new similarly massive aqueducts at Rome in AD 38. © Copyright Louise Dando-Collins.

#9. Exterior of the Roman amphitheater at Arles, France. Caligula presided at gladiatorial contests at similar amphitheaters. This one is still used today, with locals watching bullfights, bull runs, plays, and concerts sitting on the same terraces that Romans occupied two millennia ago. © Copyright Louise Dando-Collins.

#10. Rome's Trevi Fountain receives it waters from the last surviving original Roman aqueduct, the Virgo, which was damaged by Caligula when building a new amphitheater on the Field of Mars. © Copyright Louise Dando-Collins.

#11. Marble bust of the emperor Claudius, uncle of Caligula. Here Claudius wears the ceremonial oak crown, as Caligula did when he crossed the Bay of Puteoli. NY Carlsberg Glyptotek, Copenhagen. Photo: Ole Haupt.

#12. The well-preserved stage of the Roman Theater, Orange, France, including a statue of the emperor Augustus. All Roman theaters featured elaborate stages, even the temporary theater on Rome's Palatine Hill where Caligula was assassinated. © Copyright Louise Dando-Collins.

#13. Modern replica of trireme warship, mainstay of Roman battle fleets. Similar ships escorted Caligula when he traveled East with his parents as a boy, and when he traveled as emperor to Sicily and along Italy's west coast. © Copyright Wolfson College, Cambridge, UK.

#14. In the 1930s, after Caligula's lake ships were recovered at Lake Nemi, they attracted tourists from around the world. Here, with a companion and with the first ship and lake behind her, Millicent, wife of American media magnate William Randolph Hearst, pays a visit. © Copyright Bridgeman Images.

#15. The recovery of Caligula's ships was celebrated here on a British cigarette card showing the first ship and a brass rail-holder featuring the heads of Lake Nemi deities Virbius and Egeria. © Copyright Bridgeman Images.

# INTRODUCTION

In the past, I have researched and written a great deal about Caligula while documenting, in a number of books, the military of imperial Rome and the lives of members of the Caesar family, but until now Caligula has always played a supporting role.

Since the election of Donald Trump as president of the United States of America, numerous commentators around the world have compared Trump and Caligula, as demonstrated by examples in this work's final chapter, bringing Rome's third emperor into a new, modern focus and causing many old distortions, mistruths, and misunderstandings about Caligula to resurface.

With this book, I have set out to address those distortions, mistruths, and misunderstandings, so that a more accurate picture of the young emperor can be arrived at. Since it was President Trump's election that, in part, sponsored this work, I will use the final chapter to address modern comparisons between Trump and Caligula.

Today, the name Caligula registers with most people of a certain age: those of us able to remember back to the 1976 British television adaptation of Robert Graves's novels *I, Claudius* and *Claudius the God,* and to the gory 1979 movie *Caligula.* Many Roman historians and biographers have been content to stand by the mad, sex-crazed image of Caligula that has come to us from sources ancient and modern, although in 1989 and 2003 academic biographers did attempt to redeem Caligula by painting a picture of a young emperor who was neither mad nor sex crazed. Yet, some of Caligula's recorded acts do appear to have been the products of an unhinged mind, and demand exploration and analysis.

Some accounts of Caligula's life are exaggerated and biased. His second-century biographer, the sensationalist Suetonius, and third-century historian Cassius Dio, for example, both of whom are major sources on Caligula, repeated gossip, clearly exaggerated some aspects, and sometimes withheld or twisted facts to paint the emperor in a bad light. The philosopher, writer, orator, and civil servant Lucius Annaeus Seneca the Younger, who was sentenced to death by Caligula, understandably never had a good word to say about him.

Publius Cornelius Tacitus, with his *Annals* and *Histories*, provides us with detailed coverage of Roman people and events through much of the first century. Tacitus is a key source for the lives of Caligula's parents, and was clearly a fan of Caligula's father, Germanicus. While he gives us revealing tidbits about Caligula in several of his works, unfortunately, the chapters of the *Annals* covering Caligula's four-year reign have not survived to modern day.

Still, it is possible to put together the jigsaw pieces to form an accurate picture of Caligula's life and influences. Flavius Josephus, the first-century Romano-Jewish historian, tells us a great deal about Caligula's murder; about Caligula's Praetorian prefect and mentor, Macro; and about Caligula's chief assassin, Chaerea. Josephus's writing in relation to these men is so detailed that he is likely to have spoken with people who knew them.

Philo of Alexander gives a rare firsthand account of several traumatic personal audiences he had with Caligula. Pliny the Elder tells stories from when, as a teenager, he lived at Rome during Caligula's reign. Other Roman sources, such as Frontinus, tell us about some of Caligula's public infrastructure innovations, and surviving first-century papyri, inscriptions, and coins provide fascinating insights. A study of Roman religious practices also offers motives for some of the young emperor's most notorious acts.

In addition to assessing these ancient sources, and my own research, I have been able to consider the excellent observations of recent historians, covering not only Caligula's life but also Rome's army and navy, and the habits and attitudes of Romans in the first century. I have also been able to draw on modern archeological finds. For example, in 2008, archeologists at Rome unearthed the Palatine Hill tunnel where it's believed Caligula was assassinated, a tunnel whose very existence had been disputed by earlier archeologists and historians.

As a starting point for research into Caligula's life, study of the Roman military helps explain and clarify many aspects of Caligula's life and decisions. The distinctions between the roles of the Praetorian Guard and the German Guard, for example, as well as Rome's military recruiting and training practices, Caligula's recruitment of new units, Roman military bridge-building practices, the standard Roman religious ceremony on a beach prior to a military amphibious campaign, and so on. These all impact Caligula's story.

What of the accusation that Caligula was mentally deranged? Suetonius writes that, early in his rule, the young emperor came down with a "brain sickness" that seemed to drastically change his personality. Tacitus also refers to this "brain sickness." Yet, during the early months of his reign, Caligula acted very properly and was adored by the populous, with his acts lauded. Seemingly overnight, he became changeable, capricious, and cruel. His symptoms, as described by Roman authors, have led to numerous theories about the nature of that illness. As will be explained later in this work, there is a modern medical diagnosis that fits Caligula's behavior.

Despite a catalog of genuine crimes, outrages, and horrors that can be attributed to him, Caligula has been the subject of misrepresentation down through the centuries. Take, for instance, the story that Caligula made his horse a senator. That didn't happen. He did threaten to make a consul of his favorite chariot-racing horse, named Incitatus. This appears to have been both a symptom of his impatience with the Roman Senate and an example of his "off" sense of humor. Possibly as a joke at his own expense, he did appoint Incitatus to the priesthood that administered a religious order.

Caligula wasn't even the young emperor's name. He began life as Gaius Julius Caesar Germanicus, and the Roman world came to know him as the emperor Gaius. "Caligula" was an affectionate nickname his parents used for him as a child. But when Gaius was emperor, nobody called him Caligula, especially after one instance when a centurion was disciplined for daring to publicly refer to him by that name.[1] And, after Gaius died, with his successor deliberately trashing his memory, his enemies and critics tagged him Caligula to belittle him. For my part, only because the world has come to know the emperor as Caligula do I refer to him as such on an ongoing basis in this book.

Caligula became infamous for leading as many as 250,000 Roman soldiers on a campaign against Britain, a campaign that ended with Caligula's apparently crazy order for the troops to gather seashells on the French coast as victory trophies. Writers down through the ages have touted this as evidence of Caligula's insanity, to the point that, along with King Canute's legendary attempt to stop the waves, it's rated as one the greatest follies in human history. However, just as King Canute—in actuality the Danish king of England, Denmark, and Norway Cnut the Great—used the order for the waves not to touch him to demonstrate to his courtiers that he *wasn't* all powerful, Caligula's histrionics on the French beach also have a very rational explanation, as will later be explained.

Caligula is notorious in the popular imagination for holding wild straight and gay orgies. As a boy, Caligula was forced by his pedophile adoptive grandfather, the emperor Tiberius, to have gay sex, and sometimes group sex with Spintrians, a class of male prostitutes who specialized in threesomes. Caligula so hated that experience that one of the first things he did when he became emperor was to have all Spintrians banned from Rome.

Suetonius also claimed that Caligula had incestuous relationships with all three of his sisters. Some modern scholars are prepared to accept this, but others have put up sound arguments to prove that this was another example of anti-Caligula propaganda.

As for Caligula engaging in Bacchanalian orgies with gaggles of women, not even the most prejudiced ancient sources claim he did that. Once he came to power, Caligula was indeed widely promiscuous with the wives of leading senators, in part to humiliate their husbands. He even stole one bride away from her husband on her wedding night. But he was never on record as participating in group sex when emperor. And once he married last wife Caesonia he appears to have been rigidly faithful to her for the remainder of his short life.

The story that he cut a baby from his sister Drusilla's body while she was alive was a modern Hollywood invention. Drusilla died as the result of illness, and as far as we know wasn't pregnant at the time. This myth, along with much of the blame for Caligula's modern-day sex-crazed image, can be laid at the feet of the over-the-top movie *Caligula*. It's no coincidence that the film was financed, produced, and co-written by Bob Guccione, publisher of *Penthouse* magazine. Guccione and fellow script-writer, the author Gore Vidal, set out to make their Caligula character as mad and sexually depraved as possible, with Guccione publishing a dedicated Caligula edition of *Penthouse* in 1980.

This is not to say that Caligula was a benign ruler. Far from it! Many men and women perished at his command, sometimes as the result of his whims, sometimes through a desire for vengeance, and, toward the end, through pure paranoia.

All this said, Caligula's story is not solely the story of one young man thrust into the spotlight and given absolute power. Caligula's reign cannot be seen in isolation. The milieu of murder and mayhem that Caligula grew up in conditioned him to find ways to survive as numerous family members fell around him. For years, he lived in dread of the executioner's knock on the door. This apprenticeship in survival set up his paranoid reign. One first-century author wrote that Caligula taught himself to read the faces of those around him, so that from an early age he guardedly observed all around him to discern who was lying and who wasn't, whom he could or couldn't trust.

The fact that Gaius Julius Caesar Germanicus, this relative of Julius Caesar and Mark Antony, survived to reach the throne was in fact a miracle. From among his relatives—three of whom also became emperor—his great-uncle, his grandmother, his father, his mother, his elder brothers, two of his sisters, his last wife, his daughter, several cousins, his uncle, his aunt, and his nephew would all be murdered or reportedly take their own lives. Caligula's family of the Caesars was by any measure a fatal one, and the line would be extinguished with the death of Caligula's nephew, the equally notorious later emperor Nero.

Caligula's story begins just days short of his second birthday, when, despite his youth, he was to have an impact on Roman affairs...

# I

# NURSLING OF THE LEGIONS

In his pregnant mother's arms, a boy who was just days short of his second birthday watched, wide-eyed and terrified, as soldiers rioted in front of them. The time: late August AD 14. The place: the summer military camp of four legions, or regiments, of the Roman Army of the Lower Rhine. The tented camp sat within a stone's throw of a relatively new township that occupied a small, oval island close to the west bank of the Rhine River. Then called Oppidum Ubiorum, that town would grow into today's German city of Cologne. For the fifty-two years since its inception, the town had been home to the German tribe, the Ubii, who'd been encouraged by Roman general Marcus Vipsanius Agrippa to move from east of the Rhine to the western side and become part of the Roman Empire.

On this midsummer's day, the commander-in-chief of all the eight Roman legions on the Rhine, who was just twenty-nine years of age, was absent from the camp. His name was Germanicus Julius Caesar, and he was a Roman prince. The grandnephew of Augustus, Rome's first emperor, and nephew and adopted son of Tiberius, Augustus's heir apparent, Germanicus was the father of the small boy who found himself surrounded by rioters at his Rhine headquarters. That boy's name was Gaius Julius Caesar Germanicus. Because he wore a small, legionary-style red tunic and sandals made for him by legion artisans, the boy had picked up an affectionate nickname—Caligula—which means "Little Boot." This cute little tyke became "the pet of the troops" says Seneca, who knew him in adulthood, so much so that the soldiers had come to think of the child as their mascot, their lucky charm.[2]

Caligula's father, the handsome, athletic, charismatic Germanicus, possessed massive popularity with the Roman people. Says Suetonius,

"Germanicus, many writers record, had won such intense popular devo-tion that he was in danger of being mobbed to death whenever he arrived at Rome or took his leave again."[3] Germanicus's popularity, in fact, would fan the protest in the Cologne camp from a situation of murderous discontent into one of a potential military coup. Conversely, it would be his infant son's popularity that enabled Germanicus to regain control of his troops.

Days before this, word had reached the Rhine legions that after a reign of forty-five years the emperor Augustus had died at Rome. Augustus had brought decades of stability and surety to an empire that had been rocked by years of civil war originating with Julius Caesar. Minus the solid foun-dation that Augustus had represented, like a house built on sand, his army quickly became unstable in the Balkans and on the Rhine. Within the ranks of the Army of the Lower Rhine, uncertainty swiftly grew into rebellion.

Germanicus had been in neighboring Gaul at the time, supervising the annual tax collection. His two eldest boys, who were not yet teenagers, were back at Rome, living at the Palace of Germanicus on the Palatine Hill with their grandmother Antonia. The mother of Germanicus, Antonia was the youngest daughter of Mark Antony. At Rome, those elder boys were being schooled with other imperial children. In May, Augustus had sent Caligula to his mother, Agrippina the Elder, from Rome accompanied by several attendants including a doctor, telling Agrippina to keep the doctor if he proved useful.

Suetonius tells us that Caligula suffered from epilepsy in childhood, and some modern historians have postulated that this was why the emperor had included a doctor in the child's traveling party. However, childhood epilepsy typically doesn't make an appearance until around the age of three, and at the time of Caligula's trip from the capital to the Rhine, he was only twenty-one months of age. The inclusion of a doctor was likely to have been merely a regular precaution.[4]

Germanicus had not immediately returned from Gaul to Cologne when he learned of Augustus's death. He was in the territory of the Belgae—roughly encompassing Belgium today—where he had Belgic leaders swear allegiance to Tiberius as the heir to the Roman throne before continuing with the tax collection. It was only when brought news of the trouble at the legion base that Germanicus cut short his mission in Gaul, riding back to the Rhine at the gallop.

Germanicus was to learn that the mutinous outbreak had originated within the ranks of the 5th *Alaudae* Legion and 21st *Rapax* Legion, whose men had been recruited from Roman citizens in Spain and Syria. First to revolt from the authority of their officers was a levee of new men recently sent from Rome by Augustus to bring the units up to strength. Legion recruits were usually draftees but always Roman citizens, whereas these troublemakers were freedmen, former slaves, who'd been given Roman citizenship in return for two decades of well-paid legion service, at a time when the Rhine frontier was under threat. On the back of the news of the emperor's death, these recent recruits began to agitate for shorter service, increased pay, and punishment of their often-cruel centurions. The discontent quickly spread to veteran troops within the two units, and then to the remaining legions at the Cologne camp, the 1st Legion and 20th *Valeria Victrix* Legion.[5]

Unpopular centurions were mobbed by their own men. Savagely beaten, they were thrown over the camp's high walls or into the Rhine. One unpopular centurion fled to the general commanding the Lower Army, Aulus Caecina, begging for help. As soldiers wielding swords surrounded the pair, the general, fearing for his own life, let them drag the unfortunate centurion away. Seeing his commander in trouble, a high-spirited young tribune drew his sword, forced a passage through the throng, and led Caecina to safety. That tribune's name was Cassius Chaerea. Remember that name; in years to come Chaerea would play a leading role in the life, and death, of Caligula.

For several days, the rank and file ran the camp, posting sentries and issuing watchwords themselves while their powerless officers remained in their leather tents with Germanicus's wife and son. Finally, commander-in-chief Germanicus returned from Gaul to settle the affair.

"Germanicus Caesar has returned!" went up the cry, and hundreds of soldiers surged out the camp's main gate to greet their chief.

They met him with their weapons sheathed and looking sheepish. As Germanicus walked in through the open wooden gates followed by his small entourage of aides, he found thousands more men conglomerating on the camp's main street. Rather than greeting him with a friendly hail, most of these men held their tongues or murmured conspiratorially among themselves. A veteran of more than thirty years' service rushed forward and took Germanicus's hand. Instead of kissing it as the general was accustomed, the fellow thrust the royal hand into his mouth.

"Feel my toothless gums, Caesar!" the soldier implored. "Send me into retirement!"

"Look at my legs, Caesar!" cried another old legionary. "They're bowed with age. What use am I to the army now?"

As soldiers began to surge around him, encouraged by the boldness of the veterans, with many yelling at him now, Germanicus called to them, "Form up in your cohorts, comrades, so that I can address you!"

"We can hear you better as we are," came an insubordinate reply, as many soldiers stubbornly folded their arms.

Turning to his personal trumpeter in the entourage behind him, Germanicus ordered, "Sound 'Advance the Standards.'"[6]

The trumpeter lifted his long, slim, curved instrument, and a trumpet call rang out. In response, the standard-bearers of cohorts and legions obediently ran to the camp shrines where their unit standards were kept, and brought them to the parade ground. Again Germanicus's trumpeter blew a call at his chief's command. This time it was "Assembly." Reluctantly in many cases, twenty thousand legionaries fell in by 480-man cohort, or battalion.

At the front of the assembly, Germanicus mounted the reviewing mound, known as the tribunal. Despite being a member of the imperial family, he had the common touch and could talk and joke with people at every level, which endeared him to all. That day, however, he found a far-from-receptive audience. In silence, the assembled troops listened as he told them that his adoptive father, Tiberius, would now become their emperor, and all would be well with the empire. Then he turned to their mutinous behavior.

"Comrades," he said, looking around them, "what has become of soldierly obedience, of the glory of military discipline? Why have you driven out your tribunes and centurions?"[7]

In response, men yelled complaints about the cruelty and greed of their officers, with some baring their backs to show him wheals from whippings. Many complained about being overworked and underpaid. Aged veterans begged him to let them retire before they died in uniform, paying them the retirement bonuses that Augustus had promised them. This all soon became a deafening clamor, but among the complaints, Germanicus heard more troubling calls. For these men weren't opposed to Germanicus; they were opposed to the system that kept them locked into military service well after they felt they should have been allowed to retire. They were opposed to what they saw as the uncaring establishment that administered that system. These men were convinced that the famously kindhearted Germanicus was a different caliber of leader.

"If you wish for empire, Caesar," came one voice, "we'll give it to you!"

This was greeted with cheers, and soon the complaints were being drowned out by enthusiastic calls for Germanicus to declare himself emperor, and by promises that his claim to the throne would be backed to the hilt by his legions. For Tiberius was widely disliked. Germanicus wouldn't listen to such seditious talk, but was shouted down. Jumping from the tribunal, he attempted to depart. But troops broke ranks and surged around him, with some threateningly drawing their swords.

"I would rather die than cast off my loyalty to my father," Germanicus declared, referring to Tiberius. Drawing his own sword, he made as if to plunge it into his own chest.

"No, Caesar!" men cried, grabbing his arm and staying the blow, as the young general had expected.

But, calling his bluff, some soldiers urged him to follow through with the threat to do himself in. A legionary by the name of Calusidius offered his own weapon to Germanicus. "Here, use my sword, Caesar," he said, no doubt with a leering grin. "It's sharper than yours."[8]

Germanicus's staff now surrounded him and protectively hustled him to his tented HQ pavilion, where he was reunited with his wife and son. That wife, Agrippina, was an elegant twenty-eight-year-old woman of royal birth. She was the daughter of Augustus's late right-hand man, the general Marcus Agrippa, and Augustus's daughter Julia—which made Agrippina Germanicus's cousin.

With Germanicus's grandfather being Mark Antony, Augustus's defeated rival in the bloody struggle for the Roman throne, the marriage of Agrippina and Germanicus had united several great, warring Roman houses. But it had also been a love match—Germanicus and Agrippina were absolutely devoted to each other, as the Roman public well knew. Receiving rapturous welcomes wherever they appeared in public, they were the John F. Kennedy and Jackie Kennedy, the Prince Harry and Meghan Markle, of their era.

Now, in his tent, Germanicus conferred with the Lower Army commander and the four generals in charge of the Cologne legions, as they discussed the mutiny and the best way to quickly resolve it. Germanicus's major concern was that, as soon as the aggressive German tribes east of the Rhine became aware that Rome's legions were in revolt, they could cross the river and invade Roman Gaul while its defenses were down. As the generals spoke, word arrived that the mutiny's ringleaders had sent messengers upriver to the four legions of the Army of the Upper Rhine based at Mogontiacum, today's German city of Mainz, urging them to join the Lower Army in revolting, pillaging Cologne, and then plundering all of Gaul.

To nip this in the bud, a letter to the troops was written by Germanicus. He knew that many of their complaints were valid. The older soldiers had signed up for sixteen-year enlistments, but eight years before this, Augustus had extended them to twenty years. Now, at a stroke, Germanicus restored the sixteen-year enlistment period. Men who had served more than twenty years were granted immediate discharge. Those who'd served for sixteen years were discharged on condition they make themselves available for service during emergencies in the Evocati, Rome's part-time reserve, a sort of National Guard.

Germanicus also agreed to pay the promised retirement bonuses, using his own money and that of his generals to fund them. He then hurried upriver to the legions at Mogontiacum, a base that had been established by his late father, Drusus the Elder, and featured a stone tower dedicated to Drusus, who had died in the area. There, Germanicus announced the same concessions he'd granted the Lower Army.

This seemed to put an end to the mutiny, enabling young Caligula to celebrate his second birthday with his parents and without fear. But within weeks, the peace was shattered. A party of senators arrived from Rome to confer with Germanicus, and the rumor spread around the camp like wildfire that the senators had come to cancel Germanicus's concessions—which they had. Again the legions erupted. The senator heading the party was saved from the mob only when the 1st Legion's eagle-bearer protected him. Germanicus dispatched the senators back to Rome with an escort of auxiliary cavalry who hadn't joined the mutiny—the members of auxiliary units weren't Roman citizens; citizenship was their reward after twenty-five years' service.

The camp the senators left behind was once more in turmoil. Germanicus's own officers now accused him of blundering in granting concessions to the mutineers in the first place. The situation, they said, was out of hand. One general declared to Germanicus, in front of his wife and child: "You may value your own life cheaply, Caesar. But why keep a little son and a pregnant wife among madmen who've outraged every human right? Let them at least be sent to safety."

"No!" declared Germanicus's loyal wife, Agrippina, who was no shrinking violet. Years before, her grandfather Augustus had praised her intelligence but had cautioned her to drop her haughty, effected manner of writing and speaking. As Germanicus strove to talk her into leaving, she firmly, haughtily shook her head. "I'm a descendant of Augustus," she said, "and I'm perfectly capable of facing danger!"[9]

His wife's determination not to leave his side brought Germanicus to tears, but he was convinced now that his subordinate was right and the safest course of action was to evacuate his wife and child. Embracing Agrippina, he

told her that Caligula and she must leave at once, accompanied by the wives
of the other generals in camp. He was sending her to Augusta Treverorum,
today's Trier, capital of the Treveri tribe, a Roman ally that provided some
of Rome's best cavalry. Their departure was a pitiable sight—Agrippina,
carrying Caligula, followed by the other wives of the senatorial class, walking out the gate without an escort, many of them sobbing.

Mutinous troops, emerging from their tents to see what was going on,
quickly became incensed when they learned that Agrippina and Caligula
were being sent away—to the Treveri, to foreigners! Besides, many men
believed that Caligula had actually been born in this legionary camp, which
gave the soldiers a special feeling of attachment to him. Later, Caligula's
birthplace would be disputed, but most authorities came to agree that
he was born at Antium, today's city of Anzio on the west coast of Italy.
Suetonius says that Caligula himself would treat Antium as his birthplace.[10]

While some men ran to block Agrippina's path, others hurried to
Germanicus's tent to protest. There, surrounded by the agitated multi-
tude, Germanicus scolded the troops, reminding them of their past victories, which had been under his personal command in the case of the 20th
*Valeria Victrix* Legion during the Pannonian War. He then very cleverly
worked on the soldiers' professional jealousy. Two years earlier, Roman
general Publius Quinctilius Varus had perished with three entire legions
when he'd led them into a German ambush in the Tuetoburg Forest east of
the Rhine. After the Varus Disaster, as it was to become known, Augustus
had forbidden his armies to operate beyond the Rhine. This had rankled
with proud Roman legionaries, who were itching to avenge their comrades
of the lost legions, and Germanicus knew it. Now, he told the mutineers
that Rome's allies the Belgae had offered to invade Germany for Rome and
punish the German tribes responsible for the Varus Disaster.

When Germanicus's troops predictably roared their disapproval of
this idea, he urged them to restore their allegiance, throw out the ringleaders of the mutiny, and follow him on a campaign against the Germans
to avenge their comrades. Normally, Rome's legions campaigned against
her enemies between March and October every year, but for the past two

campaigning seasons, while the legions on other frontiers marched for blood and booty, the men on the Rhine had been spending the summers digging entrenchments, doing fatigue duty, becoming stale and bored, and feeling impoverished. Germanicus's plea had the desired effect, exciting his troops into a change of mood.

"Punish the guilty, Caesar, and pardon the rest of us who've erred," came the call, "and lead us against the enemy!"

"Recall your wife," others yelled, "and let the nursling of the legions come back to us. Don't let them be handed over to the Gauls like hostages!"

Raising a hand, he told them that the approaching winter and the needs of postnatal confinement care in the hands of expert midwives meant that his wife must go to Augusta Treverorum, but he would recall his little son to the camp. "The rest," he said, "you can settle yourselves."[11]

This concession, with young Caligula astutely used as a bargaining chip by his father, brought cheers from his men, who immediately turned on the leaders of the mutiny in their ranks. These ringleaders were dragged in chains by the very men who'd been following their lead just minutes earlier, to the commander of the 1st Legion, for summary trial. As that general watched, and the troops stood with drawn swords, each accused man was placed on a platform in front of them by a senior tribune.

"Guilty or not guilty?" called the tribune.

If the mob called "Guilty!" the tribune pushed the man from the platform to the troops below, who eagerly hacked him to pieces. In this way, Germanicus's own troops dealt with the mutineers in their ranks and terminated the unrest. "The soldiers gloated over the bloodshed as though it gave them absolution," Roman historian Tacitus writes.[12]

But now Germanicus had to keep up his end of the bargain and lead his legions on a campaign east of the Rhine, against the express command of the late emperor and without any authorization from the Senate at Rome.

## II

# CALIGULA AT THE BRIDGE

In late AD 14 and over the spring of AD 15, Caligula's father, Germanicus, kept his word to his troops. Sending the older soldiery into their overdue retirement, he led the remaining men of the eight Rhine legions on several lightning campaigns in Germany, with Caecina commanding the Lower Army and Gaius Silius, to whom Germanicus was related by marriage, commanding the Upper Army. Time and again, Germanicus's offensives caught the Germans by surprise. But after each bloody defeat, the tribes rallied under their war leader, a thirty-three-year-old prince of the Chatti tribe. His German name was Hermann, but the Romans knew him as Arminius, a name gained when serving as a commander of German auxiliaries in Rome's Army of the Lower Rhine. It was Arminius who'd led the ambush and annihilation of Varus's legions.

During these campaigns, Germanicus's troops located and buried the remains of Varus's butchered legionaries, captured Arminius's pregnant wife and father-in-law, and, most importantly to Romans, recaptured one of the three sacred eagle standards of the lost legions. The Roman people were overjoyed, and the Senate voted Germanicus a Triumph, the traditional parade of a conquering general through the streets of Rome. This was the first Triumph awarded since that celebrated by Augustus forty-four years before.

Germanicus's successes, and his now superstar status with Romans, forced Tiberius to tread lightly. For, despite having adopted Germanicus at Augustus's behest, Tiberius neither liked nor trusted his nephew. After hesitating during the summer of AD 14, the now fifty-seven-year-old Tiberius had ascended the throne, becoming Rome's second emperor. Ever since then, he'd been warily watching Germanicus's activities.

Robert Graves, author of *I, Claudius* and noted translator of Suetonius's *Lives of the Caesars*, was of the view that Tiberius never understood Germanicus and Germanicus never understood Tiberius.[13] Certainly, Tiberius could not bring himself to believe that Germanicus had no ulterior motive for his sudden incursions into Germany. Germanicus saw this as a way of cementing the Rhine legions' loyalty to Rome and Tiberius, while Tiberius and his closest advisers saw it as a means of Germanicus cementing the Rhine legions' loyalty to Germanicus, in opposition to Tiberius. Highly suspicious of the young general, Tiberius gave grudging praise for Germanicus's successes but was quick to criticize him when he learned that Germanicus had involved himself in the burial of the remains of Varus's dead.

For his AD 15 campaign, Germanicus had taken four legions and an equal number of supporting auxiliaries into Germany by water, with the remaining four legions of his combined Rhine armies, under his deputy Caecina, crossing the Rhine via a more direct route, using a temporary bridge of boats thrown across the great river by Roman military engineers. In the late summer, with the campaign concluded, Germanicus sent half his troops back overland with Caecina, returning with the remainder by sea.

Caecina's route westward toward the Rhine took him through marshlands by a series of narrow causeways that the Romans called Long Bridges. German leader Arminius knew that Caecina would be reluctant to abandon his crawling baggage train—it was no coincidence that baggage trains were called the *impedimenta*—which included all the legions' artillery, supplies, and booty. Caecina's withdrawal would be slowed accordingly, giving Arminius time to regroup his bloodied fighters and hurry to attack the Romans as they passed along Long Bridges, where the legions would be strung out and exposed.

Meanwhile, Germanicus's wife, Agrippina, had given birth to their first daughter. Also named Agrippina, the girl would be called Agrippina the Younger by modern historians. Today, the city of Cologne proudly claims to be the child's birthplace, yet Suetonius was adamant that both of Germanicus's elder daughters were born in Gaul, and Trier seems the most likely location of Agrippina the Younger's birth, despite her later affection for Cologne. In the spring of AD 15, as soon as Agrippina's confinement was over and she was well enough to travel, she returned with her new baby to rejoin Caligula at the military camp. By that stage, Germanicus had departed for the latest incursion into Germany.

In the late summer, Agrippina was at Cologne when word arrived that Germanicus was on his way back from Germany by sea and Caecina's army was approaching overland. And then a more troubling message arrived—Caecina's legions were fighting for their lives at Long Bridges. As the Romans slowly battled their way along the causeway against Germans who splashed their way through the marshes to attack both flanks, more Germans fell on the baggage train at the rear of the column.

Caecina tried to organize the baggage train's defense, but his horse was pierced by several German spears and fell, dumping him. He was in danger of being overwhelmed when men of the 1st Legion quickly surrounded and saved him and then counterattacked. It seems that Germanicus later endowed the 1st Legion with the *Germanica* title as a reward for saving the day in this action, for it became the 1st *Germanica* Legion.[14]

Only now did Caecina decide to sacrifice his baggage. As Germans swarmed all over the abandoned carts and wagons, looting them, Caecina's exhausted troops were able to push on to solid ground and throw a defensive perimeter around a campsite, only to be surrounded there by the rampaging Germans. Arminius subsequently led an assault that broke through the Roman defenses, but the legions rallied and drove them out of their walled camp. The following day, Caecina led a breakout toward the Rhine.

All this fighting had put Caecina's arrival back at the river well behind schedule. At the Cologne camp, as the days passed and there was no sign of, or word from, Caecina's army, senior Roman officers began to fear that it had been wiped out. This meant that the Germans could now be expected to be heading for the Rhine, which they would be able to cross via the Roman bridge of boats. Not only would this imperil Cologne, it would open the way for the Germans to invade Gaul. The Roman commanders decided to be safe rather than sorry and destroy the bridge.

It was at this point that Germanicus's wife, Agrippina, intervened. She refused to let the bridge be destroyed. For this would have cut off Caecina and his twenty thousand men, whom she was confident were still on their way to the river. Agrippina was, says Tacitus, "a woman of heroic spirit," and, to permit the safe return of Caecina's legions, she stood at the bridge's eastern end, holding the now three-year-old Caligula's hand and attended by her female servants. There, she waited, almost willing the legions' return. Finally, men from Caecina's army began to appear from the forests east of the river, helping wounded comrades to the bridge. As they passed their commander-in-chief's wife and son, Agrippina distributed clean clothes and medical supplies among the men, praising and thanking them in the name of "Caesar Caligula."[15]

When word of this reached Tiberius at Rome, with the report from sycophants that "Agrippina now had more power with the armies than officers, than generals," the emperor was beside himself with anger. "All this was inflamed and aggravated by Sejanus," says Tacitus. Lucius Aelius Sejanus was Tiberius's prefect of the Praetorian Guard, a persuasive, manipulative thirty-seven-year-old who would soon become one of the most notorious figures in Roman history and a key figure in young Caligula's life.[16]

The Praetorian Guard had been created and disbanded during Rome's republican era before being revived by Mark Antony during the civil war that put Octavian on the throne as the emperor Augustus. After defeating Antony, Augustus retained the unit as a military police force—at this point in history the Praetorian Guard did not perform the role of imperial bodyguard. As his personal protectors, Augustus created what we call today the German Guard, an auxiliary unit of legion size and structure.

This *Germani Corporis Custodes*, literally the "German Body Guard," was made up of tall, strong, bearded Germans from the Batavi, Frisii, Baetasii, and Ubii tribes. Unlike legionaries, none of these Germans were Roman citizens. Not all members of the German Guard were stationed at Rome simultaneously. At any one time, three cohorts, 1,500 men, occupied the German Guard barracks in a fort in Rome's 14th Precinct, west of the Tiber, providing the emperor's close guard at Rome and when he was traveling. Their remaining cohorts were billeted at towns in central Italy, marching to and from Rome as the cohorts periodically rotated.

Augustus had deliberately chosen non-Romans as his bodyguards. The loyalty of the men of the German Guard was not to Rome but to their pay-master, the emperor, who paid them very well. He briefly abolished the German Guard in AD 9 following the Varus Disaster in Germany, when he suddenly doubted all German loyalty, but soon reinstated them. As it was to turn out, the German Guard would remain steadfastly loyal to every emperor it served, which was why the emperor Vespasian would abolish them in AD 69 when he took the throne by force, after they'd fought fiercely for his pre-decessorand killed his brother.

Only after the German Guard's abolition would the Praetorian Guard also take on imperial bodyguard duties. In Tiberius's reign, the Praetorians and the German Guard were the only military units permitted by law to be stationed in Italy, with the legions and all other auxiliary units based in the provinces, well away from Rome.

Augustus had appointed two prefects to command the Praetorian Guard simultaneously. They took turns in the top job, with only one in charge at a time; it's possible they served one month on, one month off. At the time of Augustus's death, those two men were Sejanus and his father, Seius Strabo. In AD 15, Tiberius gave Strabo the lucrative posting of pre-fect of Egypt, which paid 400,000 sesterces a year, quite an advance on the 900 sesterces then annually earned by a common soldier in Rome's legions.

This left Sejanus in sole command of the Praetorian Guard. Sejanus's mother came from a distinguished senatorial family, while, like Sejanus, his father was an equite, a member of the Equestrian Order. These equites, or equestrians, have been misleadingly called "knights" by latter-day historians. They weren't members of any order of chivalry. In effect Rome's middle class, they ranked between the senators and the plebeians, with their status harking back to the early days of the Roman republic when the more-affluent citizens reported for military service in times of emergency with their own horse. To be promoted to senator, you first had to be an equite.

Sejanus had served as a tribune with the legions before being transferred to the Praetorian Guard. In the view of Tacitus, Sejanus had "a
thorough comprehension of Tiberius's character." Playing to Tiberius's
strengths and weaknesses, Sejanus wasted no time gaining the emperor's
trust, becoming, as the equivalent of his secretary of defense, his principal
adviser, and his primary manipulator.[17]

Following his incursion into Germany, Germanicus and his legions
returned to their Rhine bases. There Germanicus went among the men in
their barracks, comforting the wounded, chatting with the rank and file,
and paying for replacement of the equipment and personal belongings his
men had lost in Germany, again from his own pocket. The popularity of
Germanicus and Agrippina among the Rhine legions continued to soar,
and Tiberius's discontent with his feisty daughter-in-law and the "son" that
Augustus had forced on him continued to ferment.

With the talk at Rome being all about Germanicus's successes in
Germany, Tiberius put on a public front of approval, awarding three
of Germanicus's subordinate generals the top military honor to which
they could aspire, Triumphal Distinctions—the personal trappings of
a Triumph, without the Triumphal parade that was its centerpiece. As
Germanicus issued orders for the construction of a thousand new warships along the Rhine, many of them flat-bottomed for shallow river
use, Tiberius made his own plans. First he sent one of his closest senatorial friends to "assist" Germanicus. Suspecting the senator was there
to spy on him, Germanicus put the fellow in charge of a fortified supply
base east of the Rhine, in his rear and out of the way, while he himself
led the latest incursion into Germany. Then, to lessen Germanicus's
popularity with the troops, late in the year Tiberius countermanded
his son's order regarding the length of legionary service, returning it
to twenty years. Germanicus's legions, engrossed in his German campaigns, may have grumbled, but they accepted Tiberius's extension of
their service.

In the spring of AD 16, as Germanicus was preparing to launch his next German campaign, the emperor sent two thousand men of the Praetorian Guard to the Rhine, ostensibly in support of Germanicus but more likely to keep an eye on him. Meanwhile Agrippina was pregnant again. In Gaul that September, she would give birth to another daughter, Julia Drusilla, who would become known as Drusilla.

Germanicus's AD 16 German campaign was massive. Including the largest amphibious landing operation in Roman history, it involved his thousand newly constructed ships. Twice, Germanicus faced off against Arminius. In the summer, at the Battle of Idistavisus beside the Weser River, Germanicus led eighty thousand Roman troops in defeating fifty thousand German tribesmen. "It was a great victory, and without blood-shed to us," says Tacitus. Nonetheless, Arminius managed to escape on horseback, obscuring his identity by smearing his face with his own blood.[18]

When Arminius regrouped the German tribes months later, Germanicus again dealt them a bitter defeat, this time at the Battle of the Angrivar Barrier. Before charging massive German earthworks at the head of the two Praetorian Guard cohorts that Tiberius has sent to him, Germanicus deliberately discarded his helmet. He went into battle bare-headed to ensure that no Praetorian officer, using the excuse that he hadn't recognized Germanicus in the heat of battle, would plunge his sword into him on the stealthy orders of Praetorian Prefect Sejanus.

Despite the Roman victory, the campaign was not without set-backs. For one thing, Arminius again escaped. Then, on the return of Germanicus's ships from Germany, they were hit by a storm that broke up the fleet. Some ships were wrecked; others were blown along the German coast. A few ships were blown all the way to Britain, where British chief-tains came to the aid of the soldiers and crew aboard. These men would come back to the Rhine talking about terrifying sea monsters and other horrors in Britain.

Although Roman loss of life as a result of the storm was not reported as great, the loss of ships, equipment, and personal belongings was substan-tial. Once again Germanicus made up the losses from his own, seemingly bottomless, purse. In part compensation for the materiel losses, in the late days of the campaign his troops located a second of Varus's lost eagle standards. News of this again inspired Romans at home to celebrate Germanicus.

As the young general began planning an AD 17 German campaign, he received a letter from the Palatium, the imperial headquarters on the Palatine Hill at Rome that served as a combined White House and Pentagon, and from which the word *palace* derives. Tiberius had been writing to Germanicus for some time, suggesting he wrap up his campaigning and return to Rome but never going as far as ordering him back to Rome. Now he urged Germanicus to call it a day, promising to appoint him a consul—which would require him to be at Rome. Germanicus replied by requesting another year in which to finish the job in Germany and hunt down Arminius.

Tiberius wrote back urging Germanicus to let his adoptive younger brother Drusus, Tiberius's natural son, take over the Rhine command and share some of the glory. Called Drusus the Younger by latter-day historians to distinguish him from his late uncle Drusus, Germanicus's father, this Drusus attracted the nickname of "Castor." Because there was yet another Drusus in this story—a son of Germanicus and elder brother of Caligula—I will refer to Tiberius's son Drusus as Castor from this point forward to avoid confusion.

As Tiberius was aware, Germanicus was fond of Castor, and, rather than deny him an opportunity, Germanicus finally bowed to Tiberius's wishes, telling Agrippina they were returning to Rome. Germanicus, Agrippina, the now four-year-old Caligula, one-year-old Agrippina the Younger, and babe-in-arms Drusilla traveled back to Rome.

# III

## SHARING HIS FATHER'S TRIUMPH

May 26, AD 17, was a public holiday at Rome. The stands around the Circus Maximus, the city's primary chariot-racing venue, overflowed with people, and the city streets were lined with excited, expectant men, women, and children, who were held back by 9,000 troops of the Praetorian Guard and 4,500 of the City Guard. Modern historians estimate that, at that time, the city's population was at least a million people and probably more. They, and people from throughout Italy, had come to watch Germanicus Caesar celebrate his Triumph.

Suetonius records that the people of Rome had been so excited on Germanicus's return from Germany that, prior to taking his Triumph, the entire population, of all ages and sexes, had deserted the city to line the road for twenty miles beyond it to cheer his arrival. Meanwhile, two cohorts of the Praetorian Guard had been ordered to escort him to the city boundary, but, against orders, all the cohorts had marched out to meet and greet him.[19]

Country people who'd flocked to the capital had filled the inns in the city and suburbs and then sought vantage points. The Circus Maximus alone could hold more than 150,000 spectators. Just as on chariot-racing days, people would have arrived well before dawn to secure the best positions. They had come to witness Rome's first Triumph in decades. It would be an event and an experience that Germanicus's son Caligula would never forget. For, little Caligula was to participate in this Triumph with his father.

Roman Triumphs were the predecessors of the hometown victory parade of the winning Super Bowl and World Cup team, an opportunity for the public to get close to and celebrate their heroes. In ancient Rome, the Triumph had a strong religious aspect. It began in the temple precinct

18

on the Field of Mars, outside Rome's sacred original city boundary—the *pomerium*. There, traditionally, the Senate welcomed the returning general, who would apply for his Triumph and yield his army command. In Germanicus's case, this was a mere formality. He then donned the regalia of a triumphing general—a purple cloak; a tunic embroidered with the golden palm—a Roman symbol of victory; and a crown made from laurel leaves. The triumphing general was only supposed to wear this regalia on the day of his Triumph, but Julius Caesar had worn his as the mood took him, with Suetonius claiming he always wore his laurel crown to hide the fact that he was balding.

Clad in his Triumphal regalia, Germanicus joined his children as the parade formed. The triumphing general rode in an elaborately decorated golden *quadriga*, a large four-horse chariot, and, normally, his children rode on horseback behind the quadriga. Breaking with tradition, Germanicus was taking his children in the chariot with him. Four-year-old Caligula would be accompanied by two-year-old Agrippina, baby Drusilla, and Germanicus's two eldest boys—eleven-year-old Nero Germanicus Caesar and eight-year-old Drusus Germanicus Caesar.

It would have been a tight fit for them all in the quadriga, with the older children charged with looking after their younger siblings. As for the slave who in earlier times had reputedly stood in the chariot holding a crown over the general's head and whispering to him that he was only mortal and not to think of himself as a god, there is no record of such an additional occupant in Germanicus's quadriga.

As tradition required, the members of the Senate led the way on foot as the Triumphal procession began, waving to the cheering crowd as they went. The order of the parade would have been something like this . . . Germanicus and his children followed the senators in the quadriga, with Germanicus's generals and aides riding on horseback behind and trumpeters walking beside the golden chariot to periodically sound a fanfare. It's likely that the two recovered eagle standards of Varus's lost legions came next, escorted by priests and selected centurions dressed in ceremonial white, their passing bringing thunderous applause from the crowd.

Then followed representative units from Germanicus's Rhine armies, marching behind their standards and singing ribald songs that lampooned their general, as permitted by Triumph tradition. Hollywood has invariably featured pounding drums when depicting Roman spectacles and legionaries on the march, but in reality, drums played no part in the Roman military. Musicians were part of every legion, but these were trumpet and horn players who sounded signals.

Behind the troops trundled scores of wagons loaded with German shields, standards, armor and weapons, trophies from Germanicus's conquests, and huge paintings depicting various aspects of the campaigns— battle scenes, the floating Rhine bridge, the Roman fleet. Last of all came German prisoners in chains, headed by Arminius's wife, Thusnelda, with their now two-year-old son and Thusnelda's father and other captured tribal chieftains. Traditionally, the most senior prisoner would be garroted following the Triumphal parade. This had been the fate of Vercingotrix after Julius Caesar's Gallic Triumph. But Germanicus would be executing no one; Thusnelda and her son would be sent to the naval base city of Ravenna on Italy's northeast coast, where the boy would be raised as a Roman.

From its Field of Mars starting point, the parade passed through the Circus Flaminius piazza, beside the Tiber. This circus possessed no permanent grandstands; wooden stands were erected around its perimeter for special events. It's likely that, given the months of detailed preparations for the Triumph of Germanicus, such stands had been built and were now full of Germanicus's cheering fans. Traditionally the parade then entered the old city by crossing the sacred city boundary at the old Servian Wall via the Porta Triumphalis, which means the "Triumphal Gate."

Normally this gate was opened only to permit a Triumphal parade to enter the city, although a rare exception had been made for the funeral procession of Augustus three years prior to this. No modern authority has been able to fix the location of the Triumphal Gate with certainty, but the prevailing opinion is that it was one of the two gateways in the double-arched Porta Carmentalis, not far from the Circus Flaminius, which still stands.

Once inside the old city, the procession apparently did a lap of the Circus Maximus, following the sand-covered course of the U-shaped chariot-racing track as the people packing the stands cheered, applauded, and waved. Germanicus and his beaming children waved back. The route taken through the city, past the crowds on the pavements and the people waving from rooftops, varied from Triumph to Triumph, but it always used the Triumphal Way and Sacred Way before passing through the Forum and terminating at the steps to the Capitoline Mount. The triumphant traditionally climbed the steps on his knees.

On the mount, at the massive Temple of Jupiter *Optimus Maximus*—meaning "Jupiter Best and Greatest"—the Senate joined the general, with a feast for the elite following there and a larger feast taking place for the public in the city below. The Triumph of Germanicus was the greatest day Rome had seen in the memory of many; it was a day that Romans would long remember. And, as time was to prove, it left Caligula with a thirst to experience another Triumph—with himself as the triumphant general.

# IV

## HIS FATHER'S VIOLENT DEATH

Germanicus and a once-more pregnant Agrippina sailed for the East in the summer of AD 17 to base themselves in the province of Syria. Tiberius had appointed Germanicus commander-in-chief in the East. Caligula and his little sisters, Agrippina the Younger and Drusilla, were in their parents' large entourage when it departed Rome. Caligula's elder brothers remained at the Palatium, supervised by their great-grandmother Livia Augusta, Augustus's widow and Tiberius's mother.

By all accounts, Livia had never liked Germanicus or Agrippina, and she would have treated their children coldly, in the same way she has mistreated their club-footed uncle Claudius, Germanicus's younger, apparently dim-witted brother. Livia despised weakness, and was no doubt scornful of Caligula because he suffered from epileptic fits, with the boy probably first displaying symptoms in AD 15–16. In many cases, epilepsy doesn't last into adulthood, and this seems to have been the case with Caligula. Roman doctors of the first century had a list of more than one hundred natural medicines they could use to treat a variety of ailments, including one for epilepsy. We don't know what this medicine consisted of, or whether it was effective.

Caligula's epilepsy prevented him from being taught to swim, as his protective parents feared he would drown if he suffered a fit while in the water. Some of their caution was no doubt induced by experience; before Caligula was born, they'd lost another son, also named Gaius, when he was around eight years of age. All the other children of the imperial family were taught to swim. Augustus had even taught several of his grandsons personally. So, as Caligula's siblings enjoyed swimming, he was forced to sit and watch.

It's likely that Germanicus's mother, Antonia, was also in the party heading east, intending to return to Rome at the end of the trip rather than remain for any length of time with Germanicus in Syria. No ancient source mentions this, but several details hint at the possibility. To begin with, while sailing to Syria in a flotilla of ships from one of Rome's Italian fleets, Germanicus and Agrippina would visit Actium on the west coast of Greece on September 2. There, at a shrine to Apollo, they would mark the 31 BC Battle of Actium between Germanicus's grandfather Mark Antony and Agrippina's grandfather Augustus. Mark Antony was Antonia's father, so she, too, would have been keen to visit the site.

In addition, the previous year had seen the death of King Antiochus III, the cruel and unloved ruler of the kingdom of Commagene, an eastern Roman ally located in today's central Turkey. The king's son Antiochus was only a toddler and much too young to take the throne, so Germanicus was going to install a Roman *propraetor* to govern Commagene, "to inspire hope of a gentler rule under Rome," says Tacitus.[20] That governor, Quintus Servaeus, apparently traveled out from Rome in Germanicus's party. We know that the young prince of Commagene, Antiochus, along with his little sister Iotapa, would be raised at Rome by Caligula's grandmother Antonia. So, it is probable that, while in Commagene, Germanicus collected the two children, after which Antonia would take them back to Rome with her. Caligula would mix with both these children at Rome while growing up.

Germanicus and his party made numerous stops as they coasted east at a leisurely pace, first around the Adriatic, then the Ionian, Aegean, and Mediterranean Seas, being welcomed with elaborate honors and cheering crowds wherever they went. At one such halt, at the island of Rhodes, Germanicus bumped into Gnaeus Piso and his wife, Plancina Munatia, who were also heading for the East. Plancina was a close friend of Tiberius's mother, Livia, and Tiberius had just appointed Piso to be Syria's new provincial governor. The Senate had given Germanicus special powers that meant he outranked all Roman governors in the East, but Piso was an arrogant man who, according to Tacitus, could barely bring himself to be civil even to the emperor. Piso's home at Rome shared the Palatine Hill with the imperial palaces, which seems to have contributed to his elevated self-esteem.

Piso had no intention of taking orders from Germanicus, which, some friends of Germanicus were to say, was exactly what Tiberius wanted. Anxious to reach Syria ahead of Germanicus, Piso sailed from Rhodes in rough weather, only for the cargo vessel in which he was sailing to run aground. Germanicus sent triremes from his flotilla to pull Piso's ship free. After the sleek warships with three banks of oars hauled Piso from the rocks, he sailed on without a word of thanks. Once he reached Syria, he set about winning the loyalty of the Roman troops stationed there with bribes and favors.

Germanicus, meanwhile, was in no hurry. With an abiding interest in history, he was playing the tourist while the birth of his latest child approached. On the Greek island of Lesbos, Agrippina took up residence with her doctors and staff to await the birth of a girl who would be named Julia Livilla. Officially known as Julia, she is referred to as Livilla by latter-day historians to differentiate her from other Julias in the family, including Augustus's daughter Julia, who had been married to Tiberius for a time.

Leaving Agrippina on Lesbos and taking five-year-old Caligula with him, Germanicus went touring, starting at the city of Assos. On the Biga Peninsula opposite Lesbos, Assos offered the only good harbor in the area for Germanicus's flotilla. At Assos, Caligula spoke a few words to the gathered locals on behalf of his father, probably at the city's five-thousand-seat theater, declaring, "I will hold your city in remembrance and under my protection."[21]

At the Temple of Clarion Apollo near the city of Colophon on the same Ionian coast, Germanicus consulted the renowned oracle who presided in the dark crypt beneath the temple. The "oracle singer" drank the waters of a sacred pool before singing Germanicus a response to his question. The oracle's prediction to Germanicus was never revealed, but Tacitus wrote that it was rumored to have forecast his "early doom." Neither Tacitus nor Pliny the Elder took oracles seriously, with both remarking that early doom was the usual prediction of all oracles.[22]

Undaunted, Germanicus traveled on, visiting areas in Thrace, the city of Byzantium, and parts of the province of Asia, no doubt always to ecstatic welcomes from the locals. As he did, he sent orders on ahead to Piso in Syria to have the 10th *Fretensis* Legion join him as escort for his official travels through Armenia and other lands to the north of Syria. When Piso failed to comply and the legion didn't turn up, Germanicus set off for Armenia anyway, accompanied just by his friends and staff, and probably escorted by marines from the flotilla that had brought him to the East and would not return to Italy until the spring. As this trip was not without its dangers, Agrippina and the children would have gone on to Epidaphna, near Antioch, the Roman capital of Syria, taking up residence there in the villa that was to serve as Germanicus's headquarters in the East.

To cement Armenia as a Roman ally and a bulwark against Parthia, Germanicus marched in and placed a Roman-approved king, Zeno, on the country's throne, in a grand public coronation ceremony at its capital, Artaxata. Farther south, he formally made Commagene a new Roman province, leaving Servaeus as governor. Germanicus also brought the neighboring kingdom of Cappadocia deeper into the Roman fold. In AD 17, the country's aging king, Archelaus, had been summoned to Rome by Tiberius; he died there soon after. Germanicus now made Cappadocia a Roman province, installing a friend of equite rank, Quintus Veranius, as governing Roman prefect.

Once Germanicus reached Syria and reunited with his wife and young family, he lived for some time at the winter camp of the 10th *Fretensis* Legion at Cyhrrus, experiencing problem after problem with new governor Piso, who obstructed him at every turn, even embarrassing him in front of foreign kings at a banquet at Epidaphna. "Though it angered Germanicus," says Tacitus, "he still bore with patience," and tried to work with Piso.[23]

In January AD 19, Germanicus traveled down to Egypt to take measures to alleviate a famine. With the sailing season still two months away, he apparently traveled overland via Judea—Tacitus says he visited several provinces on this trip. Germanicus's brother Claudius would later say that, while in Alexandria, Germanicus addressed the local citizens "in

words more clearly stamped as his own" than of Tiberius.[24] Germanicus
then donned civilian clothes, detached himself from his staff and bodyguards, and, entirely alone, again became a tourist, sailing up the Nile
from Canopus to visit Egypt's antiquities.

At the vast ruins at Thebes, an Egyptian priest deciphered ancient
inscriptions for him, telling of an army of 700,000 men led by Pharaoh
Ramses that had conquered North Africa, Persia, and much of the Middle
East. Germanicus visited the pyramids and the statue of Memnon, and,
before turning back, traveled up the Nile as far as Elephantine and Syene,
then the southern limit of the Roman Empire.

Once Germanicus arrived back in Syria, he would have told his wife
and children about the ancient wonders he'd seen, and this is likely to have
inspired Caligula's later fascination with Egypt. Once back in Syria, too,
Germanicus found that his Egyptian trip had been reported to Tiberius,
and a letter was awaiting him from the emperor. Under a law instituted
by Augustus, no Roman senator or senior equite could visit Egypt without
the express permission of the emperor. And Germanicus had not sought
Tiberius's permission, apparently thinking the law didn't apply to him.
But Tiberius did think it applied to him. First rapping Germanicus over the
knuckles for going about in casual dress in Egypt, he "pronounced a very
sharp censure" of his adopted son for going there without his permission.[25]

Germanicus no doubt suspected Piso of reporting him to Tiberius.
Additionally, on his return to Syria, he found that all the instructions he'd
given to the legions and cities of the region prior to going to Egypt had
been repealed or reversed by Piso. Germanicus finally lost his temper,
and he and Piso had a savage argument, after which Piso declared that he
would depart Syria. But then, in the late days of summer, Germanicus suddenly fell ill, and Piso, his wife, son Marcus, and their staff tarried in the
Syrian city of Seleucia to await the outcome of Germanicus's illness.

Germanicus, suspecting he'd been poisoned, and learning that Piso's
wife, Plancina, had associated with a known Syrian poisoner named
Martina, had searches undertaken for signs of witchcraft. The search
unearthed human remains hidden in and under palace walls and floors,

as well as incantations and spells written on lead tablets along with Germanicus's name, burnt wood smeared with blood, and other signs of the sorcerer's arts. Spies from Piso were also detected at Epidaphna, sent to determine his state of health, and this angered Germanicus most of all.

"If I must gasp out my last breath under my enemies' eyes," he declared, as he struggled to breathe, "what then will be the lot of my most unhappy wife, of my infant children?"[26]

His health rallied, but shortly after, he again fell desperately sick. Convinced that Piso was behind this, Germanicus dictated a letter to him, renouncing his friendship and ordering him to quit the province. Piso and his family subsequently boarded a ship, but lingered in the waters near Syria, seemingly believing that Germanicus would die. At Epidaphna, the young prince's strength was ebbing away. On October 10, Germanicus's wife, friends, and staff clustered around his bed, as, aware that he had little time left to live and certain that he was the victim of a murder plot that had been born in Rome, with failing breath Caligula's father commanded his friends to set his wife and six children before the people of Rome to remind them of their loss, and to avenge him.

"Vengeance must come from *you*," he gasped, "if you loved the man more than his fortune."

Each of his friends, senators, and equites took his right hand in turn and swore an oath: "I would sooner lose life than lose revenge."

Calling Agrippina close, he implored her, "Swear by my memory, and on the heads of our children, that when you return to Rome, you will cast aside your high spirit and submit yourself to the cruel blows of fortune, and won't anger political rivals who are stronger than you."[27]

Germanicus, who knew his wife well and knew that her temper and haughtiness could get her into trouble, was telling her to let his male friends engage in the political infighting on his behalf. He whispered a few last words to his wife, with others present assuming he was warning her against antagonizing Tiberius. And then Germanicus Julius Caesar, heir apparent of the Roman imperial throne, passed away. He was just thirty-three years of age.

It had taken many days for news of Germanicus's illness to reach Rome. When reports first arrived that Germanicus had fallen gravely ill in Syria, the city had come to a standstill, with the people "stunned and distressed," according to Suetonius. All business ceased, and the population rushed to the Capitoline Mount to offer prayers and sacrifices for his recovery at the temple to Jupiter. Then, when word came that their prince was indeed recovering, the joy was overwhelming, with people going about the streets at night, celebrating and chanting:

> "Here's an end to all our pain,
> Germanicus is well again!"[28]

And then, not many days later, it was learned that he had died. "When the news of his death finally broke," says Suetonius, "neither edicts nor official expressions of sympathy could console the populace."[29] Romans ran riot, taking out their wrath against the gods, stoning temples, upsetting altars, tossing the statues of their household deities into the street. The public grief would last for months, with the normally joyous days of the Saturnalia Festival in December darkened by the protracted mourning.

The shock spread beyond the ends of empire. "His death was lamented by all men everywhere," says Flavius Josephus, whose family lived in Jerusalem at the time. He records foreign kings shaving off their beards and shaving their wives' heads. The king of Parthia, Rome's longtime foe in the East, reportedly also entered a period of mourning, such was the international respect for Germanicus.[30] Just as today, when popular figures who die suddenly in their prime—be they presidents or singing stars—attain legendary status and lasting fame, Germanicus would for hundreds of years be remembered as the archetypal noble Roman and the greatest emperor Rome never had.

Surviving ancient sources lavish praise on him, even those who would be highly critical of his son Caligula. Cassius Dio describes Germanicus as the bravest against the foe yet gentle with his countrymen. Suetonius writes, "Germanicus is everywhere described as having been of outstanding physical and moral excellence." Tacitus laments Germanicus's early loss to Rome, saying, "He would have attained military glory as much more easily as he had excelled Alexander (the Great) in clemency, in self-restraint, and in all the other virtues."[31]

In the nineteenth century, most historians' views of Germanicus as a general and statesman were negative, with some pointing out that he had come within a hair's breadth of defeat in several of his battles. However, the same can be said of Julius Caesar. More recently, historians have concluded that Germanicus was a bold, brave, and able general. He was never defeated in battle, he put Rome back on the front foot on the German frontier, and, most important, he gave Romans back their pride after the humiliation of the Varus Disaster. Such was the lasting luster of Germanicus's name that it would attach itself to his son Caligula, his brother Claudius, and his grandson Nero.

At Rome, the shock generated by the death of the young national hero would soon give way to a rage for revenge.

# V

## A MURDER TRIAL

The Senate voted numerous honors to the dead hero and heir to the throne, including triumphal arches dedicated to Germanicus in Rome. One of these, a spectacular triple-span Arch of Germanicus, would form the entrance to the Flaminian Circus for hundreds of years to come. Another Germanican arch was already being built, topped by his statue, flanking the Temple of Mars Ultor—meaning Mars the Avenger—in the Forum of Augustus. This had come as a result of the Senate in AD 18 voting Ovations to Germanicus for his Armenian exploit. They'd similarly voted an arch to Tiberius's son Castor, who had done nothing more than accept the surrender of German king Maroboduus while Germanicus was in the East. Maroboduus had unsuccessfully opposed Arminius, the young German leader who'd evaded Germanicus time and again. As it happened, Arminius had died around the same time as Germanicus, slain by his own people.

Honor was heaped upon honor for Germanicus. By order of the Senate, more triumphal arches would be erected in memory of Germanicus on the Rhine and on Mount Amanus in Syria, as well as a cenotaph in Antioch and a mound in Epidaphna. The equites named their benches at the theater—the first fourteen rows next to the orchestra—Germanicus's Benches and vowed that his image would lead the annual equites' parade in July in perpetuity. In numerous towns throughout the empire, including Pompeii in Italy and Arausio and Medialanum Saintonum in Gaul—today's French cities of Orange and Saintes—the local authorities would dedicate more triumphal arches to Germanicus, paid for by rich locals. Many Roman towns would have raised statues of Germanicus at their own expense, as indicated by Amelia, sixty miles north of Rome in Umbria. There, in

1963, a larger than life bronze statue of Germanicus in his armor, which had originally been covered in gilt, was unearthed outside the main town gate—it had probably stood atop the gate.

But the honors for Germanicus could not dispel the growing public anger. There was, says Tacitus, "a universal eagerness to exact vengeance on Piso." Mobs prowled Rome's streets at night, chanting, "Give us back our Germanicus!" The same message was scrawled across the walls of the city. With Romans close to revolt, and many accusing Tiberius of having Germanicus murdered, it was announced that Piso and his wife, Plancina, had been summoned back to Rome, with both to face trial in the Senate in relation to Germanicus's death.[32]

Piso resisted at first, assembling a motley military force in Cilicia to defy Germanicus's friend Gnaeus Sentius, who'd taken command in Syria on the prince's death. Hugely outnumbered by Sentius's loyal legionaries, Piso finally buckled and agreed to return to Italy. Even then, Piso took his time returning. Sending his son Marcus on ahead to Rome to seek an audience with Tiberius, who received him cordially, Piso dawdled in Illyricum. There, Tiberius's son Castor was now in charge, and Piso hoped to win his favor, which he seemed to do.

"The death of Germanicus need not be the ruin of anyone," Castor told Piso publicly.[33] Castor was married to Germanicus's only sister, Livilla, and, as chance would have it, on the very day that Germanicus had died in Syria, Livilla had given birth at Rome to twin boys, cousins to Caligula. One of Castor's twins would die quite young. The other, who was named Tiberius Gemellus and would become known as Gemellus, would come to figure significantly in Caligula's future prospects, although no one could have then imagined it.

Seven-year-old Caligula was by this stage on his way back to Rome with his mother and sisters. Agrippina had cremated Germanicus in the Forum at Antioch before a stunned crowd. Tacitus wrote that friends of Germanicus claimed his corpse displayed signs of poisoning—blue lips and blotched skin, which are consistent with poisoning by the deadly plant belladonna, commonly available in the East.[34] Equally, friends of the emperor claimed there were no such signs, although Dio, writing two hundred years later, was convinced that poison had been involved, as were most Romans.[35]

Ignoring the perils of the winter seas, Agrippina returned from the East by ship in January AD 20, bringing the hero's ashes home. After pausing at the Greek island of Corfu, she and the children landed at the port of Brundisium, today's Brindisi, on the toe of Italy, in early February. Also aboard one of the ships of Agrippina's flotilla was Martina, the Syrian poison expert, in chains. Arrested by Sentius in Syria, Martina was to be lodged under lock and key in Brundisium until the trial of Piso and his wife at Rome; clearly Germanicus's friends feared that the woman might be interfered with by agents of the accused if immediately sent to Rome.

As for Agrippina, a massive crowd had gathered from all around the region to witness her arrival, even clinging to the rooftops of Brundisium. Tacitus reports that an audible groan ran around the waterfront as she was seen to step ashore, surrounded by her children, followed by her sobbing female servants, and clutching Germanicus's ashes. Tiberius had sent two cohorts of the Praetorian Guard to Brundisium, and they provided an escort as Agrippina and the children then took the ashes all the way to Rome and interment in the Mausoleum of Augustus, on foot, with tribunes and centurions of the Guard bearing the casket containing Germanicus's ashes on a bier resting on their shoulders.

Tiberius ordered the magistrates of Calabria, Apulia, and Campania to pay official honors as the somber procession passed, on roads lined with grim-faced civilians in dark mourning clothes. At Tarracina, forty miles southwest of Rome, the cortege was met by a party from Rome headed by Germanicus's distraught brother Claudius and his adoptive brother, Castor. With them came Germanicus's eldest children Nero Germanicus and Drusus Germanicus. The boys would have had a tearful reunion with their mother and siblings at Tarracina, where they also saw their new sister, Livilla, for the first time.

The two sitting consuls and much of the grieving population of Rome came to meet the cortege outside the city, but Tiberius and his mother,

Livia Augusta, were conspicuous by their absence, as was Germanicus's mother, Antonia. Tacitus says it was generally felt that Tiberius and Livia prevented Antonia from leaving the Palatium, an act which only added to the odium surrounding the emperor.[36] Once Germanicus's remains had been consigned to the Mausoleum at night, witnessed by a massive crowd in torchlight on the Field of Mars, all attention turned to the upcoming trial of Piso and Plancina.

Friends of Tiberius in the Senate pushed for the Piso—Plancina trial to take place out of the public eye, but, with the public mood being strongly against him, Tiberius vetoed this. Such were the feelings for Germanicus and his family, and against Piso and his family, that Piso experienced great difficulty finding senators who would act as his advocates in the case. After six turned him down, a relative of Piso and two ex-consuls who were close to Tiberius took on the onerous task.

After a friend of Tiberius unsuccessfully tried to hijack the prosecution, the case against Piso and Plancina was put together by three of Germanicus's friends who'd been in the East with him and had returned for the trial—former consul Quintus Veranius, the man installed by Germanicus as governor of Cappadocia; Quintus Servaeus, whom Germanicus had a appointed governor of Commagene; and Publius Vitellius, who'd served on the Rhine with Germanicus as commander of the 2nd *Augusta* Legion before going east with him. The three prosecutors lost their key witness even before the trial opened: Martina the poisoner died in mysterious circumstances at Brundisium. Tacitus says it was rumored that she was found with poison hidden in a knot of her hair, although her own body showed no signs of poisoning.[37]

When the case got under way at dawn one spring morning in the unimposing Curia, the Senate House below the Capitoline Mount, Piso was delivered in a closed litter, escorted by an armed Praetorian tribune and through a massive crowd held back by the Praetorian Guard. Piso would sit throughout the trial with a rolled-up letter at his side. Many would speculate that this went back to AD 17 and contained instructions from someone to harass Germanicus. But who was that someone? Tiberius? His mother? Sejanus?

The Senate House was packed as sixty-year-old Tiberius personally presided. He opened proceedings with an address that, in the eyes of many vengeance seekers, favored Piso, for the emperor declared that he considered the accused innocent until proven guilty. With no direct evidence linking Piso or Plancina to Germanicus's death, the prosecutors could only present circumstantial evidence. On that first day, each of them testified to what they'd seen and heard, detailing Piso and Plancina's disrespectful and insubordinate behavior toward Germanicus, and brought forward several other witnesses to these events.

Tacitus tells us that among those to give evidence against the couple was Antonia, Germanicus's mother and Caligula's grandmother, although he doesn't reveal what she said.[38] It was highly unusual for a woman to give evidence in a case before the Senate, and even rarer for that woman to be member of the imperial family. Antonia, highly respected, possessed great intellect and great courage, as she was to demonstrate to Caligula's benefit in coming years. As it's likely she'd accompanied Germanicus and Agrippina on their voyage to the East before returning independently to Rome a year prior to her son's death, Antonia seems to have testified to seeing Piso and Plancina treat Germanicus rudely and disrespectfully when they met at Rhodes, en route to the East, and once they arrived in Syria.

During that afternoon, while the prosecution witnesses continued to give evidence, Piso's wife, Plancina, discreetly paid a visit to the house of Livia, the emperor's mother, which was just a short distance from her own home on the Palatine Hill. At that meeting, Livia gave Plancina a guarantee she would protect her, as long as Plancina dissociated herself from Piso. That night, when Piso was brought back to their Palatine home after a day in court, Plancina informed him she was separating her defense from his; she was in effect throwing him to the wolves. Piso was devastated and considered tossing in the towel, but his sons Gnaeus and Marcus convinced him to fight on, for their sakes as much as his.

On the second day, the prosecution set out to prove that the accused had destroyed Caligula's father "by sorcery and poison,"[39] but the evidence was slim. Members of the throng outside, fearing that Piso was going to escape the charge, flooded to the Forum, where Piso's marble statues stood among those of his fellow ex-consuls. Dragging down Piso's statues, the mob hauled them to the top of the Gemonian Stairs and then cast them down—the traditional fate of traitors. When Tiberius learned of this, he suspended the sitting until the Praetorian Guard had returned the statues to their plinths. Only then did he allow the hearing to resume.

The prosecution wrapped up its case by day's end. Tiberius then adjourned the House for six days, after which the advocates for the defense would have three days in which to present their case. As everyone retired for the night, the mood was somber in the Germanicus camp, with many fearing the prosecution had failed to prove its case. At home that night, Piso wrote a document and sealed it. He ate a meal and then went to bed, in a bedroom separate from that of his wife. The following morning, Piso was found dead on the bedroom floor, in a pool of blood and with a sword beside him. His throat had been cut.

Tiberius announced to a shocked Senate that morning that Piso had taken his own life and then read a short letter that he said had been penned by the accused. "I call on the immortal gods to witness," Piso wrote, "that toward you, Caesar, I have acted loyally, with similar respect for your mother." He went on to beg Tiberius to spare his sons Gnaeus and Marcus and lamented that he hadn't taken Marcus's advice when he'd counseled him not to accept the post of governor of Syria when Tiberius offered it. At no point did Piso state that he intended to take his own life. Tacitus says that, in his younger days, he himself had spoken with aged senators who'd been convinced that someone had been sent to kill Piso. As for the mysterious letter held by Piso in court, it disappeared.[40]

Tiberius proceeded to wrap up the case, calling on the Senate to exonerate Piso's sons. He then shocked many by saying that, at the request of his mother, he was asking for a full pardon for Plancina. The senior consul present, Aurelius Cotta, recommended that the emperor's requests be acceded to and then proposed a series of punishments for the dead Piso, involving his name and estate. Tiberius even watered down that proposal. In the end, the Senate pardoned Plancina and Marcus but confiscated Piso's estate, only to give half to the pardoned Marcus. The Senate also required Piso's eldest son, who shared the same first name with his father, Gnaeus, to change his name. Becoming Lucius Piso, he would twice figure in dramatic episodes in Caligula's life in years to come.

"This was the end of avenging the life of Germanicus," says Tacitus. With Piso's life snuffed out, Tiberius was able to shut down the affair. The road ahead for the wife and children of Germanicus was about to become deadly.[41]

# VI

## NURSING A VIPER

With their father's death, Nero Germanicus, Drusus Germanicus, and Caligula were seen by the Roman people as heirs to the throne, but Tiberius's natural son Drusus the Younger, or Castor, was the heir apparent, and Tiberius made Castor the guardian of Germanicus's boys. Nero Germanicus shared his father's best qualities, and the Senate officially lauded both Caligula's teenage brothers, who were serious, intelligent boys. But Tiberius declined to approve honors for them, and Praetorian commander Sejanus planted spies among their servants. Seven-year-old Caligula, on the other hand, amused Tiberius. The boy liked to sing and dance. Seeing him as no threat, Tiberius left him in his mother's care.

Sejanus had his eyes firmly on the throne. To achieve his goal, he intended eliminating all rivals, which, in particular, included the family of Germanicus. With their patron dead and the friends of Sejanus in the ascendancy, Germanicus's former clients were whittled away from his widow until just one brave equite would continue to pay his respects to Agrippina. Tacitus says that Sejanus deliberately set out to destroy what he called "the party of Agrippina." He began with the general Gaius Silius, for whom "the friendship of Germanicus was fatal," says Tacitus. Prosecuted in the Senate on false charges, Silius took his own life, hoping to preserve his family.[42]

Seeing the fate of the widely esteemed Silius, some former friends of Germanicus promptly ceased making visits to his widow. Several years later, one friend, Titius Sabinus, would be infamously trapped into speaking ill of Tiberius while agents of Sejanus hid, listening, in the space between ceiling and roof above. Others, like Quintus Servaeus, one of the prosecutors in the Piso trial, saw the proverbial writing on the wall, or supposed he did, and joined Sejanus's camp.

Sejanus even set out to separate Agrippina from her circle of female friends. Silius's wife, Sosia Galla, a relative and close friend of Agrippina, was exiled at Sejanus's direction. Sejanus then employed noted orator Domitius Afer to lead a successful prosecution with trumped-up charges against Agrippina's cousin Claudia Pulchra. When Domitius bumped into Agrippina one day following this, he stepped out of her way, looking embarrassed.

"Don't worry, Domitius," said Agrippina, before quoting Homer. "It isn't you I blame; it's Agamemnon." By "Agamemnon," she meant Tiberius. For she was convinced that Tiberius was behind the campaign against her.[43]

Strong-willed Agrippina decided to grab the bull by the horns. Going to Tiberius and finding him sacrificing to Augustus, she barged in and interrupted him, declaring that her cousin Claudia's only mistake was to admire her. Tiberius rebuked her for her haughtiness, quoting Greek verse as he reminded her she was no queen. Agrippina soon after contracted a serious illness, and, as she lay in her sickbed, Tiberius paid her a visit. For a long time, she lay silently crying, before begging Tiberius to choose her a new husband to relieve her loneliness. He didn't reply, but as she recovered, Tiberius, fearing a political motive behind her request, left her a widow. Agrippina became a powerless and friendless pariah.

Sejanus had meanwhile further promoted his ambitions by beginning an affair with Caligula's aunt Livilla, sister of Germanicus and ambitious wife of Tiberius's son Castor, immediate heir to the throne. Sejanus apparently convinced Livilla that they could jointly rule the empire as a new Antony and Cleopatra, for, in AD 23, Livilla helped Sejanus poison Castor and then convinced Tiberius that he'd died from natural causes. But Sejanus's request to then marry Livilla, and thus become part of the imperial family, was turned down flat by Tiberius. When Tiberius then anointed Caligula's brothers Nero Germanicus and Drusus Germanicus as his heirs, Sejanus set his lethal sights on them and their mother.

Devious Sejanus subsequently convinced Tiberius to invite Agrippina to dinner, knowing that each loathed and mistrusted the other. Sejanus then sent senators to Agrippina to warn her not to eat the apples at the emperor's banquet. When Tiberius offered her apples, traditional last course of a Roman meal, tactless, fearful Agrippina declined, leaving the emperor suspecting that she thought he was trying to poison her. As Sejanus had planned, this infuriated Tiberius and further alienated her from him. But as Germanicus's widow, Agrippina was still immensely popular with the Roman public. With her arrest likely to spark riots, Sejanus held back on taking action against her . . . for the moment.

Tiberius, weary of Rome, withdrew in AD 26 to the Isle of Capri, off the Italian west coast near Naples, where a dozen spectacularly placed imperial villas overlooked the sea. Taking staff, courtiers, and bodyguards of the German Guard with him, Tiberius left Sejanus in charge at Rome, although all final governmental decisions continued to rest with emperor. Tiberius would never again set foot in Rome.

Robert Graves, in his novel *I, Claudius*, paints a colorful but inaccurate picture of thirteen-year-old Caligula at this time: "He's treacherous, cowardly, lustful, vain, deceitful, and he'll play some very dirty tricks on you." While these qualities could be attributed to Caligula once he took the throne, in reality while Tiberius was still alive, Caligula kept his vices under wraps. In fact, up to this point, Caligula had been carefully displaying "exemplary" and "dutiful" behavior, according to Suetonius, as his every move was governed by Tiberius's commands and observed by Sejanus's spies.[44]

Caligula had learned to trust very few people and to let nothing slip about his thoughts or true nature. According to Philo of Alexandria, a Jewish philosopher who would meet Caligula and deal with members of his court, as a defense mechanism Caligula developed the ability to read faces. "He was very acute at comprehending a man's innermost designs and feelings from his outward appearance and expression," says Philo.[45]

Tiberius would also have taken an interest in his adoptive grandson and ward's sexual education. Young men of the Roman elite were expected to be sexually accomplished when they wed, but their brides, unless married previously, were expected to be virgins. To give them experience, families arranged for their sons to go to bed with high-class whores. In Caligula's case, his instructress in the secrets of the bedroom was a prostitute named Pyrallis, and, according to Suetonius, he fell in love with her. Suetonius also says that, just before his sixteenth birthday, Caligula was found in bed with his twelve-year-old sister Drusilla, by Antonia, their grandmother.[46] If this was true, Antonia would have scolded them severely but kept her discovery a secret, to protect both children from Sejanus. This information would have been enough to have the pair charged in the Senate with incest.

Did Caligula actually go as far as having sexual relations with Drusilla? Josephus, who was a child during Caligula's reign, was convinced of it, but offers no corroborating evidence. Suetonius, writing four decades later, was the only classical source to accuse Caligula of incestuous relationships with all three of his sisters. The occasional modern scholar has been prepared to accept that claim at face value, but others disagree. Even the claim that Caligula and Drusilla had sexual relations "need not be taken seriously," says Caligula scholar Anthony Barrett.[47]

As for triple incest: "The claim that the emperor committed incest with his three sisters is misinformation," says German scholar Aloys Winterling. He adds, "Its hollowness is easily proved." In support of his argument, Winterling points out that neither of the two main ancient sources on Caligula who actually knew him in person, Seneca and Philo, made any reference to such supposed incestuous relationships. As Winterling also highlights, both these writers "heap invective on the emperor" in their writings, yet never include incest among their accusations, despite making clear their hate of him.[48]

Seneca was himself later accused of having illicit sexual relations with two of Caligula's sisters, Livilla and Agrippina, and found guilty in the first instance. Even if he would not have wanted to slander two women of whom he was fond, that shouldn't have prevented him from accusing Caligula of bedding Drusilla. Seneca made no such accusation.

In AD 28, two years after Tiberius's relocation to Capri, Sejanus convinced the emperor to allow his close relative Aelia Paetina, who was either Sejanus's sister or cousin, to be wed to Caligula's uncle Claudius. With his influence over Tiberius now unchallenged, Sejanus felt confident enough to move against Caligula's mother and twenty-two-year-old big brother Nero Germanicus. Drusus Germanicus, Caligula's other brother, was, we are told by ancient sources, jealous of big brother Nero, whom he felt was their mother's favorite. Sejanus had Agrippina and her eldest son placed under house arrest, with Praetorian centurions stationed outside their doors.

The indications are that Agrippina was kept at her own country retreat, a villa in Herculaneum, not far from Pompeii. House arrest was almost as bad as imprisonment, for, on Tiberius's orders, in addition to being prevented from leaving their place of residence, those undergoing house arrest were permitted no contact with other prisoners or even allowed books to read. Agrippina's loneliness only increased.

In the Senate the following year, Sejanus again moved against Caligula's eldest brother, Tiberius's now heir apparent, having him accused of homosexuality. Convicted by the compliant Senate in AD 29, Nero Germanicus was removed from house arrest and sent to the prison island of Pontia, today's Ponza, off the west coast of Italy. At the same time, Caligula's mother, Agrippina, was dispatched to the rocky, barren prison island of Pandataria, also off the west coast.

On Tiberius's orders, both were transported to the ships that were to convey them to their prison islands in closed litters and wearing manacles on their wrists and fetters on their ankles. Passersby weren't even permitted by the Praetorian Guard escort to look at the litter. So, as the litter passed, civilians had to turn their backs. Worse was to come for Agrippina: on her arrival on Pandataria, a Praetorian centurion gave her a whipping that took out one of her eyes.

Caligula was now put under the care of one of his female relatives. Suetonius says that for a brief time he was put into the hands of his unpleasant great-grandmother Livia Augustus, who hated Germanicus, Agrippina, and their children. It was Livia, if you remember, who'd been accused of commissioning Piso and Plancina to harass and finally murder Germanicus. Tacitus, however, indicates that Livia was already dead. If that wasn't the case, Livia was soon to pass.[49]

On Tiberius's orders, seventeen-year-old Caligula was granted priestly offices previously held by his late uncle Castor and was called upon to give Livia's funeral oration. The youth surprised listeners with an accomplished oration. With Livia deceased, Caligula lived with his sisters and grandmother Antonia at the Palace of Germanicus, which, Josephus says, made up one of the wings of the larger Palace of Tiberius.[50]

The following year, AD 30, Tiberius increased his influence over the lives of Germanicus's surviving children, who were all now his wards. First, he ordered Caligula's sixteen-year-old sister Agrippina the Younger to marry Lucius Domitius Ahenobarbus, a much older man and a distant relative of Augustus. The couple wed in Rome, without Tiberius being present to give away the bride. Around the same time, Tiberius ordered eighteen-year-old Caligula to Capri. On the island, Tiberius performed the boy's coming of age ceremony, now two years overdue, which involved the first ceremonial shaving of his youthful beard, and then informed him that he would now be living permanently on Capri with him.

With the youth a veritable captive, the debauched emperor proceeded to teach Caligula all his depraved sexual habits with both women and boys, and indentured him into the profession of cruelty by making the boy watch tortures and deadly gladiatorial contests. Tiberius had built a "sporting house" on Capri, which consisted of a villa with a swimming pool. Here he would indulge his pedophilic desires, including having boys swim under him in the pool and nibble at his genitals. All indications point to Caligula being sickened by this lifestyle, but he'd learned that, to survive, he must always be agreeable to whatever Tiberius wanted. "Never was there a better slave, or a worse master!" someone is said to have remarked of the pair. Suetonius claims that Tiberius gloated, "I'm nursing a viper for the Roman people."[51]

Caligula wasn't the only victim of the emperor's sexual deviations. Tiberius had gathered a coterie of young men on Capri, the sons of the elite, with the promise to their fathers that they could expect career advancement for sending him their boys. One such youth was the tall Aulus Vitellius. Two years Caligula's junior, he was another future emperor of Rome. Vitellius spent his youth among Tiberius's male prostitutes who specialized in threesomes—called Spintrians by the Romans—from which he gained the nickname "Spintria." "The story goes that he secured his father's first advancement to public office," says Suetonius. That father, Lucius Vitellius, was made a consul by Tiberius in AD 34 and governor of Syria the following year—his reward for pandering his own son to Tiberius. As for Aulus, while he would become a married man and father, he would later develop an abiding passion for his slave boy lover Asiaticus.[52]

Caligula was thrown into this milieu with young Aulus, who became his friend, and Marcus Lepidus, a great-grandson of Augustus whose ancestor of the same name had shared the triumvirate with Augustus and Antony. Allegedly among Caligula's partners in the sexual activities supervised by Tiberius, Lepidus, although six years older than him, became Caligula's best friend. One of the male prostitutes linked to Caligula during this period was the handsome Mnester, an entertaining young freedman who would soon show promise on the stage as a mime actor.

Another of the noble youths caught in Tiberius's depraved net was Valerius Catullus, whose ancestor, another Valerius Catullus, a contemporary of Julius Caesar, Pompey, and Cicero, had been a noted first-century BC poet. Young Catullus would later boast (following Caligula's death) that he buggered Caligula during these years, and his father's reward from Tiberius had been a consulship in AD 31. Young Catullus would go on to become a member of the elite College of Pontiffs, which, ironically, governed Rome's religion and morals.

# VII

## CALIGULA'S GRANDMOTHER BRINGS DOWN SEJANUS

Sejanus, having removed Agrippina and Nero Germanicus from the picture, now moved against Caligula's remaining brother, Drusus Germanicus, who was married to Aemilia Lepida, sister of Caligula's good friend Marcus Lepidus. Based on information provided by Aemilia, and which was no doubt frightened out of her, one of Sejanus's lackeys, the senator Cassius Severus, accused Drusus of plotting against Tiberius. The young man was locked in a dungeon cell at the palace. The centurion and freedman in charge of his guard recorded his every word and movement, even down to the names of the freedmen who brought him food, all of whom were encouraged to either beat him or frighten him one way or another. Now, of Germanicus's sons, only Caligula remained free.

AD 31 proved to be the culmination of Sejanus's campaign for total power. Having convinced Tiberius to make him one of the consuls for the year, he dispatched a Praetorian centurion to Caligula's brother Nero Germanicus on Pontia. The centurion showed Nero a noose and told the prisoner he had a choice—take his own life, or the centurion would take it for him. Nero committed suicide. Sejanus then sent Tiberius a report that Nero had killed himself, without mentioning the centurion's role in the affair.

Caligula must have been terrified by the news of his brother's death. Suspecting that Sejanus had agents among his servants, he never uttered a word about his family's fate. Those agents would have tried to trick him into saying something detrimental about Tiberius, however Caligula was clever enough to avoid every trap. But the tide was turning against Sejanus. In the early spring, from Rome, Caligula's grandmother Antonia secretly sent Tiberius a letter containing compelling evidence of Sejanus's plan to murder Tiberius and Caligula and take the throne for himself and Castor's widow, Livilla.

Tiberius, isolated on Capri, had always trusted his sister-in-law. Convinced by Antonia's evidence and terrified that he could be acting too late, he plotted Sejanus's surprise arrest in Rome. In October, he gave the delicate and secret mission to Quintus Naevius Cordus Sutorius Macro, prefect of Rome's *Vigiles Urbani*, commonly known as the Night Watch and least senior of all the military and paramilitary units stationed at the capital. Fifty-two-year-old Macro was the only man Tiberius felt he could trust to counter Sejanus and save him.

Macro discreetly returned to Rome, where he appointed a subordinate, Laco, to command the Night Watch. On the evening of October 18, as Macro expected, he encountered Sejanus outside the Senate, which had been in session since dawn. As was always the case during sittings, the Senate House was surrounded by troops of Sejanus's Praetorian Guard. Macro carried a sealed document, and he told Sejanus this was a letter from Tiberius to the Senate announcing that Sejanus was to be forthwith granted the same powers of veto over Senate decisions that the emperor himself possessed. This right of veto had previously been vested only in the heir to the throne. Excited by this, Sejanus entered the Senate to share the news with senatorial friends.

Macro then went to the tribune commanding the Praetorian cohort on duty at the Senate House and showed him another letter from the emperor. This instructed all members of Rome's military to obey any command by Macro, who promptly ordered the tribune to march his troops back to barracks and confine them there. In a move synchronized by Macro with Laco, as the Praetorians marched away, troops of the Night Watch marched in and took their place. Macro, entering the Senate, handed the first letter to presiding consul Memmius Regulus, whom Tiberius trusted; Regulus's consular colleague was a known Sejanus supporter.

Opening the letter, the consul read it to the House as Sejanus listened expectantly. But the letter was not what Macro had led Sejanus to expect.

After a benign preamble, it contained a call from the emperor for Sejanus's immediate arrest. Now the Senate turned on Sejanus. "All with one voice denounced and threatened him," says Dio, "some because they had been wronged, some to conceal their friendship with him, still others out of joy at his downfall."[53] Consul Regulus asked a single senator whether Sejanus should be arrested, and when he agreed, Regulus had the Night Watch troops seize Sejanus and put him in chains. Regulus, Laco, and the magistrates escorted a stunned Sejanus through the crowd outside to the nearby city prison, the Tullianum.

As Sejanus tried to cover his head and protect himself, members of the public lashed out at him. According to Seneca, they almost tore Sejanus limb from limb, leaving very little for the public executioner.[54] A little time later, with the Praetorians continuing to obey Macro's command to remain off the streets and refraining from interfering with proceedings on Sejanus's behalf, the Senate felt secure enough to reconvene in the Temple of Concord. There, they voted the death penalty for Sejanus. He was immediately garroted in the Tullianum, with his body thrown down the Gemonian Stairs. His remains would be tossed into the River Tiber.

Meanwhile, on Capri that same night, Tiberius was anxiously pacing up and down on a promontory with his eyes fixed on the mainland, waiting to see a beacon light up. If it remained unlit come dawn, he intended fleeing to the East in a waiting flotilla. To his relief, the beacon glowed orange across the water, the signal that Sejanus had fallen and that Tiberius's throne had been preserved.

At Rome, Macro took charge of the Praetorian Guard, and over the coming days undertook a purge of his own, arresting Sejanus's family and key supporters. Sejanus's eldest boy, Strabo, was executed by sword on October 24. In December, Sejanus's younger children would be garroted in the Tullianum. With Roman law prohibiting the execution of virgins, the executioner used the expediency of raping Sejanus's daughter Junilla, who was aged under ten at the time, before garroting her. The children's bodies were thrown down the Gemonian Stairs, emulating the fate of their father. Their only crime had been to have Sejanus for their parent. To some, the new regime was no better than the last.

Sejanus's former wife, Apicata, the mother of his children, took her own life on October 26, but before she died she sent Tiberius a letter in which she detailed how Sejanus and Livilla had combined to murder his son Castor. Some would comment that Apicata did this purely out of spite, and that she had invented the accusation. Several of Livilla's slaves subsequently confessed under torture to administering poison to Castor on her orders. Although Apicata's letter certainly was written in spite, the overwhelming evidence of Sejanus's progressive elimination of rivals suggests that her revelation was factual. Certainly the Roman Senate believed it.

Sejanus was such a manipulative villain that it's a wonder William Shakespeare never wrote a play around him. Shakespeare's contemporary Ben Jonson did write the play *Sejanus—His Fall*, with an unnamed coauthor who, it has been speculated, was Shakespeare. Certainly, Shakespeare's *Othello* contains echoes of Sejanus in the villainous, manipulative Iago.

Sejanus's partner in crime, Livilla, Caligula's aunt, was the daughter of Antonia, the whistleblower who'd brought about Sejanus's downfall. The following January, when the Senate condemned Livilla for ordering the murder of Castor, Antonia was so disgusted that her own flesh and blood could be so heinous as to plot with Sejanus to bring down the house of the Caesars, she had a sobbing Livilla boarded up in her bedroom. There, Livilla starved to death.

Caligula was now one of three surviving heirs to Tiberius's throne. The other two were his imprisoned brother Drusus, and Tiberius Gemellus, son of Castor and the late unlamented Livilla. Gemellus, Tiberius's natural grandson, was seven years younger than Caligula. Just as Antonia was Caligula's grandmother, she was also Gemellus' grandmother, and with both the boy's parents now dead, she brought Gemellus to the Palace of Germanicus to join the brood of young royals in her care.

But Sejanus was not the only threat to the family of Germanicus, as Tiberius had approved of all that Sejanus had done to Agrippina and her eldest sons. In AD 33, eighteen months after Sejanus's removal, Tiberius ordered Caligula's remaining brother, Drusus Germanicus, starved to death in his dungeon cell beneath the Palatium. In desperation, the youth ate straw from his mattress. To the horror of many senators, Tiberius had the jailer's diary of the youth's last tortured days, including every word he said, read aloud to the Senate.

Caligula's mother, Agrippina, who was still a prisoner on Pandataria, was told of her son's cruel death by her jailers. Sustained until then by hope, or so Tacitus supposed, she gave up and committed suicide. Not very long after Agrippina's death, Plancina, the despised co-conspirator in the demise of Agrippina's husband, Germanicus, who'd lived for another thirteen years following the death of Piso, also took her own life.[55]

Caligula, the last of Germanicus's sons, was alone and under threat. Suetonius says that he didn't utter a word when he learned of the tragic deaths of his brothers and mother, which Suetonius took as indifference to their fate and his own.[56] Caligula was, of course, acutely aware that, if he didn't appear disinterested, he was likely to share his brothers' fate. Now, when Macro the powerful new Praetorian commander acted warmly toward him, he guardedly welcomed his friendship, hopeful that he was a potential protector.

Macro, seeing Caligula's potential as a successor to Tiberius, and equally, seeing the youth's vulnerability, soon set up an affair between his wife, Ennia Naeva, and Caligula.[57] Ancient sources were divided on this affair, with some, based on his later behavior, feeling that Caligula lasciviously initiated and conducted it behind Macro's back. Others believed that Macro set it up and then pretended ignorance of it to manipulate the youth, and modern historians share this view of the situation. "The version in Philo and Suetonius that the initiative was Caligula's and that Macro was ignorant of the affair must be rejected in favor of the stories in Tacitus and Dio," says historian Arther Ferrill, adding, "Ennia, Macro's wife, seduced Caligula with the Prefect's blessing."[58] Caligula biographer Anthony

Barrett thought along similar lines, with Aloys Winterling also proposing that Ennia initiated the affair.

The balance of probabilities is that Caligula was indeed not the initiator, but was, rather, the pawn in this affair. Crucially, he was demonstrably taking care to avoid incurring Tiberius's suspicion, or worse, his wrath. Suetonius does tell us, and, probably accurately in this instance, that Caligula became besotted with Ennia, the same way he'd been besotted with the prostitute Pyrallis, even giving Macro's wife a promise in writing that if he became emperor he would marry her. Whether Macro had masterminded the affair or not, now he had Caligula under his control, securing his own future.[59]

Tiberius decreed that Caligula must marry, choosing as his grandson's bride Junia Claudilla, daughter of respected senator Marcus Junius Silanus, who, now in his fifties, had been a consul in AD 15. We know nothing about Junia's age or appearance, so she may have been as young as thirteen at the time, which was the legal marrying age for Roman women. Caligula would not make her pregnant until two years into their marriage. Tiberius, who still refused to re-enter Rome, presided over their wedding, which included a public festival, at Caligula's coastal birthplace, Antium, with Capri becoming the newlyweds' home. Caligula's sister Drusilla married the same year, also on Tiberius's orders; her spouse was a much older man, Gaius Cassius Longinus, a consul in AD 30.

Tiberius didn't have many years of life left. To survive, all Caligula had to do now was keep out of trouble and outlive his adoptive grandfather. Trouble, however, was about to find him.

# VIII

## YIELDING THE UPPER HAND

In the spring of AD 36, Marcus Julius Agrippa, grandson of the late King Herod of Judea and later to become known as Herod Agrippa, arrived at Tiberius's court after fleeing the city of Jamnia in Judea. He was soon to play a leading role in the life of Caligula. Forty-seven-year-old spendthrift Agrippa owed money throughout the East, and Tiberius came to learn that he'd yet to repay a large loan to Gaius Herennius Capito, who, as a personal procurator to the emperor, managed estates around Jamnia that Tiberius had inherited from his mother, Livia. Capito, a former military tribune and now also a part-time prefect of retired veteran soldiers of Rome's Evocati military reserve, had even sent some of those veterans in chase of Agrippa, who had succeeded in escaping by ship to Italy.[60]

Tiberius initially gave Agrippa a warm welcome, but, on hearing from Capito, he banned the prince from his presence until the debt was repaid. So, the handsome, sociable Agrippa borrowed the money from Caligula's grandmother Antonia and repaid Capito. Once the debt to Capito was cleared, Tiberius welcomed Agrippa back to his court and recommended that Antonia employ him as tutor to Caligula's cousin Gemellus, which Antonia did.

Agrippa had been brought up in Rome from the age of four. His father Aristobulus IV, one of Herod the Great's sons, had been executed by Herod in 7 BC, after which Agrippa and his brothers Herod and Aristobulus had been sent to Augustus to be raised as good Romans. Living with Tiberius and his family, Agrippa and his brothers had been schooled with Caligula's uncles Claudius and Castor, to whom they became close.

Despite later proving to be a devout Jew and being a member of Eastern nobility, Agrippa had taken on Roman dress and ways, including the habit of being clean shaven, and fitted neatly into imperial court life.

During those years, he'd come to know young Caligula well. Caligula, for his part, had soon come to like and trust Agrippa, thinking of him as a father figure. Their bond was so strong that, when they shook hands on meeting, Caligula would have "yielded the upper hand."

The handshake had great significance to Romans. As a form of greeting, it goes back thousands of years, well before the foundation of Rome. It's thought that it evolved from a desire to demonstrate that one had no weapon in the right hand, which was the sword hand, and therefore harbored no evil intent. Hollywood would popularize a Roman handshake showing each participant gripping the other at the wrist; however, this derives from a carved stone image of two grasped hands that was exchanged by cities as a symbol of friendship.

The Romans came to practice the same handshake that we know today, with the hand of each participant interlocked and upright. But if you wanted to show great respect to another person, you would offer your hand palm up, so that the other person shook your hand in the dominant position with their palm down. This was known as "yielding the upper hand."

Caligula would have yielded the upper hand to Agrippa because he was a man he liked and respected, yet who was at arm's length from the lethal internal politics of Rome. The feelings were reciprocated, and each man would remain loyal to the other to the end of Caligula's life, despite Agrippa putting pressure on the relationship in AD 36 and Caligula doing the same late in his reign.

Not only had Tiberius brought Caligula to live with him on Capri, he'd done the same with Caligula's cousin Gemellus, and Gemellus's personal staff, including his new tutor Agrippa, came too. This allowed Caligula to renew his firm friendship with Agrippa. One day in March AD 36, Agrippa and Caligula went on an outing in a two-horse chariot, called a *biga*, driven by one of Agrippa's servants. Once out of the hearing of Tiberius and his staff, the pair spoke of many things. At one point, apparently as the chariot's horses were resting and the two men stood looking at the view, with their driver sitting at their feet, Agrippa ventured to raise the subject of Tiberius.

"I pray to God," said Agrippa with exasperation, "that Tiberius may soon go off the stage and leave the government to you. For you are in every respect more worthy of it."[61]

Caligula, accustomed to keeping his thoughts to himself, made no direct reply. Instead, he probably changed the subject, and the conversation moved on to other things.

This same year, Caligula's wife, Junia, died in childbirth, and their child died with her. Whether Caligula grieved for Junia, we are not to know; the ancient sources tell us nothing about their relationship. Caligula, at twenty-four, was now a widower, but Tiberius proved in no hurry to arrange a new marriage for his grandson.

Modern writers tell us that Tiberius spent the last eleven years of his life as a recluse on Capri. In fact, during spring and summer, Tiberius would take his court from Capri to various villas in Italy, sometimes on the west coast, sometimes in the Alban Hills. In September AD 36, six months after the incident where Agrippa had told Caligula he would make a better ruler than Tiberius, the emperor was sojourning on the Italian mainland at a villa at Tusculum in the Alban Hills, just sixteen miles from Rome.

This villa was so large that it had its own hippodrome. A feature of the villas of Rome's ultra-rich, this type of hippodrome mostly served an ornamental purpose, being only wide enough to permit horse races rather than chariot races, with its terraces laid out with plants. Following lunch, Tiberius frequently took a walk around this hippodrome. One hot afternoon in the late summer, accompanied by members of his entourage, including Caligula and Agrippa, Tiberius was about to stroll around the hippodrome when Caligula's continued existence was unexpectedly threatened, through the agency of Agrippa and his freedman Eutychus.

Agrippa had freed Eutychus, whose name means "Lucky," and given him a position of trust. But the fellow's luck had run out; after being caught stealing clothing from Agrippa, he'd languished in prison in Rome, awaiting Tiberius's judgment as a member of the imperial freedman establishment. In hopes of escaping punishment, Eutychus had informed City Prefect Lucius Piso, who was in effect Rome's chief of police, that months before, while driving Agrippa and Caligula in a chariot, he'd overheard Agrippa tell Caligula that he wished that Tiberius was dead and that Caligula was emperor.

This Piso, the city prefect, was the eldest son of Piso and Plancina, the accused murderers of Caligula's father, Germanicus. He was also an intimate friend of Tiberius, having been appointed a consul by him in AD 27 and, more recently, receiving his city prefecture after a two-day binge of eating and drinking with Tiberius and the senator Pomponius Flaccus, another of Tiberius's intimates.

Apparently keen to incriminate Germanicus's surviving son Caligula and win Tiberius's favor, Piso sent Eutychus to Capri for a hearing before Tiberius. With the emperor infamous for putting off appointments and hearings, the prisoner sat in a dungeon cell on Capri for months. Agrippa, keen to have the case cleared up, and unaware of the specifics of Eutychus's accusation against him, had urged his patron Antonia, Caligula's grandmother, to have Tiberius hear the freedman's case. Antonia was all the more trusted by Tiberius after she'd alerted him to Sejanus's ambitions. So, when one night after dinner at her quarters at Tusculum she walked beside the emperor's sedan chair as he was being carried away, she was able to convince him to give Eutychus a hearing.

The prisoner was brought from Capri, escorted by Praetorian commander Macro and men of the Praetorian Guard, who administered Rome's prison system. When the prisoner reached the villa, he was presented to the emperor just as Tiberius was about to do his post prandial circuit of the hippodrome. Tiberius was now seventy-eight years old, tall, bony, bald, and stooping, with plasters covering sores on his pale face.[62]

"What do have to say about this man who gave you your freedom?" he demanded of Eutychus, indicating Agrippa, who stood with Caligula.

"Oh, my lord," Eutychus replied, "this Gaius and Agrippa were once riding in a chariot when I sat at their feet. Among the other things they discussed, I heard Agrippa say, 'Oh, I wish the day would soon come that this old fellow would die and name you his successor as governor of all the world. Gemellus his grandson wouldn't be a problem—you could get rid of him, and the world would be happy, and I'd be happy.'"

Anger could be seen rising in the aged emperor. "Bind this man!" he ordered Macro, before turning and stomping away on his walk.

Macro was left stunned. He couldn't believe that the emperor meant Agrippa, but Tiberius had been looking at him when he gave the order. So Macro and the others waited as Tiberius completed a circuit of the hippodrome. As the emperor was returning, Macro called, "Caesar, could you repeat more distinctly what you said? Which man am I to bind?"

Tiberius's eyes flared with rage. "To be clear," he came back, "this is the man I meant you to bind." He nodded toward Agrippa.

"Which man?" asked Marco, still in doubt.

"Agrippa!" snapped Tiberius.

At this, Agrippa protested his innocence. "Sir, would you believe this fellow? I'm the man who grew up alongside your son, the man who's educated your grandson . . ."

But Tiberius had made up his mind, and with a wave of the hand he dismissed Agrippa, and Macro chained him and hustled him away, bound for prison at Rome. Josephus, who details this incident, writes that the freedman's words had rung true with Tiberius because, although he'd previously ordered Agrippa to be respectful to Gemellus, it seemed to him that Agrippa had attached his allegiance to Caligula.[63]

All through this exchange, Caligula had remained silent. Not a word did he offer in Agrippa's defense. In the interest of self-preservation, his lips remained sealed. Fortunately for him, Eutychus didn't accuse him of agreeing with Agrippa in the chariot, and that saved him, although Tiberius must have now suspected Caligula's loyalty, must have wondered why Caligula hadn't reported Agrippa's subversive conversation. From now on, Caligula knew, he would be walking a tightrope. The slightest slip, and he would be done for.

Agrippa, for his part, was unimpressed that Caligula hadn't stood up for him, but at least he didn't implicate the young man. Still dressed in the expensive purple tunic that he'd been wearing at the time of his arrest, and chained by his right wrist to the left wrist of a Praetorian soldier—the normal procedure for moving prisoners—he was being taken from the grounds of the villa on the first stage of a tramp to Rome, when he passed a slave of Caligula's called Thaumustus, who was carrying a pot of water. Realizing that his escort intended to make him walk through the heat of the afternoon all sixteen miles to the capital, Agrippa called to the young slave.

"Thaumustus, will you let me drink?" After the slave did so, Agrippa said to him, "Boy, this service you've done me will be to your advantage. As soon as I'm clear of these bonds I'll pay Gaius to free you—the same Gaius who's failed to give me the same help now I'm in chains that he did before."[64]

Once Agrippa reached Rome, he wasn't lodged with common prisoners in the city prison at the base of the Palatine. Instead, Macro had him locked in a room at the Praetorian Barracks, the *Castra Praetoria*, erected in the east of the city by Sejanus in AD 23. As recent archaeology has found, the rooms of the barracks, while not in the same class as the palace rooms that Agrippa was accustomed to, were clean and functional, with simple mosaics in their black-and-white tiled floors. At least this was a step up from the cold, wet stone floors and walls of the prison.

Back at Tusculum, Caligula's grandmother interceded on Agrippa's behalf. Knowing she would make no headway with Tiberius, Antonia spoke with Macro. "Can your soldiers not treat Agrippa kindly?" she asked the Praetorian commander.[65]

In response, Macro arranged for the centurion in charge of Agrippa to be of a friendly disposition and to eat with the prisoner to give him company. Agrippa also was permitted to bathe in the Praetorians' bathhouse and to receive visits from a friend and two of his freedmen, who brought his favorite foods and clean clothes. For the time being, Agrippa would have to grin and bear it and hope that Tiberius died before ordering his execution.

Meanwhile, at Tusculum, Caligula was considering desperate measures to save his friend. According to a story Caligula himself later told, one night, his affection for Agrippa, his hate for Tiberius, and his secret determination to avenge his father, mother, and brothers combined to see him slip into Tiberius's bedroom with a concealed dagger. Suetonius says that Caligula's intent was to plunge the blade into the emperor while he slept, but once he saw the slumbering old man, all he felt was pity. A simple failure of courage was the more likely cause of his abandonment of the plan. Caligula withdrew without doing the deed.[66]

# IX

# FIRST THROUGH THE DOOR IS EMPEROR

In March AD 37, six months after the incarceration of Agrippa, Tiberius, now seventy-seven, doddery and ailing, relocated with his court to the Italian mainland as was his springtime habit. This time he was staying at the grand Villa of Lucullus at coastal Misenum on the mainland. Built high on the promontory of Misenum by its original owner Marius the consul and taken over by the famous first-century BC general Lucullus, the sprawling villa had sweeping views of the town, naval base, and bay below where warships were frequently out on the water exercising their crews.

As had been the case for years, Tiberius's large entourage included both Caligula and Gemellus. According to Philo of Alexandria, Tiberius had frequently thought of doing away with Caligula in recent times, the same way he'd done away with his brothers Nero and Drusus, but Macro the Praetorian commander had assured the emperor that Caligula was honest and reliable. When Tiberius continued to harbor dark thoughts about the boy after the Agrippa incident, Macro put his name, and neck, on the line for Caligula.

"I'll stand security for him," he one day told Tiberius. "After all, haven't I given sufficient proof that I'm a friend to both Gaius and to Gemellus, since I was the one who carried out your intentions regarding the downfall of Sejanus?"[67]

Crucially, Macro swore to Tiberius that Caligula was genuinely fond of his cousin and would yield to him if Tiberius chose to make Gemellus his successor. Besides, according to Dio, Tiberius harbored doubts about Gemellus's legitimacy, fearing he may not have been Castor's boy at all but, rather, was the result of Livilla and Sejanus's affair.[68] Ultimately, says Tacitus, Tiberius couldn't summon the resolve to name one or other of the young men as his successor, and, two years earlier, had written a will leaving his estate divided equally between the two.[69]

Now, unwell and knowing he didn't have long to live, Tiberius early one morning came to the conclusion that he would "let Jupiter decide" who would succeed him. He instructed his chamberlain Euodus to summon both Caligula and Gemellus at exactly the same time, without telling them why he wanted to see them. Tiberius's plan was that whoever came through the door first would be the next emperor. Tiberius confided to staff that, in his heart, he hoped that Jupiter would send Gemellus through the door first.[70]

But teenager Gemellus decided to have breakfast before he answered his grandfather's summons. When the door to the emperor's chamber opened, it was Caligula who walked in. Accepting this as "Jupiter's will," Tiberius sighed and informed Caligula he would be the next emperor. When Gemellus finally arrived, Tiberius burst into tears, and, embracing the boy, informed him that he had just anointed Caligula as his successor.

Tacitus says that, as the tears flowed and he clutched Gemellus, Tiberius said to Caligula, "You will kill him, and another will kill you."[71]

Philo says that Tiberius made Caligula promise to treat Gemellus well and keep him safe once he took the throne.[72] Dio tells of a warning that Tiberius gave Caligula that day, or shortly after, about how he should treat the members of the Senate. "Show no affection for any of them, and spare none of them. For they all hate you (when you are emperor) and they all pray for your death, and they will murder you if they can."

Caligula may have later invented this advice, yet it reflects Tiberius's contempt for and dread of the Senate by that stage and was probably factual. Dio agrees that Tiberius did indeed decide to make Caligula his successor at this time, after which the old emperor seems to have informed other members of his court, including Macro, of his decision. However, crucially, the emperor did not change his will.[73]

Soon after this, Tiberius fell seriously ill after wrenching his shoulder throwing a javelin in a contest at Misenum. For days, he lay ill in his bed at the Villa of Lucullus. Then, on March 16, he was pronounced dead by his doctor. There are several differing ancient accounts of his death, including that Tiberius died of natural causes. Others tell a different story, which add up to the following: Tiberius's imperial seal ring was removed, and, led by Macro, courtiers and staff hailed Caligula emperor and commenced to celebrate, only for Tiberius to stir and ask for food. Shock and horror replaced joy until, on Macro's orders, Tiberius was smothered with bed-clothes. The celebrations resumed.

At Rome, news reached the imprisoned Agrippa via his friends that the previous day Tiberius had died at Misenum, and he told the centurion of his guard, who lessened restrictions on him. Word then arrived that Tiberius was alive and well. The centurion, believing that Agrippa had tried to deceive him, was close to executing him. Talked out of it, the centurion instead weighed him down with heavy chains. The following day, March 18, the Senate met, announced that Tiberius had indeed died, and hailed Caligula as emperor.

# X

## HAIL, CAESAR CALIGULA!

The cry went up at Rome and around the Empire: "The son of Germanicus is emperor!" At the age of just twenty-four, Gaius "Caligula" Julius Caesar Germanicus was emperor of Rome, with the Senate adding Augustus to his name to signify his accession to the throne. The young man was now in control of an empire that extended from Spain through the modern countries of France, Belgium, Holland, Germany west of the Rhine, Switzerland, Italy, the Balkans, and all the modern nations south of the Danube, as well as Greece, Turkey, Syria, Lebanon, Palestine, Egypt, Libya, Tunisia, and all the islands of the Mediterranean.

On a personal level, Caligula now owned Tiberius's properties. The palaces on the Palatine were now his. All twelve imperial villas on Capri were his, although, understandably, Caligula was never recorded again setting foot on Capri, his veritable prison for years. Caligula would make several country villas his own. One was located at Antium, his birthplace. Another sat beside Lake Nemi in the Alban Hills. He would also visit a seaside villa at Baiae on the Bay of Naples, which would be favored by his nephew Nero when emperor, and also stay at yet another villa farther down the coast on the island of Astura.

From his mother, Caligula inherited the *Horti Agrippinae*, her sprawling gardens flanking the western bank of the Tiber at Rome, near the Vatican Valley. These gardens contained several villas and would become a favorite retreat for Caligula. He also apparently inherited his mother's villa at Herculaneum, near Pompeii on the Bay of Naples, where Tiberius had kept her under house arrest at one time—for, one of Caligula's first acts as emperor was to have that villa torn down, erasing it from existence. The scars of his mother's persecution ran deep, as he was to prove in coming years.

Having grown to despise Tiberius, Romans expected Caligula's reign to bring a new enlightened era. Suetonius writes that Romans around the empire were swept up by "the memory of Germanicus and compassion for a family that had been all but wiped out by successive murders." Caligula's accession to the throne seemed, said Suetonius, "like a dream come true."[74] This is supported by an official inscription at Assos, the city visited by Caligula and his father twenty years before: "Since the coronation of Gaius Caesar Germanicus Augustus, which all mankind had hoped for, the world has found no measure for its joy . . . The happiest age of mankind has arrived."[75]

Assos sent a delegation to Caligula at Rome "to visit him and offer their best wishes and implore him to take care of it (Assos), even as he promised our city upon his first visit to the province in the company of his father."[76] No doubt hundreds of similar delegations from throughout the empire descended on Rome to see the new emperor.

The people of Campania saw their new sovereign close up as Caligula led Tiberius's slow-moving funeral cortege from Misenum to Rome in the second half of March, walking all the way. Suetonius reports that the public displayed "extravagant joy" as Caligula passed. It would be more than week before he entered Rome with his grandfather's remains, along a road lined with the public. Women cried out affectionately to the youth, calling him "pet," "baby," "chicken," and "star" as they wished him and his reign well.[77]

Once the cortege reached Rome on March 28, Caligula delivered Tiberius's funeral oration to a massive crowd on the Field of Mars. Following his cremation, Tiberius's ashes were lodged in a casket in the Mausoleum of Augustus alongside those of Augustus, Livia, Germanicus, and other family members. The Senate met that same day and the next. Macro had been busy behind the scenes, preparing the consuls and influential senators for Caligula's arrival, and now the Senate formally set aside Tiberius's will, in which the empire had been divided between Gaius and Gemellus.

Caligula appeared in the Senate with cousin Gemellus at his side. First announcing that he intended honoring those legacies in Tiberius's will that were intended for legionaries and Praetorians, he then announced that he was formally adopting Gemellus as his son and heir. Caligula also declared that, as Gemellus's legal father, he would officiate at Gemellus's delayed coming of age ceremony on the Capitoline Mount, which he did shortly after. These were astute political moves that brought Caligula ringing praise in the Senate and in the street and bear the mark of Macro's influence.

With the formalities over, the young emperor withdrew to the Palatine and took up residence in Tiberius's palace, which became known as the Palatium of Tiberius and Caligula. As his first official act, Caligula wanted to order the immediate release from imprisonment of his good friend Agrippa, but his grandmother Antonia counseled him to wait awhile—otherwise, she said, it would seem as if he was celebrating Tiberius's death by releasing a man he'd condemned.

Caligula swiftly found a way around this. Perhaps on the advice of Macro, and certainly in a move approved by him, Caligula decreed a general amnesty for all who had been exiled or imprisoned by Tiberius or were awaiting trial. This blanket amnesty increased Caligula's popularity with the Roman people and served the purpose of securing Agrippa's release while avoiding criticism. Caligula promptly ordered Agrippa brought to the Palatium, where he had him shaved, clothed, and then presented with golden chains weighing the same as the iron chains he'd lately been wearing in prison. Caligula had more gifts more his friend—many more.

Caligula granted Agrippa half of King Herod's former territories in the Middle East, which had been governed by Agrippa's uncle Philip the Tetrarch until his death in AD 34. To this Caligula added the title of king, after which Agrippa would become officially known as King Herod Agrippa I. To fund Agrippa's new kingdom, Caligula gave him all the tax revenues gathered by Rome in Philip's former territories since AD 34. Caligula also seems to have gifted Agrippa an imperial residence on the Palatine—possibly Livia's house—and asked him to remain with him at Rome for the time being.

There was another Eastern royal at the palace at this time, Antiochus, son of the late king of Commagene, who'd grown up in Rome as a member of Antonia's remarkable brood of princes and princesses. Caligula

returned Commagene to kingdom status, making Antiochus its ruler—
King Gaius Julius Antiochus IV. Antiochus, a former palace playmate of
Caligula's, was now in his twenties, long-nosed, and Romanized. Caligula
even added a strip of Cilicia to his grant of Commagene so that the land-
locked kingdom stretched to the Mediterranean coast, and refunded to
Antiochus all the tax revenues collected in Commagene over the twenty
years since his father's death.

Once back in Commagene, Antiochus married his sister Iotapa and
made her his queen, emulating his father, who had also married his own sister. Using part of the money granted him by Caligula, Antiochus founded
several new cities in Commagene, naming one Germanicopolis in honor of
Germanicus and his family. Caligula could afford to give these vast sums to
Agrippa and Antiochus because the miserly Tiberius had left Rome's treasury overflowing with cash—between 2.3 billion and 3.3 billion sesterces
in Cassius Dio's estimation.[78]

Among the many leading men apart from Agrippa who benefitted
from the new emperor's sweeping general amnesty was Caligula's brother-
in-law Gnaeus Domitius Ahenobarbus, husband of his sister Agrippina,
who'd been awaiting trial charged with treason, adultery, and incest with
Caligula's other sisters. Another set free was the leading tragic poet of his
day Publius Pomponius Secundus, whom Tiberius had kept under house
arrest for seven years for being a friend of Sejanus, with Publius's brother
Quintus standing surety for him all that time.

Yet another to benefit from the amnesty was Pontius Pilate—actual
last name Pilatus —former prefect of Judea. This was the same Pilate who
presided over the crucifixion of Jesus Christ circa AD 30. According to
Josephus, Pilate had been removed from his Judean post in AD 36 by his
immediate superior Lucius Vitellius, proconsul of Syria, after ten years in
the job, and ordered home to face charges before Tiberius of massacring
Jews in Samaria.[79] It seems that Pilate had come home to Italy by sea, for
he arrived in the early spring of AD 37, once the AD 36–37 sailing season
opened, and not long after Tiberius's death. As a result, under Caligula's
amnesty, Pilate was a free man.

When, months later, one of the returned exiles came to the Palatium to thank Caligula for the amnesty, the new emperor asked the man how he had spent his time in exile. His reply could only have brought a smile to Caligula's face: "I prayed continuously to the gods for Tiberius's death and your accession, my lord Gaius," the man said. "And my prayers were granted."[80]

As part of this amnesty, Caligula also publicly burned the extensive written evidence collected by Sejanus against his mother and brothers, so that informants' names could never be revealed. As the papers burned, the emperor declared he had no desire for the informants' names to be revealed. This would bring him high praise from all levels of society. He also banned from Rome all Spintrians, the male prostitutes who specialized in sex in threesomes and who had garnered Tiberius's favor. According to an approving Suetonius,[81] Caligula could "barely be restrained from drowning the lot."

Within days of this, Caligula traveled by warship to Pandataria and Pontia, ignoring a storm, to collect the ashes of his mother, Agrippina, and brother Nero Germanicus, bringing them back to Rome for proper interment in the Mausoleum of Augustus alongside those of Germanicus. At the same time, Caligula renamed the month of September "Germanicus" after his father, and every May 24 from this point on he would lead sacrifices to the memory of Germanicus.

Caligula also conferred honors on his sisters Agrippina the Younger, Livilla, and Drusilla, and on his grandmother Antonia, although she declined the title "Augusta," a title previously held only by Tiberius's odious mother, Livia. Caligula issued coins that commemorated his father's Triumph in AD 17, coins bearing the image of his mother and the inscription "To the memory of Agrippina," and coins showing his three sisters together. All this proved immensely popular with the Roman people.

The new emperor soon cemented his cabinet around him. He retained Macro, the man who'd secured the throne for him, as his sole prefect of the Praetorian Guard and chief military adviser. According to Josephus, Macro counseled the young emperor to "adopt wise counsels," and, considering the controlling attitude he displayed early in Caligula's reign, Macro would have retained the right of approval to the emperor's other choices for top jobs.[82]

Caligula appointed his able and loyal Greek-born freedman Callistus, who'd been sold to him as a slave when Caligula was a teenager, as his chief secretary, the equivalent of a modern White House chief of staff. Apparently a handsome man—his name meant "gorgeous" in Greek—he took the full name Gaius Julius Callistus when Caligula formally granted his freedom.

Callistus's previous master had considered him useless, but after Callistus became the emperor's right-hand man, that former master was spotted by Seneca one morning standing with a crowd of Callistus's clients as they clustered outside his door before dawn. All were participating in the Roman daily client/patron ritual of paying respects and seeking favors. As Seneca watched, the former master was turned away by Callistus's doorman when all others were welcomed in. "The master sold Callistus," says Seneca, "but how much has Callistus made his master pay for it!"[83]

Callistus had a daughter, Nymphidia, who was at least a teenager at the time that Caligula came to power. Nymphidia's son Nymphidius Sabinus would later claim he was the product of an illicit liaison between his mother and Caligula, although no authority ancient or modern considers that claim valid. According to Josephus, Callistus's powerful new role as the emperor's chief secretary would make him a rich man, as much through bribes in return for favors as through rewards from a grateful emperor. Pliny the Elder would have dinner at Callistus's city house at the height of his power, noting that the former slave's dining room was fabulously decorated with thirty rare onyx columns.[84]

As his secretary of correspondence and petitions, Caligula appointed a freedman by the name of Obulus. Philo of Alexander reported his dealings with this otherwise anonymous official who ran the largest department at the Palatium, with hundreds of freedmen and slaves under his control. Obulus's staff read incoming mail and reports from provincial governors and allied kings, wrote outgoing letters and orders, handwrote hundreds of copies of Rome's daily newspaper the *Acta Diurna* for display on notice boards at Rome and throughout the empire, and wrote and dispatched orders for the movement of military units and appointment and transfer of military officers. This department also received and assessed petitions to the emperor from around the empire, and controlled who was granted audiences with Caligula, and when.[85]

The third senior member of the imperial cabinet during the first century was usually the secretary of finances, but in Caligula's case, this man had a low profile and is not identifiable. We do know that another Greek freedman, Protogenes, was to become Caligula's spymaster, managing a network of paid informants, particularly among the slaves and freedmen and freedwomen in the employ of the Roman upper classes, keeping detailed records of the activities of suspects and supervising arrests and punishments.

To run the domestic side of his Palatium as chamberlain, Caligula appointed Helicon, a former Egyptian slave given to him some years earlier by Tiberius, who had little use for the man at the time. Caligula had found Helicon witty and intelligent, and he'd kept up Caligula's spirits in darker days. Philo of Alexander met Helicon at Rome. Despising him as a Jew hater, Philo described him as "a chattering slave, the perfect scum of the earth."[86] Helicon nonetheless proved totally devoted to his emperor. Going everywhere with Caligula, he would start the day breakfasting with him, then play ball and exercise with him at the baths, then bathe with him, and then even stand guard over his bedroom, sleeping by his door. It seems Helicos also fed Caligula's fascination for all things Egyptian.

Another member of the emperor's inner circle was the freedman Apelles. A native of Ascalon in Palestine, and, according to Philo, another Jew hater, Apelles was one of Rome's most noted and popular tragic stage actors of his day. Philo indicates that Apelles was extremely handsome. In Apelles's youth, says Philo, and before turning to the stage, he'd been a male prostitute. Philo ridicules Apelles, saying that Caligula chose him as a counselor so that he "might have an adviser with whom he could make mocking jests, and with whom he might sing."[87] There is no doubt that

Caligula chose Apelles for his entertainment skills, but he also seems to have employed the actor as a sort of director of imperial theatrical shows and entertainments. With Macro's aversion to actors and dancers, it's likely that Apelles became part of the emperor's inner circle only once Macro departed the scene.

Caligula appointed Cornelius Sabinus as commander of the German Guard, his bodyguard. Sabinus was a former gladiator who fought in the Thracian style with round shield, a short sword, and a dagger. There were as many as thirty classes of gladiatorial combatant, and once trained in that style, gladiators tended to remain in the same class. Many modern authors have fallen into the error of describing Sabinus as a tribune of the Praetorian Guard. This has arisen out of the fact that Josephus, our main source on Sabinus, described him as a *chilarchos*, a term that translators have generally rendered as tribune but which, in reality, was a general Greek term for "commander." Josephus refers to Sabinus as *chilarchos* of the Germans—commander of the German Guard and equivalent of the prefect of the Praetorian Guard.[88] Whether Sabinus held prefect rank is questionable. His post may in fact have been "editor," or in effect "manager," which is a civilian rank reflecting Sabinus's nonmilitary background.

In another reference, in which Josephus described Sabinus's ultimate fate, Josephus tells of Sabinus's background as a gladiator and confirms that he commanded the German Guard.[89] Matching this with Suetonius's comment that Caligula "officered" the German Guard with Thracian gladiators, and the fact that the strict career track of military tribunes of the elite Praetorian Guard precluded gladiators serving in their ranks, it is clear that Cornelius Sabinus was indeed commander of the German Guard, as academics such as John Kerr, who has done specialist research into the Praetorian Guard, have concluded.[90]

Caligula now began a period of wise and lauded rule. He abolished the charge of *maiestas*, the loose treasonous indictment under which Sejanus and Tiberius had destroyed so many Roman lives, including those of Caligula's mother and brothers. He allowed the publication of books banned by Tiberius and Augustus, including those of the historian Aulus

Cremutius Cordus, who'd been critical of Sejanus and committed suicide in AD 25 after being charged by friends of Sejanus with writing treasonous history. Conflicted philosopher Seneca would praise the man's daughter Marcia for republishing his works once Caligula lifted Tiberius's ban, but he couldn't bring himself to praise Caligula for removing the ban.[91]

Caligula also had December's four-day Saturnalia, the Festival of Saturn, extended by a day, creating a fifth, Youth Day, which proved a widely popular innovation. The Saturnalia, which began on December 17, was the Roman forerunner of, and model for, our Christmas holiday. It was Rome's happiest holiday season of the year, a free-spirited series of celebrations including a feast where masters served their servants. As a symbol of the loosening of restrictions during the festival, the wooden shackles on the ankles of the ivory statue of Saturn in the Temple of Saturn by the Forum were traditionally loosened on December 17. The Saturnalia also involved gift giving, serving as forerunner of our modern Christmas gift-giving habit.

Next, Caligula invited every senator and equite to a vast banquet, together with their wives and children, and presented every senator with a toga and every woman with a red or purple scarf. Caligula restored democratic electoral procedures, bringing back the assembly for which the plebeians could stand. He also made it possible for more commoners to advance to the Equestrian Order, improved the legal system, and over-hauled the tax system.

He announced that his neglected forty-six-year-old uncle Claudius was forthwith elevated from the rank of equite to the Senatorial Order and would sit with him as his fellow consul for two months from July. This indicates that Caligula didn't rate his uncle a complete fool. It was Claudius's first official appointment, but it wasn't just for show. In Caligula's absence Claudius would chair sittings of the Senate while con-sul, requiring in-depth knowledge of Roman law and the rules of Senate debate. Claudius had clearly acquired this knowledge while studying and writing Roman history during his years in the shadow of more illustrious family members. Nonetheless, Claudius would anger Caligula when he was slow to have statues of the emperor's two late brothers erected after they'd been approved by the Senate.

Many of Caligula's laudable deeds during this period can be attributed to the influence of Macro, his Praetorian prefect, who became the young emperor's self-appointed guardian and now used his influence over Caligula to moderate his youthful enthusiasm. As Tiberius had found, Caligula adored the theater, singing along with performers from his seat and even getting up and mimicking their dance moves. Now that Caligula was emperor, Macro put a stop to that.

Philo tells of how, during these early months of Caligula's reign, if Macro saw Caligula looking too eagerly at dancers or coming to his feet to join them, he would remind him to act like an emperor, not a child. If Caligula laughed too much like a boy at farces and spectacles, rather than merely smiling with the dignity of his rank, Macro would scold him, and Caligula would correct his puerile antics. If Caligula became carried away with the playing of a harp player, or sang along with a chorus, Macro would lean over and give him a nudge, and Caligula would act more demurely.[92]

Should Macro see the young emperor dropping off to sleep at an entertainment, he would leave his post and wake him, with the philosophy that, "A man who is asleep is a good object for treachery." Other times he would lecture the young ruler on "the science of good government."[93] Macro frequently "reclined" with Caligula at dinner; free people in Roman times reclined on dining couches, with three to a couch on three couches around a low, square table. According to the Christian Gospels, Jesus Christ and his disciples reclined to eat, including at the Last Supper. Only slaves sat upright to eat.[94] And when Macro was reclining near Caligula and saw him act less than regally, he would whisper in his ear.

"You ought not only be unlike anyone else here," Macro lectured Caligula at one dinner, "you should surpass every other man in every action of your life, as much as you surpass them in your good fortune."[95]

In response, Caligula buckled to the will of his mentor. Unlike Tiberius, who'd been heir apparent to Augustus for years, had come to the throne at a mature age, and had been prepared for the role, until Caligula had walked through the door at the Villa of Lucullus only a matter of weeks earlier, he'd made no preparations to fulfill the role of ruler of the known world. He'd come to the throne cowered by years of fear, emotionally immature, and ready to enjoy life at last, singing, dancing, and falling about laughing. Now, by force of personality, Macro forced him to stuff the playful genie back in the bottle and act the part of an emperor, not a boy.

In April, just weeks into Caligula's reign, there was another example of Macro's domination of Caligula. The young emperor had begun to sideline his grandmother Antonia. Unable to obtain an audience with Caligula, Antonia sent for him. We aren't told what she wanted to discuss. Caligula went to her quarters with Macro at his side. When Antonia asked for Macro to withdraw, Caligula insisted he stay. It's probable that Caligula was sour with his grandmother for restraining his hand when he'd sought to free Agrippa in March. He may also have been brooding over her failure to accept the title of Augusta when he offered it. Whatever Antonia asked of Caligula now, he abruptly denied her request.

When Antonia complained, Caligula retorted, "I can treat anyone exactly as I please!"[96]

Interestingly, Macro didn't correct the emperor and didn't suggest he be more courteous to and respectful of his grandmother, as he'd corrected and admonished Caligula over other matters. This was the last time that grandmother and grandson would speak together. Within days, on May 1, seventy-three-year-old Antonia was found dead. Suetonius claims that Caligula's unkind treatment hurried her to her grave. He also repeated gossip that Caligula had hastened her death with poison. Some people would say that Antonia had taken her own life; others that she'd died of natural causes.[97]

According to Suetonius, Caligula showed his grandmother little respect following her death, didn't attend her funeral, and reclined morosely alone in his dining room and watched her burning funeral pyre from a distance— probably from a villa in his mother's Gardens of Agrippina. Another interpretation of Caligula's withdrawal from society at this time was that he was experiencing genuine grief, depression, and shock at the loss of the one person in his life who'd always been there for him.

He would behave in a similar manner the following year when he lost someone else to whom, we know, he was deeply attached. Of that period, Suetonius says, "There were times when he could hardly walk, stand, think, or hold up his head."[98] Today these symptoms are recognized as consistent with depression, which can be triggered by loss. Says one popular medical textbook about severe depression: "Activity can be agitated and restless or slow and retarded . . . sleep, appetite and concentration are disturbed."[99]

As Macro gave him some rein, Caligula bounced back, energetically throwing himself into government. Caligula was a twenty-four-year-old taking over the family business from his conservative seventy-seven-year-old grandfather. He'd come to the throne bursting with ideas and keen to create a reputation as "a promoter of all kinds of innovation," in the words of Philo.[100] To begin with, guided by Macro, Caligula kept his more ambitious ideas in check, authorizing speedy completion of the Temple of Augustus and the rebuilding of the elaborate stage of Pompey's Theater at Rome. The location of Julius Caesar's assassination, the theater had been destroyed by fire in AD 22. Among the few building projects undertaken by Tiberius, these two projects had progressed slowly and remained uncompleted at the time of his death. Conversely, Caligula also ordered work to cease on a triumphal arch for Tiberius that the Senate had previously authorized.

These initiatives were uncontroversial, didn't rock the ship of state, and won Caligula widespread plaudits, enabling him, before long, to go further, initiating more major building projects around the empire, all funded by the still very healthy imperial treasury. These new initiatives weren't opposed by Macro, apparently because all had the appearance of stemming from pious religious motives; in fact, the Senate would vote the young emperor the title "Pious" for his works.

Caligula directed the rebuilding of the walls and temples of Syracuse, Roman capital of Sicily and birthplace of legendary Greek engineer Archimedes. Among structures he ordered restored was Syracuse's Temple of Apollo. He also set in motion the rebuilding of King Polycrates's five-hundred-year-old palace on the Greek island of Samos, near Miletus and Didyma on the Ionian coast, as well as completion of the huge Temple of Apollo at Didyma. Polycrates's favored god was Apollo, who according to legend, was conceived near Didyma. This massive Didyma temple, twice the size of Athens's Parthenon and the third-largest Greek temple in the ancient world, was famed for its resident oracle, which ranked second only to the oracle of Delphi. Rededicated by Alexander the Great centuries earlier, the temple was still incomplete at Caligula's accession.

Temples now being restored by Caligula had the linking theme of Apollo, favored deity of Augustus, who'd erected a Temple of Apollo beside his palace on the Palatine. As Caligula's father, Germanicus, had consulted the oracle at the shrine of Apollo Clarian as Caligula traveled with him to the East as a boy, Apollo seems to have also been a favored god of Germanicus, and this would have influenced his son.

In his writings, Cassius Dio places the Didyma Temple of Apollo at the port of Miletus—the temple precinct was actually ten miles away, with a sacred road linking city and temple. Dio also claimed that Caligula set aside this temple for his own worship—perhaps he eventually did, but modern archeology tells us that Caligula's initial work on the temple, which included completion of the exquisitely carved columns of its platform, was completed in AD 37, during the early months of Caligula's reign and some time before he proclaimed himself a god.[101]

Having heard that Augustus had set up an ancient Egyptian obelisk in the forum at Alexandria, Caligula ordered it brought to Rome to glorify the capital. Again, Macro found no fault with this expensive project. A huge Egyptian ship, 330 feet long and 60 feet wide, was used to transport the 325-ton red granite obelisk across the Mediterranean, reaching Rome before the end of that same year. After this, the ship would sit idle at Ostia, port of Rome.

On the foreign policy front, Caligula began conservativelyapart from enthroning Herod Agrippa and Antiochus IV. Retaining many of Tiberius's gubernatorial appointees around the empire, he confirmed the current king of Armenia, Mithradates, on his throne. Among his few new appointments, he awarded his brother-in-law Marcus Vinicius, husband of his youngest sister Livilla, the plum post of governor of the province of Asia, in today's northern Turkey. The appointment would come into effect in the summer of the following year, AD 38, and Livilla would relocate to Asia with her husband. These provincial appointments were much sought after, for the influence as much as the salary, with appointees routinely giving relatives, clients, and their sons posts in their provincial administrations.

On the last two days of August, to coincide with his birthday on August 31, Caligula inaugurated the now completed Temple of Augustus, which stood behind the Julian Basilica between the Palatine and Capitoline hills. Dressed in the sort of Triumphal regalia worn by his father at his Triumph twenty years earlier, Caligula arrived to dedicate the shrine driving a Triumphal chariot drawn by six horses. A choir of hundreds of boys and girls from noble families sang the dedicatory hymn. On each of the two nights of the dedication festival, the young emperor hosted lavish banquets for the leading people of Roman society. On both days, there were chariot races at the Circus Maximus, with Caligula closing all courts and businesses and even suspending the mourning of wives by decree to ensure no one had an excuse not to attend.

On the first games day, he arranged for twenty chariot-racing heats; on the second, he held forty. Prior to this, seven races a day had been the norm, with ten a day the maximum. For chariot-racing fan Caligula, sitting in the imperial box at the Circus Maximus accompanied by his sisters and his fellow priests of the Augustan Order, the *Sodales Augustales*, this was sporting heaven.

Tiberius had abolished beast hunts at spectacles, but Caligula reintroduced them at this festival, with four hundred bears and an equal number of wild animals from Libya hunted and killed on the circus sands between races over the two days. All this entertainment was quite a birthday present for Caligula, and the public loved it.

Mnester the male prostitute had meanwhile progressed to become a leading actor on the stage. Caligula always greeted him with kisses on the cheek and watched his performances with rapt attention, expecting silence from the audience. When an audience member coughed persistently, Caligula had him dragged from his seat and brought to him. As he reprimanded the offender, he reportedly slapped him across the face.

When an equite caused a disturbance during one of Mnester's performances, Caligula had a sealed note written and then delivered to the man by a Praetorian centurion. The man was ordered to go at once to Ostia and from there sail at his own expense across the Mediterranean to Mauretania and deliver the sealed note to the country's ruler King Ptolemy, Caligula's second cousin. When Ptolemy opened the note after the man delivered it to him, he read: "Do nothing at all, neither good nor bad, to the bearer." No doubt this prank would have provided great amusement for Caligula and his guests at banquets for weeks to come.[102]

At the amphitheater, watching a contest during one of the year's *ludi*, the religious games, Caligula witnessed the chariot fighter Porius celebrate his victory by publicly freeing his slave. It was an act that brought deafening applause from the approving crowd. Caligula, indignant at the man's popularity, rose up and rushed from the amphitheater. In his hurry, he tripped over the fringe of his toga as he descended the steps, and tumbled to the bottom, as his guards and staff rushed to help him back to his feet.

Caligula, unhurt, was still focused on Porius and his public reception. "The people who rule the world," he complained as he was dusted off, "seem to take greater notice of a gladiator's trifling gesture than all their deified princes, or even of the one still among them!"[103]

# XI

ENTER THE MONSTER

Six months into Caligula's reign, in October AD 37, he was laid low by a serious illness as a pandemic swept the empire. Philo, who was then living in Alexandria, reported that the emperor contracted a "terrible disease with which all the habitable world was afflicted at the same time."[104] This disease seems to have had similar qualities to an influenza pandemic. Spreading around the Mediterranean before disappearing, it would reoccur the following summer.

Worried Romans the length and breadth of the empire offered prayers for the popular young emperor's recovery, and when it was learned that he was close to death, a vast worried crowd surrounded the Palatium. Some people were even carrying placards with offers to become a gladiator or die in Caligula's place should he recover. Fearing that he was dying, from his sick bed Caligula dictated his will, leaving his entire estate to his sister Drusilla. This has been interpreted by many to mean that Caligula intended for his friend Marcus Lepidus to rule through wife Drusilla, after eliminating Gemellus.

In November, after being at death's door for several weeks, Caligula recovered, and the public rejoiced. But he was a different man. He was now changeable, capricious, and cruel. It was if his illness had drastically affected his mind and his personality. In fact, Suetonius described him as now suffering from a "brain-sickness." According to Suetonius, Caligula was aware of this mental illness and at one time spoke of taking a break to recover from it.[105]

Today, based on the symptoms and behavior that Suetonius and other Roman writers described, medical experts have offered a variety of potential prognoses. These include temporal lobe epilepsy, hyperthyroidism,

Wilson's disease, schizophrenia, and bipolar disorder/manic depression. These will be discussed further in this book's penultimate chapter.

Caligula's staff quickly became aware of the change in his personality when they told him about the man who'd offered to become a gladiator if the emperor survived his illness. Caligula promptly ordered the man to keep his vow, sending him to the arena at the next games, releasing him when he won his contest. Another man who'd publicly vowed to give his own life for Caligula's if the emperor recovered was still very much alive. On Caligula's orders, imperial slaves helped the man keep his vow by tracking him down and throwing him into the River Tiber to drown.

Taking advantage of Caligula's vindictive new demeanor, Macro brought the emperor testimony that his cousin Gemellus had prayed for Caligula's death while he was seriously ill and was preparing to take his place if that had occurred. When Gemellus was summoned by Caligula, his breath reeked from what he said was medicine for a persistent cough. Caligula became convinced that, in reality, Gemellus had taken an antidote against poison.

"Can there really be an antidote against Caesar?" he remarked to his staff.[106]

Feeling insulted that Gemellus dare fear being poisoned by him, Caligula had Macro send a Praetorian centurion to Gemellus. The centurion handed Gemellus a sword, telling him to end his own life. Gemellus, in tears, sobbed that he had never used a sword. The centurion had to show him how to kill himself and then finished the job by decapitating the teenage heir to the throne and taking the boy's head to the Palatium as proof that he was dead.

Caligula seemed in a mood for doing away with old encumbrances. In November or December, he had his favorite sister, Drusilla, divorce Cassius, the husband chosen for her by Tiberius, and then arranged for her to wed his good friend Marcus Lepidus. He even personally hosted their wedding feast.

On December 15, at the imperial villa at Antium on the Italian west coast, Caligula's sister Agrippina gave birth to a son, the first grandchild of

Germanicus. Nine days later, Caligula joined other imperial family members for the child's *Lustratio* purification ceremony, when the boy was to be named.

The *Lustratio*'s religious rites involved a procession followed by the sacrifice of a pig, a ram, and a bull, with the objective of cleansing the newborn of any harmful spirits it may have acquired at birth. The *Lustratio* would in time give way to the Christian baptismal ceremony, with the concept of harmful spirits being supplanted by the concept of original sin. At the *Lustratio* service, Agrippina invited Caligula to give her child any name he pleased.

No doubt looking at his uncle Claudius, and with a grin, Caligula replied, "I name him Claudius."[107]

Clearly, this was taken in jest, for Agrippina gave the boy a traditional name from his father's family: Lucius Domitius Ahenobarbus. Only much later would the child take the name, from his mother's side of the family, by which he became famous: Nero.

Early in the new year, deliberately careless of what Macro thought, Caligula decided to settle an old score with Marcus Junius Silanus, his father-in-law from his marriage to Junia. Back in April of the previous year, when Caligula sailed to the prison islands to fetch the ashes of his mother and brother, Silanus had been instructed to follow in another ship. Silanus, however, was a poor sailor, and while Caligula had sailed on through a storm, Silanus had turned back. At the time, Caligula had let this pass, but now he ordered a Senate prosecution of Silanus. Several senators who were approached to conduct this prosecution declined out of respect for Silanus. Caligula, made even more furious, ordered their deaths too. Reputedly among these secondary victims was Julius Graecinus, father of Agricola, the father-in-law of noted historian Tacitus.

As for Silanus himself, he received a visit from a Praetorian centurion, who gave him what Romans considered the noble option of suicide. The alternative was to face the executioner's blade on a trumped-up charge and go down on record as a convicted criminal, with his estate confiscated and his family left destitute. Silanus cut his own throat with a razor.

Caligula emerged from his illness seemingly convinced that he was a god—a god as powerful as Jupiter himself. He'd been receiving letters from around the empire addressing him as a god—the before-mentioned inscription at Assos described him as "the new god" at the very commencement of his reign. Now, to the consternation of staff and courtiers who were accustomed to his pranks, this holy belief of Caligula's seemed real.

He ordered statues of himself erected in temples around the Roman Empire and created a new religious order, so the world could worship him. In Alexandria, one of whose five quarters was Jewish—a million Jews then lived in Egypt—Jews rioted when the Roman prefect for the past six years, Aulus Avilius Flaccus, placed statues of Caligula in their synagogues and commanded them to worship him. Philo of Alexander tells of a rusting statue of a figure in a four-horse chariot, which had originally been dedicated to Cleopatra's grandmother, being quickly resurrected by local authorities and dedicated in a public place to Caligula.

The Jewish protests exploded into bloody riots between Jews and non-Jews, and as a religious war rocked the city, Flaccus the governor took drastic measures against the people he considered the instigators of the bloodshed: the Jews. Before long, this affair would land on Caligula's own doorstep.[108]

Caligula, who played many pranks on his uncle Claudius, now played the biggest prank of all. He had Claudius divorce his second wife, Aelia Paetina, and marry their eighteen-year-old cousin Valeria Messalina, younger sister of Agrippina the Younger's husband. Messalina was a beauty, but she was headstrong and notoriously promiscuous. She would give Claudius two children: Claudia, born in AD 39, and Britannicus, born in AD 41. But once she took up residence at the palace, she commenced an affair with Cornelius Sabinus, commander of Caligula's German Guard.

In late AD 37, too, Caligula attended the wedding feast of Gaius Calpurnius Piso, a relative of the Piso who'd been condemned, at least in the court of public opinion, for poisoning Caligula's father. As Piso and his bride Livia Orestilla reclined across from Caligula at the feast, with Piso affectionately putting his arm around Livia, the emperor suddenly scowled at Piso.

"Hands off *my* bride!" he cried.[109]

Jumping up, he took the startled Livia by the hand and led her away to his bed. He then married her, boasting that he was emulating Romulus, founder of Rome, and Augustus, both of whom had taken the wives of other men. Within days or weeks of their wedding, Caligula divorced Livia. He would later exile her, on the accusation that she had again taken up with Piso. This episode could be seen as Caligula quite deliberately humiliating a member of the Piso family, the family he saw as having taken his father from him. The following May, this same Gaius Piso was inducted into Rome's most prestigious priesthood, the Arval Brotherhood, and it's likely that senior advisers such as Callistus convinced Caligula to do this as compensation for Piso's stolen bride.

Emboldened now, Caligula conducted a series of dinner parties where he invited leading men with beautiful wives to dine with him at the palace. He then made the wives parade past him so that he could run his hand over them. Selecting wives at random, he took them to his bedroom, one at a time. Returning a little later, he commented to the husbands on their wives' sexual prowess—or lack of it.

Those husbands included Caligula's close friend Decimus Valerius Asiaticus. A native of Vienna in Narbonne Gaul, today's French city of Vienne, Asiaticus was a consul in AD 35, the first citizen of Vienne to be so honored. Powerfully built, a wrestling-school prodigy as a boy, he'd also been a loyal client to Antonia, Caligula's grandmother, and had become close to Caligula as a result. Now, Caligula humiliated both Asiaticus and his wife by raping her and then criticizing her skills in bed. "Ye gods!"

philosopher Seneca would exclaim. "What a tale for the ears of a husband!" Asiaticus, a proud man according to Seneca, had to wrestle with his pride, and hold his tongue.[110]

Caligula had long disliked Aulus Flaccus, prefect of Egypt, a close friend of Tiberius. Before his appointment, Flaccus had been part of Sejanus's conspiracy against Caligula's mother. But Flaccus was a client of Caligula's good friend Marcus Lepidus and also had the ear of Macro, who dissuaded Caligula from taking any action against the governor, admonishing the young emperor for "yielding to his unbridled passions."[111]

Caligula began to brood over Macro's controlling attitude. He'd accepted this when Tiberius was alive as necessary to survive, but now that he was emperor, he increasingly resented the Praetorian commander's influence. Macro knew that he was in trouble when, approaching the emperor one day, he overheard Caligula say to those with him, "Don't smile. Look sad. Here comes the sensor and monitor, the all-wise man, the man who is beginning to be the schoolmaster of a full-grown man, and of a prince, after time has separated him from and discarded the tutors of his childhood."[112]

The atmosphere between emperor and prefect became increasingly tense, and Macro was probably relieved when, in the new year, Caligula offered him the post of prefect of Egypt. There had a been a recent precedent in such a transfer, with Sejanus's father going from Praetorian prefect to prefect of Egypt. There was a twist, with Macro being required by Caligula to remove his friend Flaccus from the job of governor once he arrived in Alexandria. The Praetorian commander nonetheless accepted, and resigned his Praetorian command. He and wife Ennia began packing.

In March that year, AD 38, as soon as the sailing season opened, Macro and his wife arrived at Ostia, port of Rome, to board ship for Egypt. Waiting for them was a detachment from Macro's previous command, the Praetorian Guard. But they weren't there to see off Macro. He was arrested and returned to Rome in chains. And Flaccus retained his post in Egypt.

There is no indication that Caligula had any evidence against Macro, but Macro knew there was no coming back from this. While under house arrest in Rome, he committed suicide, followed by his wife—Caligula's former lover—Ennia. In the wake of the couple's deaths, their children and other relatives were summarily executed at Caligula's command. Yet, instead of confiscating Macro's estate, as was the norm following the death of an accused traitor, Caligula seems to have recognized Macro's will. We know this because Macro's Italian hometown of Alba Fulcens recorded its gratitude to him for endowing it with the funds to build a new amphitheater.

In place of Macro, Caligula returned to the practice established by Augustus, appointing two men to share the role of prefect of the Praetorian Guard. The identity of one is unclear, but the other was named Clemens. This man's wife, Julia, was the sister of Julius Lupus, a military tribune, while Clemens's son, Marcus Arretinus Clemens, would himself serve as Praetorian prefect under the emperor Vespasian a quarter of a century later. That Clemens would boast that his father had served honorably as Caligula's Praetorian prefect. Neither Clemens nor his colleague in the prefecture would have Macro's influence over Caligula. Indeed, Clemens would prove a mild-mannered, pragmatic Praetorian prefect, carrying out the emperor's wishes without question.[113]

Following Macro's removal, Caligula, free now of all restraint, embarked on expensive public infrastructure projects. Six decades after this, Sextus Julius Frontinus, three times a consul and a successful general who expanded Roman interests in Britain, would serve as Rome's water commissioner from AD 97, writing a detailed history of Rome's water supply. In this work, Frontinus describes how, in the second year of Caligula's reign, the young emperor commissioned Rome's two tallest, most ambitious aqueducts.[114]

Caligula's aqueducts would become known as the New Anio and the Claudia, with their waters delivered from the Alban Hills, thirty-eight miles from Rome, via tunnels driven through exceptionally hard rock and over towering aqueducts designed to reach even the highest hillside sectors of Rome. Caligula's intent was to supply every region of the city including the Caelian, Aventine, and Palatine hills and regions west of the Tiber, which were not served by running water to that time. On completion, these aqueducts would soar 158 feet above the Tiber wharves as they crossed the river. Neither would be equaled for their size, scope, or water-delivering efficiency in the city's history. Caligula was thinking big.

With his Palatium bustling with architects and engineers, and architectural plans and sketches surrounding him, the new emperor also energetically embarked on construction of a new amphitheater on the Campus Martius, just north of the Saepta Julia—the so-called Voting Porticos. Work on this amphitheater would damage the existing Virgo aqueduct. One of the city's lowest and shortest aqueducts, the Virgo's arches began in the Gardens of Lucillus and ended on the Campus Martius in front of the Voting Porticos.

Possibly because the Virgo had been built by his grandfather Marcus Agrippa, whom he came to disown because of his lowly background, Caligula didn't repair the damaged Virgo. Instead, he rebuilt the twin temples of Isis and Serapis where they'd previously stood near the Voting Porticos, possibly because of an interest in all things Egyptian inherited from his father, or because Tiberius had torn them down.

The conservative Tiberius had demolished these temples after their priests were convicted of taking bribes. He tossed the statue of Isis in the Tiber, but Caligula rescued and restored it and had a number of ancient obelisks shipped from Egypt to decorate the precinct. Caligula himself was not known to personally follow the cult—many of whose followers were women and slaves—but an adherent of Isis in the coming years would be the short-lived emperor Otho, who was to publicly celebrate the rites in the cult's approved linen smock. Dio writes that Caligula built two temples to himself at Rome, but there is no historical or archeological evidence of this. From later indications at Lake Nemi (see chapter XXI), it is possible that Caligula associated Isis and Serapis with his own worship.

To improve the ability to reliably deliver grain from Egypt and North Africa, Caligula also ordered construction of new port facilities in Sicily and at Rhegium—today's Reggio on the boot of Italy—with moles constructed well out to sea to create sea walls encircling safe harbors. The Sicilian harbor works were apparently at Messina, known as Messana in Roman times, expanding on construction, including a lighthouse modeled on the Pharos of Alexandria, that had been carried out by Caligula's grandfather Marcus Agrippa.

While Suetonius ridicules Caligula's harbor developments as grandiose, Josephus praises them as "a work without dispute very great in itself and of very great advantage to navigation."[115] Caligula also ordered the construction of luxurious new public baths at Rome, which were to feature upper-floor apartments for rental to the upper classes.

Aware that, six hundred years earlier, the king of Corinth in Greece had considered building a canal four miles across the Isthmus of Corinth to link the Ionian and Aegean Seas, Caligula decided he would build that canal. He began by dispatching a first-rank centurion of the Praetorian Guard to survey the route; the Guard and the legions all contained officers who were trained to survey and oversee military building projects. This centurion employed Greek engineers who reported that the water level on one side of the isthmus was higher than on the other—which was untrue—and that if a canal was built, water would flood through and inundate a major island. As a result of this faulty advice, Caligula abandoned the idea. Years later, his nephew Nero would recommence the project, only for it to be again abandoned. The canal would finally be built in the nineteenth century and continues to be used today.

Caligula also devoted time to his favorite sports. A fan of gladiatorial contests, he soon emulated Julius Caesar by establishing his own troupe of gladiators. According to Pliny the Elder, all twenty members of Caligula's imperial gladiatorial troupe used his preferred Thracian style.[116] According to Suetonius, two of these men trained themselves not to blink and remained undefeated. Another, named Studiosus, or Keen, had a right arm longer than the left. As this was the sword arm, it gave him a reach advantage over opponents of similar build.[117]

While one day fencing with one of his gladiators using wooden training swords, Caligula was furious when the man took a dive, and, grabbing a dagger from one of his bodyguards, stabbed the man, before running around with a raised arm as if he'd won the golden palm award in a genuine contest. On another occasion, while observing the auctioning off of gladiators from a confiscated estate, he noticed that the elderly senator Aponius Saturninus was nodding off, so he instructed the auctioneer to take each nod as a bid. When the senator awoke, he discovered that he had successfully "bid" 900,000 sesterces for sixteen gladiators.

A comment by Suetonius has led it to be accepted by some historians that Caligula chose gladiators to serve as officers of his German Guard bodyguard. It's actually highly unlikely Suetonius meant that *every* officer in the German Guard was a former gladiator, for several reasons. With the German Guard being of legion strength, its officers were accordingly a commander, ten tribunes, and sixty centurions. Normally, as a concession to their tribes, the prefects and tribunes of German auxiliary units were of German royal blood, the relatives of chieftains. Almost certainly, there would have been unrest among the proud rank and file of the Guard if all their officers were gladiators. As previously explained, we know from Josephus that the German Guard commander in Caligula's reign was indeed a former gladiator, but it could be interpreted that Suetonius only meant the German Guard was *commanded* by a gladiator, or that *some* of the officers were gladiators.

Deciding that too many *secutores* (men at arms) were surviving in the gladiatorial arena, Caligula ordered the armor of that class of fighter reduced. When a gladiator of this sort by the name of Columbus survived a fight with a light wound, Caligula reputedly sent him ointment for the wound. It turned out to be poison and killed the man.

"I call this poison Columbinium," he told companions, no doubt with the sort of amusement that typified what Anthony Barrett has characterized as his "dark" sense of humor.[118]

Alas for Caligula, his fun and games were about to be clouded by tragedy.

# XII

## THE DEATH OF DRUSILLA

In the late spring/early summer of AD 38, Caligula made a tour of the island of Sicily, which had become a Roman province in the third century BC. Ancient sources are unclear as to exact timing of the emperor's Sicilian trip, and most modern scholars date it shortly after a tragic event that occurred in Caligula's life that June. However, Greek and Roman scholar David Woods has speculated that his trip was split by that tragic event, that Caligula was midway through the first stages of the visit when he was summoned back to Rome, and that he resumed the trip following the event in Rome. There are several reasons for accepting Woods's view.[119]

The Sicilian trip would have been planned for some time, for its highlight was to be Caligula's staging of the Athenian Games, an athletic competition similar to the Olympic Games, at Syracuse, the province's capital, and it would have taken months to organize the logistics, athletes, and program. The Sicilian visit would also give Caligula the opportunity to inspect the building works he'd ordered at Syracuse—the rebuilding of the city walls and of several temples—and to look over the harbor development work he'd set in motion at Messina.

Heading south through Campania on the Latin Road, driving his own chariot and escorted by cavalry of the Praetorian Horse, Caligula passed a column of captives—probably runaway slaves being brought to Rome to die in the arena. One old prisoner with a gray beard that straggled down onto his chest recognized the young emperor and called out to him, begging Caligula to end his life for him then and there.

"So you consider yourself alive in your present state?" scoffed Caligula, before driving on.[120]

85

From an Italian port, most likely the naval base at Misenum, Caligula and his entourage of courtiers and bodyguard troops boarded ships of Rome's Tyrrhenian Fleet, with Caligula making himself comfortable aboard the flagship. That ship, a quadrireme, was a vessel with four banks of oars and four hundred paid sailors at its two hundred oars. Contrary to the portrayal in the book and movie *Ben-Hur*, the Roman navy didn't use convicts as oarsmen, although, in an earlier era, King Herod the Great had done so with his small Judean navy. Caligula's flotilla sailed down the west coast of Italy to Syracuse, where the emperor was welcomed by the Roman governor, an officer of praetor rank, and presided over the Athenian Games.

That June, while Caligula was touring Sicily, a deadly virus hit Rome. Philo tells us that the same pandemic also affected Egypt. Among those who came down with the sickness at Rome was Caligula's sister Drusilla. When news reached Caligula that his favorite sister was seriously ill, he rushed back to Rome to be at her bedside. Drusilla never recovered, succumbing to the illness on June 10. Caligula was shattered by her death. In a state of shock, he would not let anyone touch her body for days.

Unable to face the public funeral he decreed for his sister, Caligula instructed her widower, Lepidus, to read Drusilla's funeral oration and then rushed from Rome by night. Hurrying through Campania to his Alban villa, he hid away there, playing dice incessantly with his entourage. Some would write that this dice-playing showed that Caligula cared little for Drusilla, but another interpretation could be that he was trying to push his sister's death from his mind. Now in deep mourning, he allowed his hair and beard to grow, as Roman mourning tradition required.

At Rome, Lepidus presided over Drusilla's funeral, with the prefect of the Praetorian Guard and his troops joining members of the Equestrian Order to carry out the ancient funeral tradition of running around the burning pyre. Caligula had arranged that Drusilla have her own tomb, apparently on the Field of Mars. To close the funeral, mounted youths of noble birth performed the precision "Troy" horse exercise around the tomb. By Caligula's edict, during the official mourning period, it was a capital offense for men to laugh, bathe, or dine with their wives, children, or parents. Like himself, all had to cut themselves off from their families. When he heard that a hot water seller had been hawking his product during the mourning period, he had him arrested and punished; Romans diluted their wine with hot water, and Caligula didn't want anyone drinking wine and being merry.

Once the traditional nine days of mourning had passed, Caligula moved on from his Alban villa, taking ship to Sicily and resuming his tour, hoping to take his mind off his loss. In support of Woods's theory that Caligula had commenced his Sicilian trip prior to Drusilla's death, it would have been highly unlikely for a man in deep mourning to have presided over the Athenian Games had they taken place *following* Drusilla's passing.

Suetonius tells us that, during the post-Drusilla phase of the trip, Caligula cynically scoffed at stories told to him by locals of miracles associated with various shrines he visited in Sicily. Perhaps the locals suggested he endow those shrines with large financial offerings and pray for his sister's miraculous return from the dead. We know that he visited Messina on this leg of the trip, for Suetonius reported that he departed the port city in a hurry after hearing volcanic Mount Aetna rumble in the near distance. Suetonius says this was from fear; others might suggest it was mere prudence.[121]

Once back in Rome, Caligula learned that Cypros, wife of his best friend Agrippa, had given birth to the couple's third daughter not long after Drusilla's death. As a mark of respect to the emperor, Agrippa had the child named Drusilla in remembrance of Caligula's favorite sister. Agrippa's Drusilla would grow into a famous beauty.

In Caligula's absence, the Senate had voted that four princes, three of them the sons of Cotys, king of Thrace, be granted kingdoms as client kings of Rome. To Rhoemetacles went the possessions of his late father King Cotys. To Sohaemus went the land of the Ituraean Arabs. To Cotys, Lesser Armenia. And to Polemon, son of King Polemon of Pontus, the

kingdoms of Colchis and Cilicia, his father's possessions. On the Rostra
in the Forum, on a day that had been preceded by heavy rain, Caligula,
dressed formally in a white toga and sitting beneath a silk canopy flanked
by the two current consuls, presided over the formal swearing-in ceremony of the royal quartet.

As Caligula was being carried back to his palace in a litter following the
ceremony, he noticed a build-up of mud in a side alley and exploded with
sudden fury. Among the many toga-clad officials in the entourage trailing
behind the emperor was twenty-eight-year-old Titus Flavius Vespasianus,
whom history would later come to know as Vespasian, ninth emperor of
Rome. At this time, Vespasian held the post of city *aedile*, with his portfo-
lio involving the cleanliness of Rome's alleyways.

Calling Vespasian forward, Caligula berated him for the muddy state
of the alley and ordered troops of his escort to load Vespasian with the
mud, to humiliate him; they filled the fold of his toga with it. Vespasian
learned fast: not only would he speedily have the alley cleaned up, but
eighteen months later he would be in the Senate calling for honors to be
heaped upon Caligula.

At a celebratory banquet hosted by Caligula following the royal inves-
titure in the Forum, several of the kings began arguing over which of them
was of the most noble descent. This seems to have fired up a deep-seated
inferiority complex in Caligula, for he flew into a rage.

"No, let there be one master, and one king!" Caligula declared, quoting Homer.

According to Suetonius, his courtiers had to talk him out of donning a
kingly crown on the spot. "My lord Gaius," said one, "you already outrank
any prince or king." For was Caligula not a god?[122]

That summer, Caligula sent Agrippa to Alexandria, en route to his Eastern
territories, to check on what Prefect Flaccus was up to. Even though
Agrippa maintained a low profile, riots broke out after his August arrival
in Alexandria when it was learned he'd met with unhappy Jewish leaders

and forwarded their complaints in writing to Caligula; Flaccus may have deliberately leaked this information. At the end of August, once Agrippa had departed for Judea by sea, Flaccus arrested thirty-eight leading Jews in Alexandria and then whipped, tortured, and crucified them in the Alexandrian amphitheater as part of the new annual festival celebrating Caligula's birthday on August 31.

Memmius Rufus, the consul who had escorted Sejanus to his demise seven years before, had been serving as governor of the province of Achaea in southern Greece on the appointment of Tiberius. Caligula had decided to have the huge and ancient statue of Zeus that stood in a massive temple at Olympia in Achaea, home of the Olympic Games, sent to Rome, along with others. It was Caligula's intent that, once the statue was at the capital, he would erect it after having its head remodeled on his own. So, that spring he'd sent Memmius Rufus orders to have the statue demounted and shipped to Rome. Memmius had written back reporting problems with the project; the statue resisted moving, and workmen heard laughter coming from it. They were now refusing to touch it.

Predictably, Caligula's fury erupted. He devised a novel punishment for this governor who could not—or would not—carry out his wishes. He sent for Memmius and his wife, Lollia Paulina, whom he knew was beautiful and rich in her own right. Once Memmius and Lollia reached Rome that summer, Caligula ordered the couple to divorce so that he could marry Lollia. To add insult to injury, he required Memmius to betroth Lollia to him in the formal Roman ceremony where the dowry and wedding date were agreed, gifts were exchanged, and the marriage contract was signed and then sealed with a kiss.

Noted writer Gaius Plinius Secundus, or Pliny the Elder, was a sixteen-year-old living in Rome at the time and studying under Publius Pomponius Secundus, the poet imprisoned by Tiberius and freed by Caligula. No doubt through the agency of his tutor, Pliny saw Lollia at a function just days after her betrothal to Caligula. She was, says Pliny, "celebrating her betrothal covered with alternating emeralds and pearls, which glittered all over her head, hair, ears, neck and fingers, to the value of 50 million sesterces. She was ready, at the drop of a hat, to give written proof of her ownership of these gems."[123]

Caligula put off his wedding while he finalized the deification of his sister Drusilla. That deification had been made possible by a senator, Livius Geminus, claiming on oath to have seen Drusilla ascend to heaven and converse with the gods. In return for this service, Geminus was paid one million sesterces. This enabled the Senate to decree that Drusilla was indeed a goddess, giving her the official name of Drusilla Panthea.

The Senate required that a golden statue of Drusilla be erected in the Senate House. They further directed that another be set up in the Temple of Venus in the Forum, alongside and of equal size to the statue of Venus, and that Drusilla be honored with the same rights as Venus. A separate shrine to Drusilla was also decreed, with a religious order dedicated to her, served by twenty male and female priests. Where that shrine was located has never been determined, but, as later discussed, this may have been at Lake Nemi.

On September 23, the day of inaugural games dedicated to Drusilla Panthea, Rome stopped for a day of fun and feasting. By order of Caligula, September's regular festivals were that year celebrated as mere formalities so as not to outshine this event. By order of the Senate, Drusilla's games were to be equal in scale to April's *Ludi Megalenses* honoring the goddess Cybele, and they were to take place annually on this day in the future at major cities throughout the empire.

We know from a surviving inscription that at the city of Cyzicus, capital of the province of Mysia, in today's northern Turkey, two of the kings anointed by Caligula at Rome just months before this, Rhoemetacles and Polemon, attended games dedicated to Drusilla. At Cyzicus and throughout the Greek world, Drusilla was officially described as "the new Aphrodite," with Aphrodite being the Greek equivalent of Venus.[124]

At Rome's celebration, Caligula presided over a day of chariot racing that began with a statue of Drusilla being carried around the Circus

Maximus on a carriage drawn by elephants from the imperial troupe at Laurentum, outside Rome. Then, just days after the games for the deified Drusilla, Caligula married beautiful, rich Lollia, making her his third wife.

Late in the summer, word reached Caligula via informants that Aulus Flaccus, prefect of Egypt, had encouraged Gemellus to prepare to take over from Caligula when he was ill and that he had fainted on learning of Gemellus's death. These were grounds enough for Caligula to dispatch a Praetorian detachment by sea to arrest Flaccus. Headed by a centurion named Bassus, the Praetorians boarded a light, fast warship of the Tyrrhenian Fleet squadron based at Ostia, and sped directly across the Mediterranean to Egypt. As a rule, Roman warships followed the coast to reach their destination, with only cargo ships, for whose owners profit rested on speedy delivery, usually taking the more dangerous direct route.

On an October afternoon, Centurion Bassus's warship arrived off Alexandria. Bassus instructed the skipper to wait until nightfall before going into port, so that he and his men could arrive unseen. Upon landing in the dark, Bassus and his troops were marching through the streets when they came upon a soldier of the city watch. Bassus had this man take him to his commander, who informed Bassus that Flaccus was at that moment dining at the city home of Stephanion, a former freedman of Tiberius. Telling the watch commander to prepare to reinforce him if necessary, Bassus took his troops to the house in question.

Sealing off all entrances, the centurion cunningly had one of his men change into slave dress and then slip into the house to reconnoiter. As Bassus expected, Flaccus took the disguised soldier to be one of Stephanion's slaves, and Stephanion thought he was one of Flaccus' slaves. Going back outside, the soldier reported to Bassus that, apart from several diners and ten to fifteen unarmed slaves, Flaccus was alone, with not a single bodyguard present. Bassus and his men then stormed the house, arriving in the dining room just as one of the guests was proposing a toast to Flaccus. The guest of honor was stunned, but he seemed to know why he was under arrest as Bassus's troops hustled him from the house.

Two of Flaccus's senior freedmen assistants were also rounded up, joining Flaccus for a journey to Rome aboard the ship that had brought Bassus and his men to Alexandria. The party sailed through autumnal storms to reach the capital in November, and Flaccus was quickly tried before Caligula. With his two freedmen testifying against him, his fate was sealed. Caligula found him guilty of conspiracy and sentenced him to banishment on the Greek island of Gyaros. In the northern Cyclades not far from Andros, Gyaros was then the most dreaded place of exile for Romans—just nine square miles of desolate, treeless, waterless rock.

Fortunately for Flaccus, he had Marcus Lepidus for a patron. Caligula's close friend and brother-in-law spoke up for his client and convinced the emperor to send Flaccus to the more agreeable nearby island of Andros, which was mountainous and well watered. Once again Flaccus found himself aboard a warship with a Praetorian escort. Initially, Flaccus would live in Andros town, but, feeling insecure there, he purchased a small, remote farm and took up goat farming. That way, he reasoned, he could see any troops approaching to finish him off, and make his escape. From then on, he would live in dread of a Praetorian execution party arriving to dispatch him.

# XIII

## NEVER MIND THE EXPENSE

Caligula decided that a god like himself needed a much grander palace than those already on the Palatine Hill. Augustus had been the first emperor to erect an executive mansion on this hill. On the western end of the hill, Augustus's palace was modest by the standards of later emperors. Next to it, he built a smaller mansion for his wife, Livia Augusta, called the Domus Livia, or Livia's House, whose lower floor, with magnificent frescoes depicting Roman gardens, survives to this day.

Tiberius had his own, separate mansion on the Palatine. Much larger than Augustus's abode, which became referred to as the Old Palatium, the 45,000-square-foot Palace of Tiberius perched at the northwest end of the Palatine. Occupying the greater part of the Germalus, one of the hill's summits, it consisted of its four wings, of which the Palace of Germanicus was one, ranged around a massive central courtyard. The sixteenth-century Villa Farnese of Cardinal Alessandro Farnese would be built over its ruins, with the Farnese Gardens still today covering large underground sections of Tiberius's Palatium.

When Caligula first took the throne, he took up occupancy of Tiberius's Palatium. But once he decided he needed a home fit for a god, he embarked on grand palace extensions, down to the Forum, and across to the Capitoline Hill from the Palatine via a bridge to a "lodge" that he would build for himself as an attachment to the temple of his fellow god Jupiter. As his *piece de resistance*, Caligula incorporated the temple of Castor and Pollux on the Forum to create a massive entry foyer to his Palatium. Castor and Pollux, he joked, would be his doorkeepers.

Scholars were skeptical of this foyer's existence until 2003, when archaeologists unearthed its foundations. This showed that the construction had cut across an existing street to link up with the temple. No such archaeological evidence exists for the bridge to the Capitoline Mount or the lodge there, although that does not preclude their onetime construction and later demolition. Work proceeded apace on Caligula's palatial extension to the Forum temple, with events in the late summer of AD 40 suggesting this part of the project was completed by that time.

Archaeologists believe that, as part of this extension, Caligula took over a privately owned villa, the Domus Gelotiana, which sat on the lower slopes of the Palatine near the Circus Maximus. Sometime after Caligula's death, this villa would be converted into a *paedogogium*, a boarding school for imperial pages. Its remains can still be seen today. Suetonius says that Caligula was one day at the Domus Gelotiana, using it as a vantage point to inspect equipment in the circus below, when people gathered on nearby balconies to see him.

"What about a day's racing, Caesar?" one of his subjects good-naturedly called.[125]

According to Suetonius, Caligula immediately gave orders for games to be held. The logistics for such an event would have needed significant preparation and advance warning, and a religious public holiday would have been required to allow the public to attend. Our word *holiday* derives from these Roman holy days when all public business was suspended. This all suggests that Suetonius's implication that games were held immediately strays from the facts, and that Caligula may have only agreed to the suggestion in jest.

That Caligula was a chariot-racing fan is well documented. He wasn't alone. The Roman passion for the sport can be compared with the modern passion for football. Chariot racing was in fact history's first team sport, and some Romans were known to have the name of their team engraved on their tombstones. In Caligula's day, there were four factions, or teams— the Greens, Blues, Reds, and Whites. In later eras, the number grew to as many as eight teams. Caligula was a die-hard supporter of the Greens. Dio says that their team color, frog-green, resulted in them being nicknamed "the Faction of the Leeks."[126]

Each team was controlled by a corporation whose shares were so valued that they were passed from father to son. More than a sport, chariot racing was a massive business, employing thousands, from the slaves who swept the course to the charioteers. Race day brought visitors flocking to each city staging a race meeting, with the shops, cafes, bars, and prostitutes that operated under the circus stands also doing good trade. And since gambling on chariot races was legal because the races were considered games of skill—as opposed to dice games, which relied on chance and were illegal—fortunes were won and lost on race days.

Races were held in hippodromes, or circuses, dedicated horse-racing stadiums, at cities throughout the empire, with the same racing corporations entering teams at every city. It was a privilege, not a right, for a city to build a hippodrome and conduct races; it could be done only with the explicit permission of the emperor. Most provinces had a limited number of hippodromes. Just one is known to have existed in Britain, for example; it was identified only as recently as 2010. At Colchester, the city known as Camulodunum in Roman times and first capital of the province of Britannia, this hippodrome dates from the second century. The largest hippodromes were at Rome and Antioch, capital of the province of Syria. The famous fictional chariot race in the novel *Ben-Hur* was set in the Antioch hippodrome.

Racing could take place only at the dozen *ludi*, or games, of major annual Roman religious festivals through the year, with racing going on for several days straight at the larger festivals. Some months were race free, while others, such as April, were cluttered with games. Entertainment between races included the execution of convicted prisoners of the lower orders by throwing them to wild animals, and the hugely popular beast hunts. Horseback races as we know them were included on games programs, along with races for two-horse chariots and novelty events with chariots drawn by as many as ten horses. But it was the races that involved the quadriga, the four-horse chariot, that represented the Formula 1 of ancient Roman racing.

When Caligula increased the number of races on the daily program, a move which proved immensely popular with the public, it put pressure on the racing corporations to find and maintain many more horses, substantially increasing their costs. It also put financial pressure on the men funding the games; at Rome, an individual senator would sponsor each games day, putting up the prize money for the races in return for the prestige of sitting as "editor" beside the emperor at the event.

The best charioteers, usually freedmen, former slaves, became wealthy and famous, the rock stars of their day. They began their careers young and often died young in crashes on the track. One such star driver, Fustus, died in AD 34 with fifty-three victories under his belt, at just twenty-four years of age. The best chariot horses, which racked up more than one hundred wins, also were treated like gods, with the left or inside horse, which had to make the tightest turns, the most valued. The chariot corporations ran stud farms around the empire and had their own fleets of ships fitted out to carry horses from province to province. Always on the lookout for the best steeds, they also sent agents to general horse sales. By law, those agents had first pick of horses on sale, even ahead of dealers buying horses for the Roman army.

The Roman elite also used two-horse chariots as their personal transport; these were the sports cars of the day. By the time Caligula reached the throne, he considered himself such an accomplished driver that he drove racing chariots, having a track for his own use constructed on the outskirts of Rome. Called the *Gaianum* after him, it was located adjacent to his mother's gardens in the Vatican Field, west of the Tiber.

The Gaianum was closed off to the public, and served no practical purpose other than as an emperor's plaything. It wouldn't even have been used as a horse-training circuit by the military—the imperial cavalry barracks and horse-training field were located on the opposite side of town, east of the Tiber. On his racetrack's central spine, Caligula installed the ancient Egyptian obelisk he had previously shipped from Egypt. That giant obelisk today stands in St. Peter's Square, not far from where it stood in Caligula's Gaianum, with the golden ball that topped it in his day replaced by a cross.

Caligula even had a house built for his favorite Greens chariot horse, Incitatus, complete with servants and a marble stall. Almost certainly as

one of his cynical jokes, Caligula also appointed the horse to a priesthood
and even threatened to make him a consul when the Senate annoyed him.
Suetonius cites this Incitatus episode as an example of Caligula's craziness,
but historian Aloys Winterling takes Suetonius to task: "He takes Caligula's
cynical jokes literally, thereby distorting their meaning and presenting his
behavior as aberrant."[127] The joke continued when the racehorse's house
was completed; the emperor invited friends to dinner with Incitatus and
himself at Incitatus's residence. Caligula and his merry band of intimates
no doubt thought this hilarious.

One of those intimates was Caligula's favorite star Greens charioteer Eutychus—not the same man who'd informed on Agrippa. A
cheery companion, Eutychus was often seen in the emperor's company.
Eutychus became so emboldened by his friendship with the emperor that,
on his own authority, he took troops from a Praetorian Guard cohort
that was on duty in the city one day and set them to work building new
Greens stables.

This free labor was soon withdrawn when the duty tribune, Cassius
Chaerea, found out what was going on. Blasting his men, Chaerea sent
them scurrying back to their posts. This was the same Chaerea who'd saved
the life of Germanicus's general Caecina during the mutiny on the Rhine in
AD 14. Now a senior tribune with the Praetorians, Chaerea would before
long play an even more prominent role in Caligula's affairs.

On race days, fans filled the stands of the hippodromes sporting the col-
ors of their teams and chanting the names of their favorite drivers. Rivalry
between supporters of the different chariot racing teams was, like that
between fans of different sporting teams today, often fierce. At the Circus
Maximus one day, as Caligula's Greens team was beaten in a race and the
crowd cheered for the opposition and jeered the Greens, Caligula irritably
and vindictively remarked to a companion, "If only all the people of Rome
had but one neck."[128]

Caligula admired the chariot-driving skills of his childhood friend
Aulus Vitellius. But we are told that Caligula became envious of anyone
with talent, and on top of this, Vitellius was a Blues supporter. One day

at the Gaianum, the emperor's private hippodrome, Vitellius was standing on the track, watching Caligula drive a four-horse chariot. Unaccountably, Caligula drove into him. Whether this was an accident or Caligula's idea of a joke, we aren't told. Vitellius was badly injured in the thigh, leaving him with a permanent limp.

# XIV

## CALIGULA'S NEW BRIDE

In late February or early March AD 39, Caligula divorced his latest wife, Lollia, just six months after marrying her. His excuse for the divorce was that she was barren and unable to give him a child and heir. It's likely she proved a far from willing or loving bed partner after the way Caligula had separated her from her last husband and forced her to marry him. Now, cruelly, he banned her from having any contact with other men. Around this time, too, Caligula reintroduced the capital crime of *maiestas* to the statute books. From now on, anyone who crossed the emperor could be prosecuted for treason on the flimsiest grounds.

With no interest or expertise in finance, into the second year of his reign, Caligula had emptied the imperial treasury of much of the fortune that miserly Tiberius had left there. Suetonius claims that Caligula had bankrupted the state within his first year, but it seems to have taken closer to two. To raise more money, Caligula had trumped-up charges leveled at Rome's richest men. After they were convicted in the Senate, he confiscated their property and then auctioned it off, forcing other leading men to pay inflated prices for it.

This bred countless informants who brought Caligula accusations of treason against leading men in return for a reward. Among those caught up in this flood of accusations was Caligula's uncle Claudius. When Claudius was summoned by Caligula, instead of defending himself he acted dumb, seeming not to understand the accusations or their potential consequences. The result was that Caligula dismissed his uncle as a simpleton and dismissed the charges against him. Others weren't so lucky. Showing that he'd been no angel early in his reign, Caligula now produced copies of the evidence against his mother and brothers that he'd claimed to have burned, and had the Praetorians round up all the named informants, who were convicted and punished.

To raise more money for the treasury, Caligula introduced new taxes on food, legal transactions, porters, and prostitutes and directed his Praetorian tribunes to supervise their collection. Another money-making scheme attributed to Caligula was a brothel at the Palatium, with the wives of leading men to serve as imperial prostitutes, although some scholars suggest that Caligula merely joked that he might have to resort to this if all else failed to increase funds.

In the spring or early summer of AD 39, Caligula remarried. The previous year he'd had a summer fling with Milonia Caesonia, a woman a decade his senior. In her late thirties and from an aristocratic family, Caesonia was, according to Suetonius, losing her youth and looks. The only extant image of her is on a coin issued in Judea by Caligula's friend Marcus Agrippa. This shows her with a severe face, long nose, long neck, and hair plaited in a ponytail down her neck in the fashion then popular with imperial Roman women. It's an unflattering image, but Roman coin images, including those of Caligula, were frequently unflattering, and sometimes bore little resemblance to surviving busts of the same subject.

Caesonia had presented herself to Caligula eight months pregnant—with his child, she said. A later joke of Caligula's suggests he may have harbored some doubt about his paternity, but, always conscious of producing an heir—he'd divorced his third wife supposedly because she didn't quickly fall pregnant—he quietly married Caesonia at once, but didn't formally announce it. A month later, a healthy daughter was born to the couple. Only then, on announcing the birth of his child, whom he named Julia Drusilla in remembrance of his late sister, did Caligula announce his marriage.

"In addition to the burden of sovereignty," Caligula joked to friends, "I now have to shoulder that of fatherhood."[129]

In fact, he appears to have been besotted with his daughter. Taking the baby to the Temple of Jupiter on the Capitoline Mount, he put her on the statue's knee, showing her off to Jupiter, his fellow god. He then entrusted the baby's suckling to the virgin priestesses of Minerva, the great protecting goddess. He quickly came to adore new wife Caesonia, and in turn she became one of his closest and most trusted advisers, along with the freedmen Callistus and Protogenes. Caesonia didn't even seem to mind when Caligula proudly showed her off naked to his friends.

Caesonia is likely to have reminded Caligula that one of her six half-brothers, thirty-two-year-old senator Gnaeus Domitius Corbulo, who had married a great-great-granddaughter of Augustus, had been nagging the highway commissioners and Senate over the way that the past commissioners and their road contractors had allowed the roads to deteriorate by keeping most of the allocated funds for themselves. Caligula ordered the past commissioners and road contractors to be heavily fined, giving Corbulo the task of collecting the money. It was a task that Corbulo assiduously carried out, placing the monies in a dedicated roads fund. Caligula rewarded Corbulo by appointing him to serve as a suffect consul during July and August that year.

With Caesonia now constantly at his side, Caligula progressively lost interest in the finer details of government and lost interest in Rome. He sometimes now spoke of emulating Tiberius and removing his court from Rome, in his case to Antium or Egypt, to relax and spend more time with the love of his life. No longer did he pore over legal cases, soaking up every word and every argument as he had in the past.

One day when Caesonia awoke from a nap, she asked, "What have you been doing?"

"I've been clearing my accounts," he replied. "In fact, I've done very good business since you dozed off." He added that, while she slept, he'd passed a single sentence on forty citizens whose cases he was required by law to review, without reading a word.

After signing the execution warrant for a group of prisoners from Gaul and Greece, he quipped, "Today I've subdued Gallo-Graecia."[130]

# XV

# CALIGULA'S INVASION

That spring of AD 39, with an increasing interest in the prophesies of oracles, and perhaps keen to learn what future he could expect for his marriage and child, Caligula traveled one hundred miles north of Rome to Mevania, modern Bevagna, where there was a temple to the river god Clitumnus. It was a site famous for prophesies. According to Suetonius, while there, someone—probably German Guard commander Sabinus—reminded Caligula that a number of older Batavians in the German Guard were about to retire after twenty-five years, service, creating a need to recruit replacements. It seems Caligula joked that he should personally go to Batavia to select the recruits, and this apparently resonated with something he was told by a priest at Mevania's sacred grove, sparking an idea.[131]

Amminius, son of British king Cunobelinus, had fallen out with his father and sent messages to Caligula urging him to invade Britain. Meanwhile, reports from Gaul described German tribes east and north of the Rhine as restive. Caligula set in motion a plan to lead a Roman army to quell the German threat, and thereafter make an unannounced invasion of Britain to complete the job Julius Caesar failed to finish a century earlier. Suetonius says that Caligula even sent to Alexandria for the armor of Alexander the Great from Alexander's mausoleum there, to wear while on campaign.

Some modern writers have questioned whether Caligula genuinely intended to conquer Britain, suggesting that this was just crazy bravado on his part and that he never planned to follow through with it. Others see his British campaign as a deliberate and well-planned operation. A recent study of Caligula's generalship by Lee Fratantuono concludes that Caligula was "a surprisingly competent military strategist."[132] Roman historian Tacitus certainly believed that Caligula was perfectly serious in his intent to expand the empire into Britain. "Britain was long neglected," Tacitus writes. "Augustus spoke of this as 'policy.' Tiberius called it an 'injunction.' The emperor Gaius unquestionably planned an invasion of Britain."[133]

Historian Arther Ferrill, who was otherwise highly critical of Caligula and considered him "a crazy man," believed that "Caligula actually planned to invade Britain, but he aborted it."[134] Ferrill's statement that "he aborted it" seems to hit the nail on the head. "Certainly Gaius was forced to call off the invasion," say British academics Graham Webster and Donald Dudley, authors of The Roman Conquest of Britain. Caligula biographer J.P.V.D. Balsdon likewise concludes Caligula was "forced" to call it off.[135]

The military preparations that preceded the operation, which would take close to a year to complete, were detailed and meticulous. To begin with, orders went out from Caligula's Rome HQ, the Palatium, requiring two brand-new legions to be created, in the recruiting grounds of a pair of existing units, the 15th Apollinaris Legion, which had originally been raised in Cisalpine Gaul, and the 22nd Deiotariana Legion from Galatia. Both original legions were permanently stationed in the Roman East. The two new units, the first new legions raised by Rome in many decades, would increase the Roman army's then complement of legions from twenty-five to twenty-seven.

Confusingly to some, these two new units would also take the numbers 15 and 22. They were to be enlisted, equipped, trained, and commissioned over the autumn and winter of AD 39–40 in readiness for a spring campaign in AD 40. In addition, every provincial governor across the empire received orders from the Palatium to levy new auxiliary units and send them to join the Rhine legions for the offensive.

Most of this would not cost Caligula a sesterce. In that era, no legionaries were recruited in Italy. Every legion had its own designated recruiting ground in the provinces. The practice of the time was that the cost of raising new military units and recruits was borne by each governor, from his province's resources. A key role of the governor's adjutant, a junior magistrate of *quaestor* rank, was the administration of military recruitment in his province. Every town in the empire had to maintain a list of eligible citizens aged seventeen to forty-six who had registered for call-up as required by law. When orders were issued from the Palatium to the provinces for new enlistments, the selected provinces' quaestors dispatched their *conquisitors*, or recruitment officers, to gather up recruits.

Provinces routinely stockpiled armor, weapons, and ammunition in readiness for equipping new enlistments, and this suggests why the recruiting grounds of the existing 15th and 22nd were chosen—the requisite recruits and war materiel were apparently in abundance there. And just as, over the summer of AD 39, the conquisitors were very busy in every province, Rome's allies across the empire were answering Caligula's call by raising new non-citizen cavalry units and auxiliary light infantry from slingers to spearmen. What's more, they were paying for their equipment from their own treasuries. In addition, Caligula "collected military supplies of all kinds on an unprecedented scale," says Suetonius.[136]

Military recruitment was also going on in Italy. Caligula increased the Praetorian Guard from nine cohorts to twelve during his reign, and there can be little doubt the three additional cohorts were raised as part of his empire-wide recruitment for the northern campaigns of AD 40. During this era, Praetorian troops were recruited only in Italy, with their centurions transferred from both the legions and existing Praetorian cohorts. Most Praetorian recruits were draftees.

Because the Guard rarely took part in military campaigns in which they could enrich themselves with booty, Tiberius had upped their pay to three times that of legionaries. Praetorians also received larger retirement bonuses and served shorter enlistments. In the Praetorians' case, the cost of recruitment, equipping, and training was borne by the separate military treasury established by Augustus at Rome in AD 6.

Caligula's northern expedition was no slapdash, spur-of-the-moment affair. "The massive preparations preclude the notion," says Barrett, "that the northern expedition was anything other than a campaign that had been seriously planned."[137] Among the logistical details of the invasion plan was a naval base established at Gesoriacum, today's Boulogne-sur-Mer on the French coast, as the staging point for the operation. To assist with navigation in the English Channel, this new base was to be equipped with a tall lighthouse just northwest of the town.

The design of Caligula's lighthouse was based on the famous Pharos of Alexandria, a wonder of the ancient world. It was swiftly and efficiently built. Towering remnants of alternating courses of brick and stone would remain outside Boulogne until the eighteenth century, with the French calling it Tour d'Ordre. Locals ultimately plundered its stone and bricks for new constructions. Meanwhile, orders went north for a fleet of sleek new trireme warships to be built for the invasion and based at Gesoriacum. Their crews would be recruited from Gallic freedmen.

With his Palatium staff overseeing the detailed preparations for the northern operation, Caligula removed from Rome to his Campanian seaside villas for the spring. From these, Suetonius tells us, he would board massive galleys with ten banks of oars for morning cruises along the coast. These galleys possessed, says Suetonius, jeweled sterns, multi-colored sails, huge baths, colonnades, and banqueting halls. "Not to mention vines and fruit trees of different varieties," he adds. Suetonius had a habit of exaggerating, so it is possible that there was just a single pleasure galley. But even one would have been spectacular.[138]

Suetonius claimed that Caligula had his luxurious galley/galleys specially built, but he failed to say where. Italian authorities on Roman ships today conclude that, with these ships, Caligula was trying to emulate his great-grandfather Mark Antony and his consort Queen Cleopatra of Egypt—who famously seduced Antony aboard an Egyptian pleasure galley just like those described by Suetonius.[139]

The products of Egyptian shipbuilders were superior to those of the Romans. For one thing, Egyptians didn't use green timber as the Romans did, and their vessels lasted much longer. In Caligula's day, a squadron of Egyptian warships captured from Antony and Cleopatra at the Battle of Actium was still based at Forum Julii, today's Frejus on the south coast of France, with Roman crews. With Caligula importing other Egyptian artifacts to Italy, it's not unlikely that he also had one or more pleasure galleys either built in Egypt or brought to him from there.

It appears that, while coasting along in one such pleasure barge, Caligula had an idea for what his critics would describe as one his most grandiose, wasteful, and downright crazy projects to date.

# XVI

## CALIGULA WALKS ON WATER

In the summer of AD 39, Caligula had a massive floating bridge built across the Bay of Puteoli between Puteoli, modern Pozzuoli, then Italy's principal west coast commercial port, and a seaside town, either the naval base of Misenum, or Bauli, where Caligula's sister Agrippina had a villa, or Baiae—today's Baia—which was then an exclusive resort town with scores of massive villas of the Roman elite including Caligula. Differing ancient sources offer the three different destinations, but, from an episode involving Herod Antipas and his wife Herodias that will be detailed shortly, we know that Caligula stayed during this summer at the imperial seaside villa at Baiae, which Suetonius gives as the southern terminus of the bridge.[140]

Caligula's floating bridge was to be two to three miles long, and would employ the Roman military's temporary bridge-building technique of anchoring boats side by side and then running a wooden deck over the craft from one shore to the other. Julius Caesar had spanned the Rhine with just such a bridge of boats. Caligula's father, Germanicus, had done the same. Their bridges had been nowhere near three miles long, but the principle was the same. In this case, a covering of compacted earth was laid on top of the wooden decking, so that those who passed over the bridge trod earth from one shore to the other across the sheltered bay. Plus, says Dio, "lodging-houses" with running drinking water were built at intervals along the bridge's course.[141]

Caligula's bridge required two rows of supporting craft, and he had hulls built specially for the purpose, on the spot. When these new boats proved insufficient, cargo ships were commandeered from nearby and added to the line at various points. Cassius Dio would rail against this use of civilian craft, claiming it significantly impacted on grain imports and as a result "a very severe famine occurred in Italy, and particularly in Rome." That this comment was probably an exaggeration will become apparent. Dio himself tells us that the ships were "assembled there in a very brief space of time."[142]

At best, the cargo vessels would have only been out of service for a week or two. The bridge was used for just three days before apparently being dismantled, and its construction would have taken only several days when built by the military—Caesar's Rhine bridge was built in a day.

For close to two thousand years historians have puzzled over why Caligula had this temporary bridge built. Suetonius says that his grandfather told him Caligula built the bridge to prove wrong an earlier prediction by court astrologer Thrasyllus to Tiberius. The astrologer had said that Caligula had no more chance of becoming emperor than riding over the gulf of Baiae on a horse.[143] However, Thrasyllus's prediction had already been debunked by Caligula—he'd been emperor for two years by this stage!

Seneca believed that Caligula set out to emulate Persian king Xerxes, who, centuries before, had crossed the Hellespont with a bridge of boats to pursue his war with Greece. Dio felt that Caligula was keen to drive his chariot across the sea, and Josephus supposed that Caligula was trying to prove he was lord of the water and as powerful as Neptune, god of the sea. Suetonius also suggests that Caligula may have built his bridge to awe the Germans before his campaign the following year, and this may have had some truth to it.

Above all, Caligula's bridge, while turned into a propaganda exercise for him and Rome, had probably begun with a very pragmatic motive. As mentioned, this type of temporary bridge was a specialty of the Roman military, with all construction work on a campaign performed not by slaves or civilians but by legionaries—not even auxiliaries were permitted to participate in military construction, with their role restricted to scouting, foraging, and maintaining guard while the legionaries toiled.

None of the ancient authorities mention either imperial slaves or civilian contractors in relation to Caligula's spectacular bridge. Indeed, Suetonius tells us that the entire Praetorian Guard was involved in this project. And, as we know, three thousand new recruits were brought into the Praetorian Guard around this time by Caligula.

Quite probably, then, the bridge had begun as a training exercise for the Praetorian troops, new and old, in preparation for the Guard's participation in the northern campaigns the following year. In fact, Suetonius tells us that several floating bridges would be built across the Rhine for the German campaign of AD 40, side by side. Even Suetonius admits that this bridge across Puteoli Bay was a "huge engineering feat," and once Caligula saw the publicity potential of the Guard's training exercise, he capitalized on it.[144]

The day that Caligula chose for the inaugural crossing of his bridge was almost certainly July 21, for reasons that will shortly become apparent. At dawn on the big day, Caligula and friends who were summering with him offered sacrifices to various gods, beginning, says Dio, with Neptune, Roman god of the sea and freshwater, to whom the traditional sacrifice was a bull. Diana may have been among the other gods to whom sacrifices were made, as there was a Temple of Diana at Baiae. Dio specifically says that Caligula also sacrificed to Invidia, goddess of envy: "So that no jealousy should attend me," Caligula announced.[145]

The young emperor had come wearing a breastplate that he said had belonged to Alexander the Great, brought from Alexandria. He topped this with a purple silk cloak glittering with gems from India. A sheathed sword was on his belt, a shield on his left arm, while on his head he wore an oak-leaf crown. Caligula mounted a brightly decorated horse, and the Praetorian Horse mounted up behind him as the cohorts of the Praetorian Guard fell in with shield and spear. Caligula then led the way across the bridge toward Puteoli. Once Caligula's procession of thousands of men had reached the far end, "he dashed fiercely into Puteoli as if he were in pursuit of an enemy," says Dio, who stated that the emperor remained in Puteoli all the following day, "as if resting from battle."[146]

On the third day of the exercise, July 23, with the waters of the bay remaining flat throughout, says Dio, Caligula led the way back across the bridge. On this second bridge-crossing day, according to Suetonius, the emperor "appeared in charioteer's costume driving a team of two famous horses," one of whom was probably Incitatus. Dio, who observed that Caligula's tunic for the day was gold-embroidered, wrote that a long train of "spoils" followed the emperor's chariot, among them Darius, son of the king of Parthia, who had arrived at Rome as a hostage in AD 37/38. This has caused some modern historians to posit that Caligula was treating this parade as a pseudo Triumph, for conquering the sea, but Suetonius scotches this idea by putting Darius in the chariot with Caligula, an act quite contrary to the traditions regarding Triumphs.[147]

The emperor's friends, relatives, and senior staff came next, riding in Gallic chariots and wearing flowered robes, with the Praetorians again riding and marching in the imperial wake, followed by the public in a massive throng. On ships near the center of the bridge Caligula halted and alighted to address his troops from a platform as the dozen Praetorian standard-bearers with their standards bearing Victoria, goddess of victory, gathered below him and the now stationary parade stretched back to the Puteoli shore.

In a speech to the troops, Caligula first extolled himself. "I am an undertaker of great enterprises," he declared. Then he turned to his soldiers. "You are men who have undergone great hardships and perils," he said, before praising them for "this achievement of yours in crossing through the sea."[148]

The emperor paid his troops a bonus for their efforts, after which he and the crowd sat down to a feast, with Caligula and many others lunching on the bridge while members of his entourage feasted in boats moored close by. The banquet lasted throughout the afternoon; as the sun set, it showed no sign of ending. All this was cited by the likes of Suetonius and Dio as yet another example of the emperor's ludicrous grandiosity and enormous wastefulness. More recent critics regard it as the act of a man who'd lost touch with reality. In fact, Caligula seems to have had several very practical reasons for staging the event.

What no ancient author chose to tell their readers is the significance of the reference to Neptune. As we know, Caligula sacrificed to Neptune at the bay. The purpose and dating for Caligula's two processions across the water become abundantly clear when you know that July 23 was the annual *Neptunalia*, the Festival of Neptune, a major event on the Roman religious calendar. In addition to being god of the sea, Neptune was Roman god of horses and patron deity of racehorses, often being depicted driving a chariot. This was why Caligula had driven a chariot, and pulled by famous racehorses at that, on the return journey across the bridge, but not on the first crossing, two days earlier.

July 21, the day on which Caligula would have made his first bridge crossing, was the last day of the *Lucaria*, a religious festival associated with the clearing of groves—the first day was July 19. This would explain Caligula's oak-leaf crown that day, and possibly the flowery outfits that Dio noted on his companions. A feature of the Lucaria was the construction of temporary leafy huts, and Dio's "lodging houses" along the bridge were probably these leafy huts. Both July 21 and July 23 were public holidays, with the Neptunalia being the larger and more important of the two events and requiring by tradition a large public feast, which Caligula celebrated on the bridge.

So, Caligula's bridge was no act of madness. It was clearly a culmination of three factors—the need for a Guards training exercise, a desire for a memorable public religious observance while Caligula was staying at Baiae, and his determination to enhance his reputation as a great innovator.

Caligula being Caligula, once the religious aspects of the day had been dealt with, fun featured high on the agenda. As the sun went down that evening, lunch became dinner, with giant oil lamps on the bridge and fires all around the bay lit to turn night into day. As the food and wine continued to flow, Dio says that Caligula became "glutted with food and strong drink" and joked, when someone remarked on how calm the waters had remained throughout, "Even Neptune is afraid of me!" And when Xerxes and his father Darius were mentioned, Caligula made all manner of fun of them, declaring, "Ha! I've bridged a far greater expanse than them!"[149]

Then, it was time for water sports. Becoming playful, the emperor pushed several companions into the water. Plus, for nighttime entertainment, he'd arranged for small craft armed with "beaks," water-line rams, to be rowed about, ramming the boats containing his friends in sea-battle style. Dio says that Caligula personally sailed about doing this. That would have been a risky enterprise considering the fact that he couldn't swim and would have required plenty of bravado. According to Suetonius, Caligula alternated between bravery and timidity, depending on his mood, so it's hard to know if he genuinely participated. According to Dio, a number of people ended up in the water, and several drowned, although he gave no names. "The majority, though drunk, managed to save themselves," he says.[150]

With the fun over, Caligula returned to his Baiae villa in time to sit in judgment on a legal case with biblical connections.

Herodias, sister of Caligula's good friend King Herod Agrippa, had married another Herod, Herod Antipas, the Jewish ruler of Galilee and Perea who'd refused to judge Jesus of Nazareth when Pontius Pilate sent the prisoner to him around AD 33. Jewish historian Josephus tells us that, in AD 39, jealous of her brother Agrippa after he'd been given half of King Herod's former territories by Caligula, Herodias convinced her husband that they should go to Italy and convince the young emperor to remove these lands from Agrippa and give them to Antipas. Agrippa, who was in Judea at the time, got wind of this and sent his trusted freedman Fortunatus with letters for Caligula, hoping to head off his rivals.

After sailing to Puteoli, both parties turned up simultaneously at Caligula's door at Baiae. Today, many of the ruined waterfront Roman villas of Baiae are visible from the surface of the waters of the bay, sitting on neat grid-pattern streets, after half the Roman town long ago sank beneath the water as the result of an earthquake. There at his seaside villa, Caligula heard Herod Antipas and Herodias put their case against Agrippa. Once he'd listened to their argument, he read Agrippa's letters.

Agrippa wrote accusing Herod Antipas of having been an ally of Sejanus in the past and of having more recently become an ally of King

Artabanus of Parthia, Rome's greatest foe in the East. As proof of the latter, Agrippa claimed that Herod had secretly built up an armory to equip
seventy thousand men. When Caligula put this claim to Antipas, he didn't
deny it. Furious, Caligula declared that this was not the act of a friend of
Rome, and banished Antipas for life to the Pyrenees Mountains town of
Lugdunum Convenarum, which today is Saint-Bertrand-de-Comminges.
Situated in the southwest of Gaul, this was a remote Roman military colony established by Pompey the Great in 72 BC, not far from the modern
Spanish border. Adding to the punishment, Caligula took Herod Antipas's
existing territory and possessions and gave it all to Agrippa.

As for Herodias, Caligula was prepared to pardon her because she
was Agrippa's sister, but haughty Herodias declared that, having shared
her husband's good fortune in the past, she would share his misfortune
now. Furious that she refused his act of clemency, Caligula also took all of
Herodias's possessions and gave them to her brother, and banished her to
Gaul with her husband. Herod Antipas would reputedly die there in exile,
and Herodias no doubt suffered the same fate. Her daughter Salome voluntarily traveled to join the couple at Lugdunum Convenarum in the winter of
AD 39/40, only to drown en route while crossing an iced-over river, with
the ice breaking beneath her and consigning Salome to a freezing death.[151]

Meanwhile, according to fourth-century writer Eusebius, Christian
Bishop of Caesarea in Palestine and counselor to Constantine the Great,
there was another notable victim of Caligula's ongoing purge of suspected
traitors at Rome at this time, another who'd played a role in Christian
history. This was the Pontius Pilate, former prefect of Judea. As mentioned
previously, he'd been sent back to Rome by Vitellius to face charges in
front of Tiberius and had benefitted from Caligula's general amnesty of
AD 37. According to Eusebius, Pilate was now banished by Caligula to
Vienne in Gaul. The reasons for Pilate's exile are unknown.[152]

It was Roman poet Virgil who invented the term "snake in the grass,"
but it was Caligula who came to personify the snake in the grass in the eyes
of Romans who, like Pilate, were at one time pardoned by him only to be
later caught up in a new, unheralded round of punishments. Caligula, for

his paranoid part, would have considered the likes of Pilate the snakes in the grass.[153]

Pilate became the second leading figure from the last days of Christ to be punished by Caligula, and the second administrator of part of the Holy Land exiled to today's Vienne. Herod Archelaus, another son of Herod the Great and uncle of Herod Agrippa, had, in 4 BC, been allocated control of half his late father's kingdom by Augustus. By AD 6, Herod Archelaus had such a poor reputation that Augustus removed him from power, summoned him to Rome, and turned Judea into a sub-province of Syria ruled by a Roman prefect, of whom Pontius Pilate was the fifth. At Rome, Archelaus had been unsuccessfully defended by Tiberius before Augustus, who exiled him to Vienne. It's believed Archelaus died there sometime prior to AD 18. Some writers suggest the story of Pilate's exile to Vienne arose out of confusion with Herod Archelaus's exile there, but, equally, Herod Archelaus's fate may have inspired Caligula's decision to exile Pilate to the same place.

Before the year was out, Pilate's story and Caligula's story would briefly converge one more time.

# XVII

## THE POWER OF WORDS

Like all upper-class Romans, Caligula had been taught rhetoric and dec-lamation as a boy. These lessons in public speaking prepared Roman men for public life, in the courts, in the Senate and lesser representative bodies, and during campaigns for election to public office. Caligula was fluent and well-read in both Latin and Greek. Strange as it may seem to us today, the custom in those times was to read books aloud, not privately and inwardly as we usually do, and this contributed to developing public speaking skills.

According to Suetonius, Caligula "showed remarkable eloquence and quickness of mind, especially when prosecuting. Anger exited him to a flood of words and thoughts. He moved about excitedly while speak-ing, and his voice carried a great distance. At the start of every speech, he would warn the audience that he proposed to 'draw the sword which I have forged in my midnight study.'"[154]

Caligula became convinced that no one was a better public speaker or legal advocate than himself, and he was reportedly jealous of the leading writers and speakers of the day. Suetonius claimed that Caligula consid-ered removing from Roman libraries the books and busts of poet Virgil and historian Livy—the latter had been his uncle Claudius's history tutor. Suetonius also says that Caligula declared that Virgil "had no talent and little learning," and thought about also removing Homer's work from pub-lic circulation. Yet Suetonius separately tells us of several occasions when Caligula publicly quoted both Homer and Virgil.[155]

"Caligula always found some cause for envy," says Suetonius, and the evidence suggests he was correct in this regard. Suetonius writes that Caligula despised all polished and elegant style when it came to speaking and writing, and considered Seneca, who'd become the leading speaker and legal advocate of the day, "a mere textbook orator," while his work was "sand without lime."[156] Yet, despite his inflated opinion of his own talents as a legal advocate, Caligula never ventured to write and publish books, unlike his uncle Claudius, who wrote copious historical works, or his father Germanicus, who was a noted writer of Greek plays and books on a variety of subjects, including a work on astronomy that was still being quoted in the Middle Ages.

Most of the writers who irritated Caligula were dead, but one living writer was within reach of his wrath. In the mood to punish someone one day, Caligula decided to condemn Seneca to death, because, in the emperor's presence, Seneca had eloquently pleaded a case and secured the acquittal of a man Caligula wanted condemned. Caligula is said to have issued an order for Seneca's execution, and Seneca himself was to say some years later, "Gaius was known to keep his word in commands of that sort." Although, what followed was to prove Seneca wrong.[157] Seneca would in fact outlive Caligula, by a quarter of a century.

In this case, Caligula was reliably the changeable weathercock. He neither arrested nor executed Seneca. A female associate of Seneca went to the emperor and pleaded for his life, telling Caligula that Seneca was suffering from an incurable illness which was in an advanced stage, assuring him that Seneca was likely to soon die. Content to see Seneca die slowly and painfully, Caligula relented and dropped his execution plan.[158]

In addition to personally acting as prosecutor in some cases, to show off his legal skills, Caligula did write and publish papers in which he refuted the arguments of defense attorneys who'd secured the acquittal of their clients. Other times, he would write and publish arguments for both the prosecution and the defense for cases currently being heard in the Senate, and summon to the Palatium an audience of members of the Equestrian Order, who were not permitted to hear Senate debates, to hear him read his work aloud.

"By Hercules!" he is said to have exclaimed after the outcome of one particular case went against his wishes. "No lawyer will be able to give advice contrary to my will!"[159] And yet, there is no record of Caligula ever ordering the reversal of a trial decision.

One senator, Domitius Afer, who was brought to trial in the Senate in AD 39 for treason, woke up to the fact that it was narcissism that drove Caligula. This was the same Afer who, years before during the Sejanus era, had led the prosecution against Claudia Pulchra, cousin and close friend of Caligula's mother. Caligula seems to have long hated Afer because of this, so, when he learned that Afer had set up a bust of him with an inscription stating, accurately, that at twenty-seven Caligula was consul for the second time. Afer, and most others, considered this praise, but Caligula's inferiority complex kicked in—he took the inscription to mean Afer was "reproaching him for his youth and for his illegal conduct," says Dio. As a result, Afer found himself charged with treason, with the young emperor personally writing the case for the prosecution and delivering it in the Senate.[160]

When came time for the senator to defend himself, instead of trying to counter Caligula's case, Afer went through the indictment point by point, praising it as a work of genius. As a consequence, Caligula set him free. More than that, within months, changeable Caligula would appoint Afer a consul. It helped Afer's case, and his subsequently revived career, that he was a client of Caligula's chief adviser Callistus. Following Afer's acquittal, Callistus asked the emperor why he'd proceeded with the prosecution against the senator in the first place.

Caligula replied, "It wouldn't have been right for me to have kept such a speech to myself."[161]

# XVIII

## PREPARING FOR WAR

Caligula invited numerous dignitaries to accompany him on his German campaign, and over the summer of AD 39 King Agrippa, King Antiochus IV of Commagene, and King Ptolemy of Mauretania arrived in Rome to join the imperial circle, which also included Caligula's good friend Marcus Lepidus and the few other senior senators that Caligula trusted, men such as Servius Selpicius Galba, a close friend of his uncle Claudius.

Cassius Dio was to be highly critical of Agrippa and Antiochus, considering them bad influences on Caligula and describing them as "tyrant-trainers."[162] Yet, while Christian writers would later be critical of Agrippa because Christians were persecuted in Palestine by Jewish authorities on Agrippa's watch, Agrippa was considered a far from tyrannical ruler by his Jewish subjects, who rated him kind and generous and dubbed him Agrippa the Great. Antiochus, meanwhile, would prove a loyal and reliable ally of Rome for decades. If anyone could have given lessons in tyranny by this time, it was Caligula.

Caligula also recalled his brother-in-law Vinicius and sister Livilla from Asia, where Vinicius had served just a single year as governor, to join his northern expedition. His sister Agrippina, whose husband was ill and unable to leave Rome, was also preparing to join the emperor's party for the northern jaunt. Livilla and Agrippina would both be in Gaul with Caligula come the fall, and Caligula's biographer Suetonius castigates him for taking women on a military campaign.

A number of modern-day historians suspect that Caligula's new wife and trusted confidant Caesonia also traveled to Gaul with him; Barrett suggests she returned to Rome once he set off from Lugdunum for the Rhine.[163] Caligula's new daughter was probably left in Rome in the care of the priestesses of Minerva and a wet nurse. His uncle Claudius was not joining the expedition; he was remaining behind at Rome to deputize for the emperor at all the games that took place during his absence.

Caligula was meanwhile irked by the fact that Caesonia's brother Corbulo and his fellow unidentified consul since July failed to proclaim a thanksgiving on his birthday on August 31. To find some cause for firing them, he criticized the pair for celebrating a customary festival on September 2 commemorating Augustus's defeat of Mark Antony at the Battle of Actium, by stressing that he was a blood descendant of Antony. He had told his closest confidants that whichever course these consuls took, sacrificing to Augustus or Antony, he would find fault with them for their August 31 error.

On September 2, he replaced his brother-in-law and the other consul with Didius Gallus and Domitius Afer—the same Afer who'd recently avoided the executioner by praising Caligula's indictment against him. No doubt as a favor to his new wife, Caligula didn't physically punish her brother Corbulo and the other sacked consul, but he did have their consular fasces publicly shattered in front of them. Corbulo's colleague was so humiliated that he went home and committed suicide. But Corbulo was made of sterner stuff—over the next two decades, he would prove to be Rome's strictest military disciplinarian and one of her most successful generals.

It was probably at this time of frustration with consuls that Caligula threatened to have Incitatus the racehorse made one. Shortly after their appointment, Caligula hosted a banquet for new consuls Afer and Gallus. As the pair shared Caligula's dining couch, Caligula suddenly burst out laughing. Perplexed, the consuls asked him what was so funny.

"I've just realized," Caligula replied, "that I only have to give the nod, and both your throats would be cut."[164]

In the summer of AD 39, before he embarked on his northern campaign, Caligula made major changes to the empire's southern boundaries in North

Africa. This seems not to have been born out of any carefully thought through policy. Rather, it came through the agency of his annoyance with two men. The first was a Piso.

Based on the writings of Suetonius and Dio, it has been assumed by many scholars that by this time the Senate had totally surrendered to Caligula's will and was willing to give him everything he wanted. Something that occurred that summer suggests otherwise. While the emperor was authorized to appoint the governors of propraetor rank to "imperial" provinces, the Senate was entitled to appoint the proconsuls who governed "senatorial" provinces, which were known as "armed" provinces because legions were stationed there. Now, the Senate appointed Lucius Piso to become the next governor of the armed senatorial province of Africa, with his appointment to commence the following year.

Senators must have known this man was the son of the Piso who'd been condemned by the Senate after being charged with the murder of Caligula's father, Germanicus, and who had himself been forced in AD 20 by the Senate to change his first name to Lucius from that of his reviled father, Gnaeus. They must also have been aware that this man, while city prefect, had facilitated the AD 36 arrest and imprisonment of Caligula's close friend Agrippa, following the accusation made by his chariot driver.

It is likely that Piso was still serving as city prefect in AD 39 and quite probable that Caligula demanded his removal from that powerful post—the city prefect commanded the City Guard and Night Watch troops at Rome. But for the Senate to then make Piso governor of Africa, in command of more than ten thousand legionary and auxiliary troops, could only have raised the emperor's hackles. And it did! In fact, Dio was to say, Caligula was in fear of Piso using these troops in a rebellion against him.[165]

Caligula didn't confront the Senate head-on in this matter. Instead, he made a cunning geographical change, dividing the one former province of Africa into two, with Piso to govern the unarmed coastal province. At a stroke, Caligula left Piso with a gubernatorial appointment while taking all military forces from him. Caligula gave control of the new "armed" province to the commander of the resident 3rd *Augusta* Legion, an officer of *legatus* rank personally appointed by the emperor.

The other individual to influence Caligula's North African policy was his second cousin Ptolemy, King of Mauretania, whose grandparents had been Mark Antony and Cleopatra, queen of Egypt. Ptolemy had grown up in Rome as a member of Antonia's circle of princes and princesses, living under her care and patronage on the Palatine. In his late forties or early fifties now, with a neat beard and mustache and artificial Roman curls, Ptolemy had been on his throne for two decades when he came to Rome that summer as Caligula's guest, apparently to join the northern expedition at the end of the summer. Caligula gave his cousin a warm welcome with full honors, and they seemed to be getting along splendidly through the summer, until one day when both attended an amphitheater to witness a gladiatorial contest.

Suetonius tells us what took place, but not where and precisely when. While Caligula followed the imperial custom of spending much of the summer away from Rome at his country and coastal villas, he seems to have returned to Rome for this event. The venue would have been either his as-yet-uncompleted amphitheater on the Field of Mars at Rome or the sixty-eight-year-old Taurian Amphitheater to the south of the Field of Mars. This latter structure, whose seating was wooden, would be destroyed in the AD 64 Great Fire of Rome, to be replaced in the AD 80s by the Flavian Amphitheater—the Colosseum, or Coliseum, as we know it.

As for the event attended by Caligula and Ptolemy, under a law of Augustus there were then just two official gladiatorial shows at Rome each year, each limited to 120 fighters. The elaborate and lengthy annual *Ludi Magni*, or the Great Games, largest, oldest, and most famous of the *ludi*, which ran over September 4 to 19, would be the most likely candidate for the games in question. These were the most important games on the Roman calendar. Dedicated to Jupiter, Juno, and Minerva, they usually began with a triumphal procession, featured gladiatorial contests and multiple days of chariot racing, and were managed by a full-time procurator on an annual salary of 200,000 sesterces. Following these games,

Caligula would almost immediately depart Rome for his northern military campaign.

With Caligula seated in the imperial box since the commencement of the program, King Ptolemy was to arrive late this day. Caligula was already in an ugly mood, as he invariably seemed to be at the amphitheater. Suetonius tells of an occasion—it may have been this very day—when the crowd began to shout, "We want Tetrinius the bandit to come out and fight!"

"They are all Tetriniuses too!" growled Caligula testily.

Before long, five *retiarii*, the net-and-trident class of gladiator, came out into the arena to fight five *secutores* armed with shield and sword. All five net-and-trident men performed badly, with their opponents disarming them. The *secutores* turned their backs to the downed and wounded retiarii as they faced the emperor's box to await a signal as to whether their opponents should be permitted to live or not. As the crowd roared its advice to Caligula, the emperor, disgusted by the poor performance of the defeated men, gave the signal for all five to be dispatched—we still don't know whether the gladiatorial death signal was a thumbs up or a thumbs down. Meanwhile, one of the condemned men grabbed a trident from the sand and rose up and stabbed all five secutores in the back. Most of the people in the crowd thought this hilarious.

Caligula didn't agree. He was outraged. "This was bloody murder!" he declared to his companions, shaking his head with disgust at this crowd that approved of such underhanded behavior, as the bodies were dragged from the arena.[166]

It was around this time during the afternoon's program that King Ptolemy made his entrance to the stadium. Wearing a rich purple cloak, he turned heads and received applause from the crowd. According to Suetonius, Caligula was incensed by his cousin's rich cloak, and by the attention it received from the Roman public that now seemed to always rile him. Caligula ordered Praetorians to immediately arrest the king, drag him away, and imprison him. Ptolemy would spend months incarcerated. Seneca wrote of visiting him while he was imprisoned. Between the time

Caligula arrived at Lugdunum in Gaul in the autumn and moved on to Mogontiacum at the beginning of the following spring, Ptolemy would be executed back in Rome on Caligula's orders.

Suetonius says it was merely envy of Ptolemy that drove Caligula to remove him.[167] Alternatively, some modern writers have suggested that Ptolemy was somehow involved in a conspiracy that Caligula would expose in Gaul in October. Caligula would also arrest another foreign ruler and ally in Rome around this time—King Mithradates of Armenia—and imprison him. Mithradates would escape the executioner, remaining a prisoner at Rome until Caligula's own death. It is likely that Caligula's arrest of Ptolemy was done on an irritable whim, yet his subsequent execution of his cousin could have been for a quite pragmatic, if greedy, reason.

The motive for Ptolemy's death is suggested by what Caligula did next. Mauretania was one of the richest of Rome's client kingdoms, and now the emperor ordered its invasion and occupation. Mauretania would be divided into two Roman provinces, but not before the Mauritanians put up stiff armed resistance, led by Aedemon, one of Ptolemy's retainers. This resistance would be swiftly put down, only to flare up again a little later and last for months. After a bloody campaign, Rome's troops would finally snuff out the resistance in late AD 40, consolidating Mauretania and its wealth into the Roman Empire, which now stretched all the way along the North African coast from Egypt to beyond the Strait of Gibraltar.

Dio was in no doubt that Caligula removed Ptolemy simply to access the wealth of his kingdom, and considering the focus Caligula would apply on squeezing cash from wealthy Gauls in the Gallic provinces in the coming months, this seems the most plausible motive for Ptolemy's rude end.[168]

# XIX

## SHOCKS IN GAUL

Shortly after September 19, AD 39, following the five days of chariot racing that culminated the long program of the Great Games, the emperor moved to the suburbs of Rome, leaving the new consuls Afer and Gallus in charge at the capital. It's highly likely that his party—now in the suburbs with Caligula—included his wife and two sisters, King Agrippa and King Antiochus of Commagene, the emperor's brothers-in-law Lepidus and Vinicius, and a clutch of senators including Galba. They would have been joined by a Praetorian prefect and the commander of the German Guard, as well as senior Palatium staff.

Josephus tells us that when Agrippa returned to Rome that year to rejoin Caligula's court, he remembered an old promise and purchased the freedom of Caligula's slave Thaumustus. This was the same slave who'd given him water when he was being taken away in chains from Tiberius's villa at Tusculum three years earlier. Agrippa subsequently sent Thaumustus to the Middle East to manage his estates there. Thaumustus would serve Agrippa until the king's death, after which he faithfully served Agrippa's son and daughter.[169]

Soon after leaving the city proper, the emperor, his courtiers, and a massive entourage including actors and gladiators, departed Italy unannounced. Suetonius thought it scandalous that actors, gladiators, women, and horses were in the imperial party, but all had their role to play in what was to follow. The gladiators in question would have been the twenty Thracians of Caligula's personal troupe, whom he would pit against all comers at games in Gaul, most particularly at Lugdunum, today's Lyon in central France, where he planned to spend the winter. The actors, too, would appear at the games, in theatrical shows.

By far the largest contingent in the imperial party was made up of troops—cohorts of his German Guard bodyguard and several cohorts of the Praetorian Guard, plus the men and horses from an ala (wing) or two of the Praetorian Horse. Perhaps as much as half the now enlarged Praetorian Guard—six thousand men—was heading north. In all, the emperor's escort is likely to have involved more than ten thousand troops. The entourage would also have included hundreds, if not thousands, of servants of the emperor and his courtiers—doctors, secretaries, cooks, bakers, stewards, valets, dressers, hairdressers, and handmaids. In the imperial court, there were even slaves whose only job was to maintain the water clocks, while others collected cobwebs as a remedy against the emperor's shaving cuts.

Caligula's route and mode of transport for reaching Gaul was not recorded by the ancient authorities, but modern scholars have tended to assume that Caligula and his party traveled overland all the way, through northern Italy to the south of France. However, we know that during his reign Caligula had the habit of using ships of the war fleet based close to Rome at Misenum. Plus, it's recorded that when the next emperor made this exact same trip to Gaul with a similarly large party not many years later, he traveled by sea from Ostia, port of Rome, to the port of Massalia in Narbonne Gaul, today's Marseille.

Ancient sources only speak of Caligula traveling overland in Gaul, and it's highly likely that he began the journey by doing the same as his successor, either moving the short distance down the Tiber to Ostia, or farther south to Misenum, to embark for a sea crossing to Massalia.

Apart from Caligula's visit to Sicily, this expedition was the first visit to the provinces by a reigning emperor in more than fifty years and would have generated great excitement among the local population—the same sort of adoration we see lavished on senior members of the British royal family when they visit countries in the British Commonwealth. As Caligula leisurely progressed through Gaul, water was sprinkled outside each town he entered to put down the dust. His column would have been strung out for miles, with Praetorian cavalrymen clearing the road of civilian traffic,

with travelers joining locals to line the roadside and watch the emperor's
lengthy cortege pass.

Caligula was carried in a litter by eight slaves. The ladies would also
have been borne in litters. The servants, like the troops, were on foot. The
baggage train trundling along at the rear would have included hundreds
of wagons carrying the furniture, eating and drinking utensils, clothing,
and other possessions of the imperial party, as well as the larger military
equipment. There would have been a minimum of five hundred pack
mules carrying the tents, grinding stones, and other heavier equipment of
the soldiers—one mule for every eight men was the norm—led by scores
of muleteers.

The troops themselves, in loose marching order, would have had
their helmets slung around their necks. On their shoulders, they had carrying poles to which were attached their cloaks, bedrolls, mess equipment, and personal items such as their military decorations and detachable
helmet plumes for parade use. A mounted Praetorian advance party would
have been a day's march ahead, choosing, mapping, and preparing camp-
sites where the tents of imperial party, troops, and servants would be
erected by troops for the night. As well, they would be foraging firewood
and fodder and gathering water, food, and wine for the imperial party
from the local communities, which had been given many months to prepare since the first instructions regarding the emperor's intended visit had
been issued by the Palatium in the spring.

Caligula's route from Marseille would have taken him first to the
provincial capital, Nemausus, today's city of Nimes, crossing the Rhone
and Gardon rivers en route. A thirty-one-mile aqueduct would be built to
Nemausus from Uzes to supply the city with running water. Today, part
of this system is preserved as the magnificent Pont du Gard, which crosses
the Gardon east of Nimes. For a long time, this aqueduct was credited to
Caligula's grandfather Marcus Agrippa, but it is now believed that construction began in AD 40, during Caligula's reign, to be completed fifteen years
later. It's likely that Caligula inspired the project during his AD 39 visit,
boasting to locals of the two massive aqueducts he was building at Rome.

From Nemausus, Caligula would have followed the River Rhone to the city of Arelentum, today's Arles. He probably then traveled northeast to Orange, called Arausio in Roman times and settled by legion veterans in 35 BC. This would have allowed Caligula to pass under a triumphal arch at Orange's northern entrance that was dedicated to his father Germanicus—as indicated by the modern recreation by archaeologists of its brass inscription letters.

Paid for by local dignitaries, the arch at Orange depicts via its weathered stones Germanicus's AD 15–16 German campaigns. Built by veterans of the 2nd *Augusta* Legion, whose recruiting grounds were in the Orange area, the arch shows war trophies including German shields, armor, horns, and boar standards, as well as several of Varus's twelve *fasces*, symbols of his rank as an ex consul, which would have been captured by the Germans at the Tuetoburg and recovered by Germanicus. Even the wrecked ships and sea monsters mentioned by Tacitus in his *Annals* account of the AD 16 campaign appear on the arch.[170]

At one of the Gallic cities through which Caligula passed, he and his party would have joined the locals in celebrating the Augustan Games of early October. Meanwhile, according to Dio, while playing dice with his friends at one Gallic city, Caligula ran out money. Leaving the others playing, he departed the room and called for the census lists of all the wealthy citizens of Gaul. He then ordered the richest of them arrested, convicted of crimes, and executed, or required to commit suicide. He then confiscated and liquidated the victims' estates, adding the money to his depleted treasury.

Returning to his dice game, Caligula chided his friends, saying, "Here you are playing for a few denarii, while I've taken in a good hundred and fifty million." That was 600 million sesterces.[171]

Indeed, his critics would declare that this expedition to Gaul was all about making money. It was found that one local, Julius Sacerdos, was confused with another wealthy Sacerdos, and executed by mistake. Caligula had no regrets and offered no apology to the man's relatives.

"Let them hate me, so long as they fear me," he responded to the news, quoting second-century BC poet Lucius Accius.[172]

Caligula's concourse took him on to the Rhone city of Vienne. If Eusebius and later sources are to be believed, Pontius Pilate was then in exile in Vienne and was forced to take his own life by Caligula, after which his body was thrown in the Rhone—in the same way that the bodies of persons convicted of treasonous crimes were thrown into the Tiber at Rome.[173] The people of Vienne will direct you to a Roman monument in their city, La Pyramide, which reputedly sits over Pilate's tomb. It takes the form of an Egyptian obelisk, atop a small arch, which originally sat on the spine of Vienne's Roman hippodrome. Considering the reported nature of Pilate's death, it's doubtful his remains would have been permitted such formal interment; under Roman law, family and friends were not permitted to retrieve and inter the remains of persons convicted of treasonous crimes.

The emperor and his party moved steadily onward and reached their destination, Lugdunum, arriving in the picturesque city no later than the third week of October. Caligula would have felt a strong connection to Lugdunum. His father, Germanicus, had been born there, and he himself would have passed through it several times as a child. Founded on the site of a Gallic town by a Roman general in 43 BC, it was the administrative center of the province of Gallia Lugdunensis and two other smaller Gallic provinces, which together covered much of today's central and northern France and Belgium.

Sitting on a river bend where the Rhone and Saone met, Lugdunum was in a key strategic location, being the junction of four major Roman roads—south to Marseille, west to Aquitania, north to the Rhine, and northwest to the English Channel. Despite its importance, the city didn't then possess a hippodrome for chariot racing. It did have an amphitheater and a fine drama theater built into the side of the Fourviere Hill, overlooking the city. Caligula would take full advantage of both during the months he spent here. Lugdunum was then home to the only imperial mint outside Rome. To guard the mint, a cohort from Rome's City Guard was permanently stationed in Lugdunum, and these 1,500 men, along with the city's population, would have turned out to welcome the emperor.

As he took up residence high on the city's Fourviere Hill, Caligula would have received the governor of Upper Germany, Gnaeus Cornelius Lentulus Gaetulicus, summoned well in advance to discuss the emperor's upcoming German campaign. It's likely that Gaetulicus was joined at Lugdunum by his father-in-law Lucius Apronius, governor of Lower Germany, who would also have been expecting to sit down with the emperor in the German war council, with the campaign involving his four legions as well as those of his son-in-law.

Gaetulicus, who'd held his current post since AD 26, was the only senior associate of Sejanus known to have escaped punishment following Sejanus's downfall—apparently because he was in Germany at the time and played no part in Sejanus's seditious activities. Gaetulicus had kept his appointment under Caligula by sweet-talking him from afar. Suetonius says that, apparently aware that one of Caligula's favorite deities while growing up had been Hercules, "Gaetulicus tried to flatter the proud young monarch by pretending that he came from Tibur, a city sacred to Hercules."[174]

Once Caligula arrived at Lugdunum, out of the blue he ordered the arrest of three members of his party—his own sisters Agrippina and Livilla and his brother-in-law Lepidus. To complete the surprise, Governor Gaetulicus was also arrested. While the first three were charged with incest and conspiring to overthrow Caligula and put Lepidus on the throne, the specific charges against Gaetulicus are unclear, although many historians today believe he was probably in league with Lepidus and planning to back his claim for the throne with his legions. This turn of events was all the more stunning because Caligula had at one time indicated that he saw Lepidus as his successor. Ironically, that may have put the idea into the conspirators' heads.

We can date these arrests to around the second or third week of October, because, on October 27, at Rome, the Arval Brethren religious order formally gave thanks for the emperor's delivery from the plot; the record is still extant.[175] Augustus had once boasted that Rome's very efficient courier service, the *Cursus Publicus Velox*—literally the State's Very Fast Runner—could deliver messages to him at Rome from the farthest reaches of the empire in no more than ten days. Allowing a week for the news of the arrests at Lugdunum to reach Rome and a minimum of a day for the Brethren to gather and act, those arrests can be seen to have taken place on or before October 19.

It's clear that Caligula had been aware of the plot for some time and had planned to lure Gaetulicus away from his Rhine legions and Lepidus and his sisters away from supporters in Rome before he arrested them. Dio says that Gaetulicus was very popular with his Rhine legions because he'd relaxed discipline during his ten years in command. It made sense for Caligula to arrest the governor well away from those soldiers. At Lugdunum, surrounded by the emperor's loyal troops, Gaetulicus was on unfriendly ground and too far from his legions for them to aid him.

Caligula promptly brought Lepidus and Gaetulicus to trial there in Lugdunum. At Lepidus' hearing it became clear that the case against the accused had been some time in the making, for incriminating letters written by Agrippina and Livilla and obtained by informants were presented. Ultra-ambitious Agrippina would be said to be behind the plot to replace Caligula with Lepidus, but the indications are that twenty-one-year-old Livilla was not entirely an unwilling or unwitting participant. When, prior to Caligula's accession, someone had said that he might one day succeed to the throne, Livilla had reportedly said, "I pray that the Roman people might be spared so cruel and underserved a misfortune."[176]

Lepidus and Gaetulicus were promptly executed. In Lepidus's case, his executioner was a tribune named Dexter, who dispatched Lepidus using an axe, not a sword, which was the usual weapon used in the execution of a Roman citizen. It was routinely the job of Praetorian centurions to carry out executions. Tribunes didn't normally dirty their hands with such duties. Meanwhile, Dexter, whose name means "skillful," was typically a name of an auxiliary soldier, and the axe was a typical German weapon. This all suggests that Dexter was a tribune of the German Guard, and conjures an image of a massive, blond, bearded German nobleman wielding the blade that took off Lepidus's head. At least an axe would have given Caligula's former best friend a relatively swift and painless death.

As for Agrippina and Livilla, Caligula spared them, banishing them to the Pontian Islands. It was probably no coincidence that he chose to exile his sisters to the same place that their mother and eldest brother had occupied, and where they'd perished. After Lepidus's body was cremated, Caligula required Agrippina to carry his ashes back to Rome before she was taken off to Pontia. As his sisters were taken away, Caligula gave them a chilling warning, reminding them that he could order their execution at any time.

"I have swords as well as islands," he told them.[177] Clearly, he wanted them to live in constant fear, just as he had done as a youth. Agrippina's young son Lucius, the future emperor Nero, then at Rome, would now be cared for by his paternal aunt Domitia Lepida. Caligula dedicated three swords to the Temple of Mars the Avenger at Rome, with a placard declaring that they were the weapons that the plotters had intended to use against him.

From among his party, Caligula appointed Galba, another future emperor, to replace Gaetulicus as proconsul of Upper Germany and commander of the four legions and auxiliary forces stationed there. It's likely that the emperor had this appointment planned even before he set off from Rome. Caligula also removed Gaetulicus's father-in-law Apronius from his post in Lower Germany, apparently without punishment. This seems to have been a "just in case" move on Caligula's part. Apronius's replacement, Publius Gabinius Secundus, would not be recorded on the Rhine until the following year, indicating that he wasn't with the imperial party in Gaul at the time of Apronius's removal.

Galba, Gaetulicus's replacement, shortly after parted company with the emperor at Lugdunum and hurried to Upper Germany to take up his new post. It seems he arrived at Mogontiacum in the first half of November, during the celebration of the fourteen-day annual Plebeian Games. Starting as he meant to continue, Galba immediately introduced tough discipline to his four legions. Suetonius tells us that Galba refused all the legionary leave applications that were normal for this time of year—once legions annually went into winter camp from October 19, one in every four legionaries was permitted to take furlough and leave camp, subject to the approval of their centurions and army commander.

Galba also implemented harsh training, and very soon after his arrival banned unseemly and unmilitary applause by troops on duty at the games, which were continuing, posting a notice on the camp notice board which read: "Hands will remain inside cloaks at all times."[178]

In Lugdunum, Caligula auctioned off the property belonging to Lepidus and his sisters, including their slaves. Gallic buyers proved so keen, and the results so profitable, that Caligula sent to Rome for furniture from Augustus's Old Palatium, and from the Palatium of Germanicus. According to Suetonius, to convey all of this furniture overland to Gaul his Palatium freedmen at Rome commandeered all manner of wheeled transport, from bakers' carts to private passenger vehicles, causing delays and shortages until they returned weeks later.

Once the furniture reached him at Lugdunum, Caligula personally acted as the auctioneer, declaring, as each item was put up for sale, "This belonged to my father," and, "This to my mother," "This to my grandfather," and "This to my great-grandfather." When a particularly fine piece of Egyptian furniture came up, Caligula announced, "This Egyptian piece was Antony's—Augustus's prize of victory."

All the while, Caligula pretended to be heartbroken at having to sell imperial property to commoners. When bidding sometimes failed to yield the price he wanted, he would declare to the packed auction, no doubt with a grin, "Such avarice! You people are richer than I am!"[179]

The sale went very well, with provincials keen to acquire rare imperial pieces, which would be shown off in their homes for generations to come. Dio says that, despite Caligula's successful money-making ventures, he never secured a surplus.[180] He seemed to spend the money as soon as it tumbled into his hands. Seneca would accuse him of squandering money on sumptuous dinners, adding, "Everybody used their ingenuity to help him" spend.[181] Invitations to Caligula's dinners in Lugdunum were so sought after that one provincial offered a bribe of two thousand sesterces, or nearly three times a legionary's annual salary, to obtain one. Caligula was so delighted when he found out that he paid the man two thousand sesterces for some trifling object and invited him to his next dinner party.

Not long after he'd done away with Lepidus and his sisters, Caligula was pacing the halls of his Lugdunum abode in the early morning hours. Suetonius tells us that he had already been afflicted with insomnia at Rome. "Three hours of fitful sleep were all he ever got . . . he tired of laying awake the greater part of the night, and would alternately sit up in bed and wander through the long colonnades, calling out from time to time for daylight, and longing for it to come."[182] Now, he was thin, haggard, and pale and had lost most of his hair. Seneca speaks of "his bald head with a sprinkling of beggardly hairs."[183]

Sleep-deprived Caligula was furious with himself for having allowed Lepidus to convince him to be lenient with various culprits. "The banishment of these men is only a kind of emigration!" he raged, as bleary-eyed staff tried to calm him.[184]

As he paced, he remembered the former exile who'd told him several years before how he'd prayed continuously to the gods for Tiberius's death and Caligula's accession. Concluding that current exiles must likewise be praying for *his* death, Caligula called for a list of all persons then in exile and ordered their execution. Top of the list was Flaccus, former governor of Egypt. Many of the exiles, like Flaccus, had persecuted or turned their backs on members of Caligula's family in days gone by. Now, Caligula would make them pay. To avenge his family, he ordered a slow death in the case of Flaccus.

"Make him *feel* that he is dying," Caligula stressed.[185]

Not long after, on the Greek island of Andros, Flaccus was on the road from his farm, heading into the town, when he saw his Praetorian execution party marching down the road from the port. Turning, he fled over rough country. But on an island, he could only go as far as the sea, and the Praetorians, giving chase, soon caught him. He was then made to stand and watch as a grave was dug in front of him.

Again Flaccus tried to escape, only to be cut down by the soldiers, who hacked into him with their swords. In the process, they inflicted numerous wounds, giving him the slow death required by the emperor. Only once he'd bled to death was his head lopped off; it would be taken back to Rome as proof of his execution. Flaccus's body was so cut up that when the Praetorians took his arms and legs to lift him into the prepared grave, the limbs parted from his body.

From executions, Caligula turned to exhibitions. At Lugdunum's amphi-theater and drama theater, he celebrated November's Plebeian Games with his Gallic subjects. Traditionally, the programs of these games involved both athletic competitions and theatrical shows. The former offered an opportunity for his gladiatorial troupe to show their skills, while the actors in the emperor's party would have been involved in the theatrical shows, with tickets to both being snapped up by locals keen to see the best that the capital offered.

Suetonius also tells of Caligula conducting "anonymous" games during the months he spent in Lugdunum. One was a competition in Greek and Latin oratory, no doubt conceived by Caligula in collaboration with actor friend Apelles, held in the city's hillside theater, which dated from 15 BC and then held five thousand spectators. Caligula required losing oratory competitors to give gifts to the winners, while those who "failed miser-ably," in Suetonius's words, were given a choice: erase their chalked up entries with a sponge, or, if they particularly displeased the emperor, with their tongues, or be flogged and thrown into the Rhone.[186]

Some modern writers have cited this episode as an example of Caligula's cruelty. But, then, perhaps it was merely an example of his dark humor. The reference to gift giving suggests Caligula staged this con-test during the Saturnalia in December, and that it was all in the name of Saturnalian high jinks.

While the emperor amused himself in Lugdunum, in Rome the Senate quickly put together a delegation. Led by his uncle Claudius, the delegation's task was to congratulate Caligula on detecting the Lepidus/Gaetulicus plot and inform him that the Senate had awarded him an Ovation for detecting and eliminating the plot. The imperial courier service sped news of this to Caligula, but far from being pleased, he was offended by the award and refused to see most of the delegation, sending orders for them to turn back before they even reached Gaul.

Like Caligula's father, Claudius had been born in Lugdunum, and this was perhaps why Caligula permitted Claudius and a handful of delegates to come to him at the city. According to Suetonius, Caligula had his uncle thrown fully clothed into the Rhine during this period for a nonfatal dunking. Modern scholars such as Lee Fratantuono place this event at Lugdunum, making the river in question the Rhone, not the Rhine, which makes sense. A December arrival in Lugdunum by Claudius is likely, suggesting that his Rhone dunking was connected to Caligula's Saturnalia oratory competition. There is no doubt that Caligula and Claudius were in Lugdunum together—an inscription found in the city places the pair at the opening of a new building.[187]

While staying in Lugdunum, Caligula issued oracular prophesies in the guise of Jupiter while seated on a tall platform. This was not, as Suetonius and Dio would have us believe, a strange or rare thing for the times. In fact, according to Petronius Arbiter, writing not many years after this during the reign of Nero, it was the norm for Rome's mostly part-time priests to claim the gift of prophesy. "Priests, animated by an hypocritical mania for prophesy," says Arbiter, "boldly expound mysteries which are too often such to themselves."[188] Caligula was one of those priests, being a member of several priesthoods, not to mention being a god with his own priesthood.

The upper classes among Caligula's Lugdunum audience therefore showed an acceptance of his prophecies, but a Gallic shoemaker in the audience called out that this was all rubbish. Caligula had the man brought forward.

"What do I seem to you to be?" Caligula asked the shoemaker.

"A big imposter," the shoemaker replied.[189]

It was probably possible to hear the proverbial pin drop as the stunned audience waited for the emperor to erupt. But it appears that Caligula only laughed and let the shoemaker go free.

# XX

## CALIGULA GOES TO WAR

In a January sitting of the Senate at Rome, novice member Vespasian rose to propose that the traitors Lepidus and Gaetulicus be denied the right of public interment of their ashes. Vespasian had learned the art of sycophancy. His motion was passed, and the ashes were scattered to the winds. In a later sitting, Vespasian would publicly thank Caligula for having hosted him for dinner at the Palatium prior to embarking on his northern expedition. In January, too, from Lugdunum, Caligula sent for foreign dignitaries to come to Rome in the summer to witness the Triumph which he intended to celebrate following his German and British campaigns.

Early in the spring of AD 40, Caligula reached Mogontiacum on the Rhine, capital of the province of Upper Germany, which he had designated as his operational HQ. He was greeted by new governor Galba, who had checked an eastern bank raid by the Chatti tribe just prior to the emperor's appearance. As Caligula impatiently awaited the arrival of all the troops he'd ordered to assemble at Mogontiacum, he ventured by chariot across one of the newly built floating Rhine bridges, safely in the rear of a legion column that was advancing with Galba.

As the column advanced twenty miles into Germany, forty-two-year-old Galba jogged along beside his emperor's chariot, carrying a shield and issuing orders to the troops as they advanced. The very fit Galba would still be leading troops at the age of seventy-two. Suetonius claims that Caligula "made some of the highest officials run for miles beside his chariot, dressed in their togas," but Galba is the only one we can identify running beside Caligula's chariot, and not in a constricting toga.

Suetonius also says that, in a defile, someone in the emperor's party exclaimed, "What a panic there would be if the enemy suddenly appeared!"

This was enough to unnerve Caligula, who, mounting a horse of one of his escorts, galloped back to the bridges. Both bridges were crowded with the baggage train and camp followers at the very rear of the column, which were in the process of crossing. So, according to Suetonius, Caligula was carried aloft, from hand to hand, back to the western bank.[190]

Bored while waiting for the arrival of reinforcements from around the empire, the emperor decided on a little sport, embarking on giant games of hide-and-seek. Sending men of the German Guard across the river with orders to hide, he subsequently mounted up and led his friends and a Praetorian Cavalry detachment to find them. Trotting back that night by torchlight with tree branches dressed as trophies, he chided friends who hadn't taken part in the game as timorous. To those who'd joined him, he awarded a novel Rangers Crown, ornamented with sun, moon, and stars. Another time, he sent local school students out at night, then tracked them down, bringing them back in chains.

Finally, the last of the newly created military units marched into Mogontiacum. Among these were cohorts of Batavian auxiliary light infantry that would be partnered with the 14th *Gemina Martia Victrix* Legion for decades to come. The commanders of these Batavian units were tribesmen of noble birth who had been granted Roman citizenship and equite status. One such new Batavian prefect sporting the valued gold ring of the equite was Gaius Julius Civilis, who, after serving Rome loyally for twenty-five years, would lead a bloody revolt on the Rhine in AD 69.

The new Batavian units didn't have far to march to reach Mogontiacum from their homeland at the North Sea mouth of the Rhine, but other new auxiliary units had to come from the far reaches of the empire to the east and south. Some of these new units arrived at Mogontiacum past the date specified by the Palatium, driving Caligula into such a rage that he summarily dismissed the commanders of the units involved; Suetonius says the slightest delay now irritated the emperor.[191]

Archeological evidence indicates that the two new legions, the new 15th and 22nd, built a base for themselves at Weisenau, a mile south of the now overflowing legion base at the conjunction of the Rhine and Main

Rivers. The men of these new legions seem to have arrived on the Rhine toward the end of AD 39, before winter fully set in, because the religious ceremony associated with their units' formal dedication took place between late December AD 39 and late January AD 40. We can deduct this in the case of the new 22nd Legion because, in addition to its unit emblem of a spread eagle that adorned its shields, it also sported the birth sign of Capricorn, the goat; each legion proudly displayed its astrological birth sign on its standards. A January 1 dedication date would have been considered most auspicious, because this day of new beginnings was when all legions annually assembled to renew their oath of allegiance to the emperor.

To differentiate these two new legions from the original 15th and 22nd, both were given the title *Primigenia*, meaning "firstborn." This may have related to the goddess Fortuna Primigenia, who had an oracular shrine at Palestrina in central Italy. Caligula's uncle Claudius had a particular attachment to this goddess and shrine, and Caligula would himself soon be on record consulting another oracle of Fortune. Equally, with Caligula known to have been especially proud of his new daughter, Julia Drusilla— his firstborn—the title may have had a link to the emperor's child.

By the first days of spring AD 40, the 15th *Primigenia* Legion and 22nd *Primigenia* Legion would have marched up the Roman road to Mogontiacum to join Caligula's assembling forces, which Cassius Dio numbers at between 200,000 and 250,000 men, making it one of the largest Roman military forces ever to come together in the one place. Taking the ten legions believed to have then been on the Rhine, an equal number of supporting auxiliaries, plus the Praetorians and men of the German Guard, a force of some 120,000 fighting men can be arrived at. Perhaps a few thousand marines from warships based on the Rhine could be added, plus auxiliary cavalry and the troops of allies, which may have increased the figure by another 50,000 men, to 170,000. If the civilians such as the handlers of the more than 15,000 mules in the baggage trains are also included, a total of approaching 200,000 men crowded into the Mogontiacum camp is not impossible.

As the units paraded before him, Caligula removed elderly first-rank centurions from their posts; some centurions serving during the first century are known to have been aged in their seventies. Caligula also awarded prizes to Galba's four legions of the Army of the Upper Rhine for being the best turned out of all his troops.

An AD 40 sesterce coin depicts Caligula addressing five soldiers equipped with four military standards, and bearing the inscription "Addressing the Cohorts," but devoid of the usual "S C" inscription for *Senatus Consulto*, which means the minting was not "Senate approved." Some numismatists have assumed that, from the inscription's reference to "cohorts," this coin depicts Caligula addressing Praetorian Guard cohorts. Praetorian cohort standards bore the winged Victory symbol, however, while the standards shown on the coin are clearly eagles, which were used exclusively by the legions. The term "cohorts" was commonly used in Roman times in reference to legions. Julius Caesar, for example, in his *Gallic Wars*, wrote of "twenty cohorts" when he was in fact referring to two legions, each of which comprised ten cohorts.

In the *Dictionary of Roman Coins*, nineteenth century British coin expert Admiral William Smyth expressed the belief that this coin celebrated the Rhine army assembly that took place immediately prior to the launch of Caligula's British campaign. Admiral Smyth appears to have got this coin's origins right, indicating that it shows Caligula with Galba and the eagle-bearers of his four award-winning legions. This sesterce was probably produced at the Lugdunum mint.

Following the Rhine assembly, the emperor ordered elements of this massive army to march west with him to Gesoriacum, on the coast. Perhaps he'd tired of Germany. Perhaps he'd always intended the German episode as a feint, with Britain his real focus. Certainly, he'd deliberately made his German expeditionary plans public well in advance—Philo records the people of Alexandria making offerings for the success of the German campaign in AD 39.[192] At the same time, Caligula's Palatium gave no hint that an invasion of Britain was intended. Yet, his shipbuilding and port facility preparations in Gaul had commenced many months in advance and should have tipped off astute observers that something was afoot in the region.

Clearly, Caligula didn't make this turn away from the Rhine and toward Britain on a whim. It was a preplanned move, but one made in utmost secrecy, even though traders to and from Britain must have become aware of the construction work at Gesoriacum and alerted the tribes of southern Britain that something was going on just across the channel. However, to later Roman historians, even the better ones, Caligula's actions displayed neither rhyme nor reason. "His impulsive ideas shifted like a weather-cock," says Tacitus, "and his grandiose efforts against Germany had come to nothing."[193] In fact, says Tacitus, "the boastful threats of Gaius Caesar ended in farce."[194]

Caligula and his army made camp outside Gesoriacum. Suetonius says that Caligula then formed up the army on the beach, climbed a lofty plat-form, and ordered his assembled troops to gather seashells as trophies of his defeat of the ocean. Down through the centuries, this has been taken as proof that Caligula was quite mad. However, according to Roman naval authority Chester Starr, "The expedition of Gaius became a subject of malicious distortion."[195] There are in fact other explanations for the expe-dition's failure and the seashells incident, and quite reasonable explana-tions at that.

Unlike fellow author Tacitus, who commanded a legion during his rise up the Roman civil service ladder, Suetonius had no personal mili-tary experience. His father was serving as a tribune with the 13th *Gemina* Legion at the time of Suetonius's birth, but it appears that Suetonius him-self studiously avoided the military officer path, initially serving as a lawyer and later becoming an imperial secretary and successful author. Suetonius would nonetheless have been aware that, prior to the commencement of a military campaign, Roman armies went through the *Lustratio exercitus*, a religious purification ceremony.

What Suetonius was either unaware of, or failed to mention, was that, if a Roman army was near a seacoast at this time, or an operation involved the sea, tradition required that the army form up on a beach for the *Lustratio*, with half of the sacrificial animals used in the ceremony—a pig, a sheep, and a bull—thrown into the sea, and half burned on a prepared altar onshore. If a fleet was involved, it anchored off the beach for the ceremony in a half-moon formation. This appears to have been what Caligula's army was doing on the French beach, undergoing the *Lustratio exercitus* prior to the planned British invasion.

Numerous modern historians think that his army now mutinied, refusing to invade Britain, exactly the same way that Claudius's army would mutiny three years later, at this very same spot, and for the very same reasons—terror created by rumors spread by veterans who'd served under Caligula's father, Germanicus, and who'd been washed onto Britain's shores during Germanicus's German campaigns. Tacitus, in describing the AD 16 return of those shipwrecked troops to Gaul, wrote: "Not a man returned from a distance without his story of marvels—terrible hurricanes, unknown birds, sea-monsters, creatures half-human and half beast—all of which they had seen, or believed in their fear." This would explain a lot.[196]

Dio tells us that, a quarter of a century after Caligula's expedition, the British tribes boasted of having actively worked to keep the Romans from their shores. He quoted British war queen Boudicca declaring: "We dealt with Augustus and with Caligula Caesar and (made) the attempt to even sail here a formidable thing."[197] This implies covert action by the tribes at the time, such as planting agents among traders to spread wild rumors in the army's camp at Gesoriacum about the sea crossing to Britain.

We know that Caligula's successor had to bribe his troops into proceeding with that invasion, and it looks like Caligula tried the same, for, according to Suetonius, he promised his men four hundred sesterces each. The money remaining in his depleted treasury would have dictated the amount. While not huge, it still represented close to half a year's wages to a legionary. Using a quote from Vigil's *Aeneid*, Caligula added, sarcastically, "Go happy; go rich!"[198]

Still the troops refused to embark. It's apparent that, in typical fashion, when bribery didn't achieve the required results, Caligula decided to humiliate his troops by ordering them to collect seashells, after which he cancelled the whole invasion plan. "When the soldiers of his army balked," says Chester Starr, "Gaius dropped the scheme of conquest."[199] Balsdon was of the same opinion.

Dio writes that Caligula then boarded a trireme and sailed out into the English Channel, later turning around and returning to shore. Dio also says that the only plus that came out of Caligula's aborted British campaign was the surrender of a British king, the son of Cunobelinus, Shakespeare's Cymbeline. Suetonius called the young king Adminius; other sources say Amminius. Dio called him Berecus.[200] Anthony Barrett suggests that Caligula may have accepted the surrender of Amminius and some of his followers at sea, and this explains the trip out into the channel.[201]

Caligula, angry with his troops for refusing to cross the channel, and particularly peeved with the older men of the legions who'd mutinied against his father twenty-four years before, and who would have circulated the rumors that had caused the aborting of his British invasion, ordered the legions to assemble in camp without arms.

His plan, says Suetonius, was to execute every man in the offending legions.[202] Only a small number of men from AD 16, perhaps a few hundred or so, would have still been serving with these legions, under new enlistments. Caligula's friends, including kings Agrippa and Antiochus, talked him out of this mass punishment, so instead, he decided to decimate these legions. Decimation involved executing every tenth man, a standard Roman military punishment for cowardice or insubordination. Julius Caesar did this to his own troops, as did Mark Antony.

According to Suetonius, when men were seen streaming to their tents for weapons, Caligula dropped the decimation plan, and, in panic, fled south. Considering how many Praetorians and German Guard troops he would have had with him as protection, this seems unlikely. Another story offered by Suetonius was that news of an uprising of German tribes sent him fleeing. Also according to Suetonius, Caligula traveled so fast that, to keep up with their galloping emperor, the Praetorians had to tie their standards to mules of the baggage train trailing behind.[203]

The latter story sounds like Suetonius hyperbole. It was unheard of for Roman military units to voluntarily part from their sacred standards.

Roman legionaries gave their lives defending those standards, and a legion that lost its eagle in battle was disgraced, and sometimes abolished. What may have happened in this instance was that detachments protecting the Praetorians' cohort and maniple standards marched with the baggage mules while the remainder of each cohort force-marched to keep up with their emperor.

Caligula loved a military parade. As he headed south for Italy, no doubt with fond memories of his father's AD 17 Triumph, he sent orders ahead for a Triumph to be organized for him at Rome. Simultaneously, he ordered the triremes built for his British invasion sent to Rome, for the most part overland, apparently to be used in his triumphal parade. Plus, says Suetonius, not only did he require the few German prisoners taken by Galba to be sent to Rome for the Triumph, he ordered tall Gauls and chieftains sent to supplement their numbers, with instructions that they grow their hair long and dye it red in German style and also take German names and learn to speak German.[204]

When met en route by another Senate delegation sent from Rome to meet him, Caligula began by being unusually courteous. It's likely he was hoping to hear that the Senate had voted him the Triumph he desired. His mood darkened when the delegation merely said that the Senate was anxious to see him back in Rome.

"I'm coming," he told them. Patting the hilt of his sword, he added. "And this is coming too."[205]

Seneca says that Caligula was back in Italy by May and in the vicinity of Rome.[206] Apparently landing at Antium and initially taking up residence at his villa there, he was still bent on celebrating a Triumph, although he wasn't going to humble himself by asking the Senate to award it to him. The traditions governing Triumphs prevented a conquering general crossing the city boundary before his Triumph, and, despite his often outrageous behavior, Caligula adhered to Roman tradition when it mattered. Setting his birthday on August 31 as the day he would celebrate his Triumph, thus giving the Senate plenty of time to formally offer it to him, over the next few months he moved around his Campanian villas, within easy reach of the capital.

On his return to Italy, Caligula's daughter, Julia Drusilla, would have been brought from Rome to Caesonia and himself. The priestesses of Minerva told Caligula that when the child, now around one year old, played with other children, she tried to scratch out their eyes.

"There can be no doubt that I'm the father then," Caligula joked in response.[207]

# XXI

# CALIGULA'S TRIUMPH

At the commencement of the winter of AD 39/40, a delegation of five Alexandrian Jewish leaders had sailed to Italy to petition Caligula on behalf of the Jews of their city. They were led by Philo, a leading philosopher whose younger brother Alexander the Alabarch, a wealthy Alexandrian merchant, had for many years managed the Egyptian estates of Caligula's grandmother Antonia and was a close friend of Caligula's uncle Claudius.

The Jewish delegation's mission was to solicit Caligula's help for the Jewish residents of Alexandria after they had come off worst in deadly battles with the predominantly Greek locals in the city, battles that followed governor Flaccus's summer of AD 38 campaign to install Caligula's statues in synagogues. This had led the locals to attack the Jews and drive them into a ghetto in one part of the city. In Philo's account, the Jews were innocent victims, but, as has emerged from a record found at Alexandria, the Jews of the city had taken their protests against Caligula's deification to Roman "gymnastic and cosmetic games" held in Alexandria in AD 38, creating disruptive riots.[208] Those games were part of the Roman religious calendar, so the Jews were seen as pitting their faith against the state religion, which could only lead to counter-riots by the locals and to the government crackdown initiated by Flaccus.

The Palatium controlled all travel to Italy from the provinces, but first the delegation had to win approval of their travel application by their local governor. With Flaccus removed, the delegation had to await the arrival of Flaccus's replacement as prefect of Egypt, Gaius Vitrasius Pollio. Once Pollio approved their travel application, he had to submit it to Rome for Palatium approval. The party clearly only received final permission to travel just as the Mediterranean sailing season was officially closing in October AD 39—the seaways were tossed by storms in winter and considered too dangerous. To obtain a jump on a delegation of Greek Alexandrian citizens who received permission to appear before the emperor to put a case against the Jews, Philo's delegation decided to make a risky winter voyage to Rome.

Philo and his companions reached Italy safely, after which they would have stayed with the large Jewish community of mostly manumitted slaves who settled on the Tiber's west bank after Tiberius had banned Jews from the city proper. Caligula had not lifted that ban, which meant the delegation had to find a way to gain an interview with the emperor outside the sacred city boundary. With Caligula being in Gaul when they arrived, the delegation had to cool their heels at Rome for months. Sometime in May or June, probably through the connection Philo's brother had with the Palatium, the Jewish delegation was taken to meet Caligula at his mother's gardens, the *Horti Agrippinae*, west of the Tiber.

Built into the side of the Janiculum Hill and extending all the way down to the river, the gardens overlooked Caligula's private hippodrome, the Gaianum. Imperial gardens were open to the public except when they were in use by the emperor. When Caligula retreated to his mother's gardens, the German Guard sealed them off, standing sentry duty in helmets, armor and German breeches," then insert "to be" between "allowed" and "outside fully armed—as they were allowed outside the sacred city boundary. This meant that when Philo and his four colleagues saw them, in addition to a dagger and their long, blunt-ended *spatha* German sword, the guardsmen were equipped with the flat, partly oval German shield and long spear.

The Alexandrian delegation would have passed these bearded, grim-faced German sentinels as they were ushered into the gardens via its one porticoed entrance. Inside, they found two huge colonnaded wings enclosing a massive central courtyard, with several summer villas sitting on the Janiculum slopes above. Seneca was to say he felt these gardens had an unwholesome air, contributed to by the fact that Caligula would withdraw there to mope. Roaming garden pathways at night in torchlight, says

Seneca, the emperor paused only to view the decapitation of one condemned eminent Roman or another in the gardens before resuming his
nocturnal prowls.[209]

Caligula was at the gardens at this time because he was determined
not to cross the city boundary and officially enter Rome until his birthday
on August 31, when he intended celebrating his Triumph. When the five
Alexandrian Jews were introduced to the emperor as he strolled in the gardens, talking animatedly with his staff, Caligula proved courteous, referring them to his secretary of petitions, Obulus, and saying he would give
them a hearing at the first opportunity. While Philo's colleagues thought
this progress, Philo was not so sure.

When summer arrived and they'd had no satisfaction from Obulus, Philo
and his colleagues followed Caligula to Puteoli on the west coast. This was
the main Italian docking point for Egypt's grain fleet, and Egyptian mer-
chants such as Philo's brother spent much of the spring and summer there,
supervising the unloading, sale, and distribution of their shipments. The
Alexandrians had learned from contacts that, there in Puteoli, Caligula was
staying in a seaside villa, but they failed to win an audience with the emperor.

Instead, to their shock and horror, the Jewish delegates learned that
Caligula had ordered his new governor of Syria, Publius Petronius, to
march half of Syria's large military establishment down to Judea and erect
a massive gilded statue of the emperor in the Jewish Temple at Jerusalem.

This order from Caligula had come in response to a dispatch from
Gaius Capito, procurator of the imperial estate at Jamnia in Judea; Caligula
had inherited both the estate and the procurator from Tiberius. Capito
had reported that Jews in Jamnia had destroyed an altar set up there to
Caligula. Philo would claim that Capito exaggerated the affair and had perhaps even been behind it, to discredit the Jews. Philo was also convinced
that the idea of erecting a statue to Caligula in the Temple at Jerusalem had
originated with two of Caligula's freedmen advisers, Helicon and Apelles,
as a deliberate slight against the Jews.

"This scorpion-like slave discharged all his Egyptian venom against the Jews," says Philo, referring to Helicon, "and Apelles his Ascolonite poison, for he was a native of Ascalon, and between the people of Ascalon and the inhabitants of the holy land, the Jews, there is an irreconcilable and never-ending hostility, even though they are bordering nations."[210]

Publius Petronius, in his gubernatorial palace in the heart of Antioch, capital of the Roman province of Syria, had been greatly troubled by Caligula's written instruction to erect this statue at Jerusalem. Philo describes Petronius as a kind and gentle man and points out that he was an experienced diplomat, having diligently served in one gubernatorial appointment after another without interruption before taking up his latest post as proconsul of Syria. Prior to going to Syria, Petronius had even made a point of studying Jewish philosophy, and he'd concluded that Jewish religious sensibilities had to be handled with kid gloves.

Petronius knew that, by setting up a statue of anyone, let alone a Roman emperor, in the Jerusalem Temple, heart of a Jewish monistic faith that banned all graven images, he would face enormous resistance from the Jews, who were prepared to die for their faith. Petronius also knew that Caligula was not a man to argue with. "He heard that the emperor's wrath was implacable not only against those who did not do what they were commanded to do," says Philo, "but who did not do it at once."[211]

So, against his better judgment, knowing that his emperor had no conception of the consequences of his actions and was flirting with war with the Jews, but knowing also that his own neck was on the line, Petronius issued orders to comply with the emperor's command. First, he set in motion the creation of a huge, gilded bronze statue of Caligula at a workshop in the ancient city of Sidon, on his province's Mediterranean coast in what today is Lebanon. According to Josephus, Petronius instructed the artisans involved to take their time—in the interests of perfection, he would have said.[212] Secondly, Petronius ordered two of the four legions based in Syria, plus all their attached auxiliary units and allied cavalry, to prepare to escort the statue down to Jerusalem once it had been completed.

Caligula, meanwhile, unaware of, or uncaring of the hornets' nest he was about to disturb in Judea, was still moving around villas on the Campanian coast and in the Alban Hills so that he didn't formally enter Rome until his Triumph at the end of August. In June, on the second June 10 anniversary of his sister Drusilla's death, Caligula almost certainly visited Lake Nemi, a freshwater lake sitting in a volcanic crater in the Alban Hills, where he had a villa.

Lake Nemi was sacred to the moon goddess Diana. It is known for its famously spectacular and magical midsummer reflections of the moon at its center, which the Romans called the *Speculum Dianae*, or "Mirror of Diana." At the August full moon, the locals paraded around the lakeshore bearing burning torches as part of the Nemoralia Festival. That ceremony still takes place today, more in veneration of the tourist dollar than of Diana.

A Temple of Diana was located in a sacred lakeside grove, and the priest of the temple was known as the King of Lake Nemorensis. In a tradition said to have been established by Virbius, first priest of the cult of Diana at Lake Nemi, the priest was always a runaway slave who'd killed his predecessor and carried a sword to defend himself against subsequent claimants. Caligula had mischievously sent a more powerful man to slay and depose the current long-reigning priest, for which Suetonius was to censure him.[213]

By law, no boats were permitted upon sacred Lake Nemi, but Caligula received a religious dispensation to anchor several vessels there. Even though no classical author mentioned these lake craft, down through the centuries at least one massive vessel could be seen through the murky lake water by locals, sitting in mud on the lake floor. Repeated attempts to raise this ship failed until 1928, when a portion of the lake was temporarily drained, revealing not one but two vessels. These two vast ships proved to be the largest known vessels from the Roman era—the larger craft was 240 feet long and 80 feet wide, the smaller, 235 feet by 66 feet.

The first ship was successfully removed from the lake bed in 1929, the second in 1932, and a museum was set up on the lakeshore for their preservation. It has long been suspected that a third, even larger boat lies hidden somewhere in the mud of the lake floor, but it has yet to be discovered. In May 1944, during World War II, the museum caught fire, and the Nemi ships were destroyed. Retreating German troops were accused of deliberately setting fire to the museum, although U.S. Army shells landing in the vicinity at the time may have been the cause.

Lead, brass, bronze, and iron artifacts from the ships have survived, as have stone objects, mosaics, and roof tiles. So, too, have huge oaken and bronze anchors. Among the artifacts are double-headed brass fittings that once held deck railings on Caligula's ships. These rail-holders feature the back-to-back heads of a bearded man and a woman, which many modern-day writers have taken to represent the classical figures of a satyr and a water nymph. They are more likely to depict Virbius, first priest of the cult of Diana at Lake Nemi, and Egeria, consort of King Numa Pompilius, founder of the Lake Nemi sanctuary. It was the king who appointed Virbius to his priestly post.

Both Virbius and Egeria were worshipped as minor deities at the lake alongside Diana. Virbius was said to have been raised from the dead by Asclepius, god of healing, while Egeria was considered the protector of pregnant women. Egeria was supposedly also imbued with the gift of prophesy—something which, we know, was of great interest to Caligula.

Fortunately, Italian authorities had performed thorough investigative work on Caligula's two ships prior to their 1944 destruction. Both flat-bottomed hulls were crafted of cedar covered with three layers of lead sheeting, while it was revealed that the wooden decks had a painted wool covering. The use of cedar was common to craft constructed in Egypt, with European shipbuilders favoring oak, suggesting that both Lake Nemi ships originated in Egypt.

The smaller ship had clearly been fitted with banks of oars that had been removed. The larger ship was a barge; devoid of oars, it would have been towed across the water by powered vessels. The smaller ship had been fitted out as a luxurious imperial houseboat, with accommodations, baths, hot and cold running water, and garden terraces in stone. The larger craft had borne a stone temple or temples. Both ships had been moored toward the northern end of the lake, two hundred yards apart, with the houseboat linked to Caligula's villa on the shore by a long, narrow wooden jetty.

That these were Caligula's ships was confirmed by inscriptions on lead piping in the houseboat, which referred to Caligula, while roof tile stamps dated the upper structures on both ships to AD 40. Experts concluded that the ships' hulls predated AD 40 and had been converted from seagoing craft for use on the lake. The Romans covered the hulls of only their *seagoing* vessels with lead, to protect them from saltwater shipworm. No such problem existed in freshwater, with Roman vessels that were built to ply rivers and lakes using exposed wooden hulls. Had the Lake Nemi ships been purpose-built from scratch, the expensive and pointless lead covering would not have been used.

Similarly, while the hulls showed they had been the work of naval architects, the above-deck works had clearly been designed by civil architects and engineers, who were also responsible for the ship's technologically advanced first-century fittings. These fittings amazed the twentieth-century experts: history's first known bilge pumps, piston pumps for the running water, and the only known example of Roman ball bearings and cylindrical bearings, which allowed two platforms supporting statues to rotate with ease. All of these engineering advancements, which would be lost to mankind during the Dark Ages before being reinvented in more recent times, bear the mark of Caligula's desire to innovate.

So, two massive seagoing vessels—probably originating in Egypt—had been hauled overland from the west coast of Italy, up into the hills, and to the lake. There, civilian contractors had stripped away unnecessary maritime fittings and created Caligula's houseboat and floating temple, with conversion work completed in AD 40. The smaller vessel may well have been one of the huge galleys with ten banks of oars that Suetonius described Caligula previously using for cruises along the Campanian coast; its fit-out was very similar to that attributed by Suetonius to Caligula's cruise ships. The larger vessel at Lake Nemi, the barge, could well have been designed to carry a very large object before being sent to the lake.

That object was quite possibly the Olympian statue of Zeus, whose transfer to Rome was abandoned by Caligula in AD 39.

Most writers have assumed that Lake Nemi's floating temple was dedicated to Diana, considering its location on Diana's lake. However, there was already a Temple of Diana on the lakeshore—its remains are still to be seen. Authorities at the lakeside naval museum, which today houses the surviving artifacts and scale models of the ships, speculate that Caligula dedicated the floating temple to Isis, based on artifacts connected with Isis found on board and the fact that he restored the Temple of Isis at Rome. Those authorities point out that, from the reign of Caligula, Isis increasingly became linked with Diana and became the patron goddess of Roman seafarers.[214]

Yet, while he displayed an interest in Egypt and restored the Temple of Isis at Rome, no evidence suggests that Caligula personally worshipped Isis. As has been shown, at the start of his reign, Caligula showed a strong attachment to Apollo before later identifying with, and competing with, Jupiter. Another god to receive his attention was Venus, with whom his sister Drusilla was officially linked. The two rotating platforms for statues that existed on the Remi ships, which are likely to have been rotated to follow the rising and setting moon, could have supported statues of two gods. Diana and Isis? Venus and Isis? Caligula and Drusilla? We can only speculate.

Caligula's intense interest in the moon is illustrated by a story told by Suetonius. Lucius Vitellius, father of Caligula's friend Aulus Vitellius, had returned to Rome in AD 39 after serving as governor of Syria since AD 35 and being replaced by Publius Petronius. Sometime after his return from Syria, he answered a summons to present himself to Caligula, on a moonlit night. During his tenure in Syria, Vitellius and his four legions had confronted Artabanus, aggressive king of Parthia, at the River Euphrates and compelled him to pay homage to statues of Augustus and Caligula and make peace on terms favorable to Rome. Artabanus had even sent members of his family, including his son Darius, to live at the Palatium in Rome as hostages to peace—the same Darius who crossed the bridge at Puteoli with Caligula in the summer of AD 39.

Vitellius had been hailed back home for this diplomatic coup, but Caligula was seen as jealous of Vitellius's achievements, and those close to Vitellius feared the young emperor planned to kill him. So Vitellius went to Caligula simply dressed, discarding all the accoutrements of a victorious general. He found Caligula on a terrace, talking in tongues to the full moon. Dropping to Caligula's feet, Vitellius cunningly worshipped him as a divinity, vowing that, if permitted to live, he would make sacrifices to the emperor.

Caligula asked, "Can you see the moon goddess beside me, Vitellius?"

Vitellius, a past master at sycophancy, as he had demonstrated by prostituting his son Aulus to Tiberius, now trembled in fake awe, and, keeping his eyes to the ground, answered in a hushed tone, "Only you gods, master, may behold one another."[215]

Caligula was so impressed that he made Vitellius one of his most intimate colleagues from that point forward. Suetonius makes no mention of where or when this exchange took place. Considering the reference to the full moon and the goddess Diana, it may well have been that Caligula remained at Lake Nemi for several weeks in June AD 40 to take in the full moon late in the month, which would place the terrace where Vitellius had his full moon exchange with the emperor aboard one of his Lake Nemi ships.

Restlessly, Caligula continued to move around the Alban Hills. He visited nearby Velitrae, modern Vellitri, which housed a shrine to Apollo. Outside the town lay the villa of Augustus's grandfather, where visitors were shown a small room the size of a pantry that was said to have been Augustus's nursery. In a giant plane tree in the vicinity, a platform like a massive children's tree house had been erected, capable of supporting Caligula, fifteen guests, and their attendants. Here in the tree house, the emperor enjoyed a picnic lunch.

As Caligula prepared for his Triumph in late August, the Senate had still to vote it to him, because, it was said, he'd told them he wanted no more honors from them. The emperor was determined to avoid the process that tradition dictated for Triumphs, which required him to meet the Senate in the Temple of Bellona on the Field of Mars and formally request his Triumph, after which the senators would lead the triumphal procession. Just as he was determined not to ask the Senate for anything, he would not share his moment of glory with the senators. Against all tradition, he could have taken his Triumph without involving the Senate. Yet, as willful as Caligula was, he clearly wasn't prepared to buck this tradition.

At the last minute, he canceled arrangements for the Triumph and announced he would instead celebrate an Ovation, two of which had been previously voted to him by the Senate. This involved a lesser form of triumphal parade in which he could walk or ride a horse rather than use a chariot, and in which the Senate did not take part. He crossed the sacred city boundary of Rome on his birthday, August 31, celebrating his Ovation with the seashells collected in Gaul displayed among his "spoils" in the parade that followed him.

We can assume that the triremes that Suetonius says were brought from the English Channel for Caligula's Triumph were also somehow involved in the Ovation parade, and possibly also the elephants from the imperial elephant troupe he'd used during Drusilla's games. We know that the German prisoners brought from Gaul, the real and the fake, trailed in his wake, while the senators who so annoyed Caligula watched from the sidelines.

But Caligula was not a happy young man as he took his seat at the games following the Ovation parade. Everyone, of every class, was irritating him. He seethed with rage with the plebeians when they extolled him with cries of, "Hail, young Augustus!" on his entry into the stadium. For Caligula, inferiority complex pricked, felt that he was again being censured as too young to rule. At the same time, he was annoyed with the leading men of society for not showing the same enthusiasm for his spectacles as he did—some had left early when he arrived late. His fury was compounded when the crowd failed to applaud his favorite performers and hailed others he disliked.

As his rage simmered, he spotted Aesius Proculus, son of a Praetorian Guard first-rank centurion, in the audience. Proculus was so handsome and well-built that he'd been given the nickname of Giant Cupid by the public. Caligula ordered Proculus dragged from his seat and thrown into the arena to do battle with a net fighter. Proculus won, to the delight of the crowd, so Caligula had him fight a *secutore*. When Proculus won that contest, too, Caligula had him dressed in rags and led through the streets in leg irons, to be jeered at by passersby, for execution outside the city. The young man's only crime had been to be good looking and popular, although Caligula's agents would have claimed that information had been received against Proculus from anonymous informants.

For a number of people in the crowd, the removal and execution of people from amid their very ranks had gone too far. Ignoring the show going on in front of them, some, and before long many, loudly and courageously called out for the emperor's secret informants to be handed over, so that they could deal with them. Dio described the situation as "an angry ruler on one side, and a hostile public on the other." Caligula, incensed, departed his own games, leaving others in charge.[216]

As if to appease the populace, for several days after this Caligula had gold and silver coins thrown from the roof of the Julian Basilica on the south side of the Forum Romanum. A massive crowd tried to snaffle the cash, and a number of people were reportedly trampled in the crush. One side of the Basilica faced the Temple of Castor and Pollux, by this time part of Caligula's palace, from which he no doubt watched proceedings with glee. Not only did he have the pleasure of seeing some of the complaining populace of Rome crushed to death, he'd had iron blanks mixed in with the gold and silver coins, so that some Romans died for a piece of worthless iron.

He also used another way to punish his subjects. Finding the commoners hadn't embraced democracy as he had hoped, doing nothing of note in the sittings of the assembly he had reinstated, and with just a single candidate standing for each vacancy, he canceled their elections, demonstrating that what he could give, he could just as easily take away.

# XXII

## THE VICTIMS MOUNT

Through the summer of AD 40, Philo and his Alexandrian delegation remained at Rome, hoping to again see Caligula and put their case to him. Now, following the emperor's return to the city and his Ovation parade, they were informed that there was a brief window in his schedule during which they could see him outside the city boundary before he again withdrew to Campania. This time, Philo's delegation would have to address the emperor in competition with the delegation of similar size that had arrived from Alexandria's Greek community, led by an Alexandrian named Apion.

The two delegations were brought to Caligula as he studied ongoing work on the new public baths he'd commissioned, beside the Gardens of Maecenas and the Lamnian Gardens, which he'd inherited from Tiberius. Northeast of downtown Rome, the gardens were beyond the *pomerium*. Maecenas, one of Rome's wealthiest men and patron of poets including Virgil, had built his gardens over a rubbish dump in the reign of Augustus. These gardens included Rome's first heated swimming pool—as opposed to a heated bath. Caligula intended being just as innovative with his new public baths complex. Philo learned that the emperor had been staying here for the past three or four days, taking an active interest in construction, and he and his fellow delegates hurried to take advantage of the opportunity for an audience.

The upper floors of Caligula's complex featured apartments. Downstairs, the public would be able to relax using exotic oils in both cold and hot baths, which Suetonius decries as utterly decadent. Caligula was also introducing crystal windows to allow light to flood into the baths while keeping out wind and rain. For a long time prior to this, Roman baths had been windowless, with Romans bathing in lamplight. Caligula critic Seneca was to live in an apartment above public baths, and he would complain about noise from the baths by day and from fellow tenants by night, which interrupted his writing. Seneca's combined baths and apartment building home may well have been this very bathhouse of Caligula.

As the Alexandrian delegations arrived to put their cases to Caligula at the building site, where construction was nearing completion, Caligula ordered all the outer buildings opened for his minute inspection. Philo writes, "As soon as we were introduced into his presence, the moment that we saw him, we bent to the ground with all imaginable respect and adoration."

"You are haters of god," Caligula suddenly declared, glaring at the Jewish delegation. "You don't think that I'm a god. Me, who's already confessed to be a god by every other nation! Yet *you* refuse me that title." He then stretched his hands to heaven and called out, invoking a Roman god. Philo the devout Jew considered his actual words too blasphemous to repeat. It was perhaps the name of Hercules that the emperor called. Caligula was known to use the common Roman cry of "By Hercules!"

This reaction delighted the Alexandrian Greek delegation, who clapped their hands with glee and hailed Caligula by his various Roman godly titles. One of the Greeks, Isodorus by name, took his opportunity to criticize the Jews, declaring that they had failed to offer prayers in Caligula's name when every other subject around the empire was offering prayers for his safety.

"Lord Gaius, we are falsely accused!" Philo and his companions retorted, going on to say that the Jews of Alexandria had offered burned offerings and prayers for his safety both when he came to the throne and when he was ill, and offered prayers of thanks after his reported victory in Germany.

"But you sacrificed to another god," he complained. "What good was that to me? You didn't sacrifice to me."

Unable to remain still for long, Caligula turned and strode into the new bathhouse. As the delegations bustled to keep up, Caligula examined the male and female baths and change rooms on the ground floor and then bounded up the stairs to inspect the apartments above. Now he addressed himself to the building managers, "blaming some points of their preparation as defective," in Philo's words, "and planning alterations and suggesting designs, and giving orders to spend more money on them." All the while, the Jewish delegation's adversaries mocked and ridiculed them, "like people at a play in the theater," says Philo. "Indeed the whole matter was a kind of farce."

When Caligula had satisfied himself as to the state of construction, he suddenly turned on the Jews and threw them a question. "Why is it that you abstain from eating pig's flesh?"

The Greek delegation roared with laughter at this, which proved unwise, for, as Philo's delegation had been forewarned, sometimes it wasn't safe for even his most intimate friends to as much as smile at his words. In fact, the Greeks' jocularity backfired on them, with imperial freedmen in Caligula's entourage indignantly cautioning them to show more respect to the emperor.

As the Greeks flushed red and fell silent, one of the Jewish delegates replied to Caligula's question about eating pig's flesh. "My lord, different nations have different laws, and there are things that are forbidden to us and our adversaries."

Said another of the Jews, "There are also many people who don't eat lamb's flesh, which is the most tender of all meat."

This brought an amused laugh from Caligula. "They're quite right, for it's not nice," he said. And then his mood quickly became serious again. "I want to know what principles of justice you recognize with regard to your constitution," he snapped.

Philo gave a studied reply, but before he could get to the matters that had brought the Jewish delegation to this meeting, Caligula literally ran off while Philo was in mid-sentence, trotting toward the main building in the bathhouse complex. The delegations, Caligula's staff, and his bodyguards were all forced to run after him. Bursting into the high-roofed building, the emperor pointed to the windows high in the walls and demanded to know why they had yet to be filled with transparent white crystal as he'd originally commanded.

Once he'd received answer, he swung on Philo and said, in a more moderate tone, "What were you saying?"

Philo quickly resumed, coming to the point of the Jewish delegation's petition. He was able to convey the general tenor of their arguments about the unjust treatment of Jews in Alexandria, although, by his dismissive manner, Caligula obviously disagreed with some of the facts as Philo presented them. And then the emperor was on the move again, hurrying toward a villa where, he said, he had commanded some ancient and admirable pictures to be placed. This time, the delegations were prevented from following by the emperor's guards. So, Philo and his four Jewish companions dropped to their knees and prayed for the success of their mission.

Presently, Caligula returned. Seeing the Jews in prayer, the emperor said to his staff, "These men don't appear to me to be wicked so much as unfortunate and foolish, in not believing that I've been endowed with the nature of Jupiter." To the delegations, he said, "You may go." And then he quickly walked away, with his entourage falling in behind.[217]

Both delegations were instructed by Palatium staff to go home to Alexandria and await the emperor's decision. Philo felt they had been lucky to escape with their lives, and so they were. The failure of people to recognize him as a god annoyed Caligula above all else. Around this time, or perhaps a little later in the year, but certainly before he could return to Alexandria for the winter, Philo's merchant brother Alexander was arrested and thrown into prison in Rome, where he would still be languishing come the new year. Whether this was connected to Philo's petition we don't know, but it is highly likely.

One day around this time, Caligula, accompanied by his regular companion Apelles the actor, was standing in front of a statue of Jupiter in the Temple of Jupiter Best and Greatest on the Capitoline Mount. Out of the blue, Caligula posed his companion a question.

"Apelles, which of us is greater—Jupiter or Gaius?"

When Apelles hesitated, Caligula ordered him arrested and flogged. It's not impossible that Apelles had been linked by informers to a murderous plot against the emperor that was then attracting adherents, which came to be known as the Rectus conspiracy. That night, Caligula dined in torchlight in the gardens of his mother, as Apelles was lashed in front of him.

"Your groans for mercy have a musical quality, Apelles," Caligula remarked, before taking another mouthful.[218]

Following this, Caligula would periodically have Apelles tortured on the rack, let him recover and encourage him to think that he'd been forgiven, and then send him to the rack again. It may have been that, rather than being linked to a plot, with Caligula taking an increasing interest in theater productions, Apelles may have disagreed with the emperor over some stage-related matter, and this led to the actor's downfall.

Apelles's place as entertainer-in-chief to the emperor was now taken by the freedman Vatinius, a dwarf and son of a shoemaker. Vatinius, "a man born to be a butt for ridicule" because of his diminutive stature, was, says Seneca, "a graceful and witty jester." His talent endeared him to the emperor, who, in return for lively companionship and repartee, made him a wealthy man.[219]

As the list of Caligula's victims kept mounting, a plot to assassinate him was taking shape—the before-mentioned Rectus conspiracy. A Stoic philosopher named Julius Canus had been involved in a running feud with the emperor for some time, and finally Caligula sent for him and disputed with him one last time over some point. It's likely that Canus was linked to the assassination plot led by a friend of his named Rectus, but, apart from his close association with Rectus, there appears to have been little evidence against him.

As the philosopher was being escorted from the audience chamber, Caligula called to him, "Canus, in case you're deluding yourself with foolish hopes, I've ordered you to be led off to execution."

In response, Canus bowed and said, "I thank you, kind prince."

Canus was lodged in the city prison, in a cell with numerous others. Not long after—ten days was the usual period between a conviction in the Senate and execution of the sentence, and Anthony Barrett suggests that Canus was officially condemned in the Senate after arrest at Caligula's command—Canus was playing draughts with a fellow inmate when a centurion and a detachment from the Praetorian Guard arrived and began selecting prisoners for execution. Canus calmly played on as the execution party was put together.

Then, the centurion turned his way. "Canus, too," he commanded.

Without a hint of concern Canus counted his remaining pieces on the board, noting that his outnumbered those of his opponent. "See that you don't falsely claim after my death that you won," said Canus to his fellow prisoner. Then, when the centurion came to stand looking impatiently down at him, Canus looked up and cheekily said, "Centurion, you will be witness to the fact that I am leading by one piece?"

Canus was hauled to his feet and dragged from the cell with the other condemned men. Then, like the others, he had his right wrist chained to the left wrist of a Praetorian soldier for the march to the execution site beyond the sacred city boundary. Outside the prison gate, Canus's friends had been maintaining a vigil ever since his arrest, and they came forward as he was led past them in the gang of condemned men.

"Why so sad?" said Canus to his friends. "You've wondered whether souls are immortal. I will soon know."

Canus's philosophy teacher, Antiochus of Seleucia, and others fell in at Canus's side, to accompany him to the execution and offer some comfort in his last minutes of life. As the party reached the Temple of the Divine Caesar on its way out of the city, Antiochus asked his friend, "What are you thinking, Canus? What's your state of mind?"

"I've decided," Canus replied, "to take note whether in that fleeting moment (of death) the spirit is aware of its departure from the body. If I discover anything, I'll visit you all and let you know." He also predicted to Antiochus that their mutual friend Rectus would also be executed, and within three days. This suggests that Rectus may have been arrested some three days after Canus. According to Seneca, the prediction regarding Rectus's fate would prove correct.

Canus lost his head that day, going to his death in classic Stoic fashion, another "who swelled the roll of Gaius's victims," says Seneca. Canus's teacher, Antiochus, would some time later claim that Canus came to him in a vision, but without offering an answer to the mystery of the state of the soul at and after death.[220]

Caligula headed back to his Campanian villas in the first week of September. Dio says he returned to Rome for the September 23 games celebrating Drusilla's birthday, which spread over two days and again featured chariot races and exotic beast hunts. As if to restore favor with the Senate, while in the capital Caligula threw a feast for the senators and their wives, with gifts for all. And then he again withdrew from society and returned to Campania.[221]

With no imperial pleasure galley any longer in the picture—as mentioned previously, one may have ended up on Lake Nemi—Caligula now employed the flagship of the Misenum fleet for his coastal cruising, as a flotilla of escorting trireme warships kept pace with it. While large, with four banks of oars and four hundred freedmen oarsmen, the flagship was a fighting ship, devoid of luxury, and Caligula would have simply used it to commute from one waterfront villa to another.

For a time, he stayed at a villa on the small, low west coast island of Astura. Only a short distance from the Italian mainland, it was reached via a long bridge, and over time the gap between island and mainland would fill in. Famed first-century BC statesman Cicero had a villa on Astura, and this is likely to have passed down through the imperial family to Caligula. Among the villa's remaining ruins are its seawall and two private stone wharves where the Tyrrhenian Fleet's flagship would have docked with Caligula—Roman warships only having a shallow draft.

Sometime in October, before the sailing season concluded, Caligula once again boarded the fleet's flagship to make a trip along the coast from

Astura to Antium, his favorite place according to Suetonius. En route, *Echineis* sucker fish, also known as remora, attached themselves to one of his ship's two steering oars, impeding his vessel but not others of the fleet, which breezed by. The flagship hove to, and divers from the crew went down to clear the obstacle. A diver surfaced with one of the strange fish in hand, then, clambering back aboard and dripping with water, he brought it to the emperor. Shaking his head, Caligula studied the odd little six-inch-long fish, which had natural suction cups on its head.

"Such an obstacle as this was impeding my progress?" he said indignantly, before remarking on the power of such a little fish in the water while being powerless out of water. The fish were removed, and the emperor sailed on. Soon, Caligula would be the fish out of water. Pliny the Elder would note that, at this point, the young emperor had but weeks left to live.[222]

Landing at Antium, he took up residence at his villa, which was so large it had a permanent staff of some 250 slaves, from boats' crews to hedge trimmers to secretaries caring for the library. There, a bored Caligula had his horoscope read by a noted fortune-teller named Sulla, who warned him that he must expect to die very soon. Overcome with paranoia, and knowing that Augustus had once consulted the oracle of Fortune at Antium, Caligula fearfully paid a visit to the same oracle.

Every oracle in ancient times had its own peculiar practices. At Antium, there were two statues of Fortuna—one of Victorious Fortune and one of Happy Fortune. The priests of the shrine wheeled these out together on a cart decorated with rams' heads. After making a suitable offering, the supplicant—in this case Caligula—had to write several potential answers to a single question that was troubling him on wooden rods, or "lots." It could be a simple "yes" or "no" answer, or something more descriptive. These were laid before the statues. Then he posed his question to the goddess.

"Of whom should I beware?" Caligula asked the oracle.

One or both of the statues inclined or moved forward, in the direction of one of the wooden rods. A priest handed the rod to Caligula, who read his answer, "Cassius. I have to beware of Cassius!"

He took this warning to refer to his former brother-in-law Cassius Longinus, Drusilla's first husband, whom Caligula had forced to divorce his sister. This Cassius was also related to that famous Cassius who'd partnered with Brutus to lead the murder of Julius Caesar. The previous year, Caligula had appointed Cassius Longinus to replace his other brother-in-law, Marcus Vinicius, as governor of the province of Asia. Taking heed of the oracle, Caligula sent a Praetorian centurion to Asia to arrest Cassius and bring him back to Rome as a prisoner. Relieved now that he had taken preemptive action, Caligula returned to Rome for the winter.[223]

By the middle of October, Petronius, governor of Syria, had arrived in Ptolemais, a southern Syrian city on the Mediterranean coast a little below Sidon. He came with a force of more than twenty thousand troops, which Petronius ordered to set up camp for the winter, as the Roman army's campaigning season formally ended on October 19. Ptolemais, a port city, offered facilities for a large army camp, and would be used for such in future campaigns by the likes of Vespasian. The impression that Petronius gave in camping at Ptolemais was that he intended entering Judea to proceed to Jerusalem in the spring of AD 41, once the new campaigning season opened, to install the emperor's statue.[224]

Once the Jewish population of the region knew that Petronius was there, and why, they dropped what they were doing and rushed to Ptolemais in their tens of thousands. Unarmed but angry they came, townsmen from Jerusalem and the other towns and cities of the region, and farmers who deserted their farms. At Ptolemais, Jewish leaders presented Petronius with a petition against erection of the statue. Meanwhile their people conducted a civil disobedience campaign that blocked the roads and disrupted daily life.

Petronius called a conference of regional leaders inland at the capital of Galilee, Tiberias, a city, named for the emperor Tiberius, that sat due east beside the Sea of Galilee. Leaving his army encamped outside Ptolemais, Petronius rode to Tiberias with his senior staff. Thousands of Jews followed him there, keeping up their civil disobedience for forty days as he tried to work out a solution with Jewish leaders, who included Aristobulus, a brother of King Herod Agrippa.

As the Tiberias talks drew out, it became clear to Petronius that the Jews would take up arms if he went forward to install Caligula's statue at Jerusalem. Rome would be facing a full-scale Jewish revolt for which Petronius would be blamed. It was a case of being damned if he did and damned if he didn't. Petronius was candid with the Jewish representatives. If it were up to him, he said, the statue project would be abandoned. But it wasn't up to him. He was under orders from his emperor.

As the talks reached a stalemate, Petronius had an idea. He had received advance warning from the Palatium that the emperor would be making a trip to Egypt in the new year, emulating his father Germanicus's AD 18 trip by passing through numerous provinces and kingdoms including Syria and Judea en route. Like his father, Caligula would be making much of the journey by sea, coasting east in a fleet of warships and docking for the night at various ports en route. As much as half his party would be traveling overland, bolstered by the addition of regional governors, kings, and their entourages at each province and kingdom they passed through. Those provinces would be expected to feed the massive imperial party while it was on their soil. And this was what gave Petronius his idea.

⁂

Soon after Caligula arrived back at Rome in early November, he received a number of letters from Petronius, sent by special couriers. As Caligula began to read, he saw that Petronius was trying to dissuade him from setting up his statue in Jerusalem by using a novel argument. Petronius informed the emperor that, in taking up their protests over the Jerusalem statue, the Jews of Judea had walked away from their farms and abandoned the latest harvest. If this strike continued for much longer, he wrote, there would be no harvesting of corn, olives, and other crops essential to the Roman diet in the region. Not only would this bring a famine that effected Rome's troops as well as the locals, it would mean that there would be no supplies for the imperial party when it came through the area the following year. He therefore begged the emperor to call off the installation of the statue, an act that would allow the harvest to be completed before the crops were spoiled.

In support of his argument, Petronius had sent imperial agents around the region to do a survey of available food supplies and to assess the likely situation into the new year should the Jewish farmers' strike continue while the threat of the erection of the emperor's statue remained. To his letter, he attached the reports of his assessors.

With rising anger, Caligula waded through most of these reports. Then he gave up and called for a pen. Pacing about, he went through Petronius's letters again, this time making marks on every page—here scoring things out, there making notations "in fury and indignation," according to Philo. Finally, Caligula cast the letters aside and clapped his hands together, summoning his freedman secretaries.

"Truly, Petronius," he growled, as if the governor were in the room, "you don't seem to comprehend that you are the subject of an emperor. The uninterrupted series of governorships you've held have made you too crafty."

He then dictated a furious letter, telling Petronius he'd paid too much attention to the feelings of the Jews and not enough to his. Caligula was no fool. He'd quickly realized that the harvest issue was a pretext and rightfully declared that neighboring regions could make up the food shortfall. He was offended most of all by the fact that Petronius had thought he could bluff him into changing his mind. "But why do I speak in this way before acting?" he dictated. "And why is there no one who anticipates my reaction? He who delays will discover that the wages of his delay are his own suffering. I'll say no more, but I won't forget the matter."[225]

The letter was duly dispatched, but Caligula stewed about the matter overnight, and the next day he dictated a second letter to Petronius.

This time he began with lavish praise for the governor, for his prudence and anxiety for the future needs of his province. After skirting around the matter of the statue, he ended by saying, "I desire you not to be so anxious about anything as the speedy erection and dedication of my statue." This letter was also dispatched to Petronius. But Caligula's anger still had not been quenched.[226]

# XXIII

## RUNNING OUT OF FRIENDS

King Herod Agrippa, one of Caligula's few remaining trusted friends, returned to Rome at this point. He intended to winter at Rome with Caligula before, it seems, accompanying him on the trip to the East in January. Agrippa was fully aware of the Jerusalem statue affair. As a devout Jew, he was roundly against the idea, but as far as we know, he had yet to express his view to Caligula. Unaware of the latest exchange of letters between Petronius and the emperor in the matter, and the day after he arrived in the city, Agrippa paid Caligula his respects at the usual dawn assembly of courtiers at the Palatium.

Agrippa was shocked by the Caligula he found. The young emperor couldn't stand still, instead pacing about and waving his arms in a most irregular fashion as he spoke to the assembly. But it was the look in the emperor's eyes that troubled Agrippa most of all. "By the excitement that shone in his eyes," says Philo, "he conjectured that he had some anger smoldering beneath." Unable to determine the cause of Caligula's anger, Agrippa began to worry that he had done or said something that had upset the emperor. Unable to think of anything he could possibly have done wrong, Agrippa decided that someone else was annoying Caligula, but couldn't work out who that could be.[227]

Agrippa felt increasingly uncomfortable, for, while others spoke to the emperor, Caligula stared distractedly at him with a morose look in his eyes. To avoid the imperial gaze, Agrippa dropped his eyes to the floor. He considered asking what the matter was but thought better of it in case he incurred the emperor's wrath.

"You look perplexed, Agrippa," said the emperor at last. "I'll relieve you from your perplexity. You've lived with me for such a long time, yet you're still ignorant of the fact that I not only speak with my voice but also with my eyes." Now his tone became sarcastic. "Your loyal and excellent fellow citizens, the only nation of men upon the whole face of the earth that doesn't esteem Gaius as a god, appear now to even be desiring to plot my death in their obstinate disobedience. For, when I commanded my statue in the character of Jupiter to be erected in their temple, they raised all their people and quit city and countryside in a body, under the pretense of addressing a petition to me. But in reality they were determined to act in a manner contrary to my commands!"

Caligula probably also informed him that Agrippa's own brother was one of the leaders of the Jewish protests. This, along with the fact that many of these people came from Agrippa's jurisdiction, proved a huge shock to the fifty-year-old and put him directly in Caligula's sights. Even as Caligula was speaking, Agrippa suffered what seems to have been a heart attack, a precursor to a sudden cardiac arrest that would kill him in Judea just three and half years later. This night in Rome, Agrippa's pallor went from pale to livid as he trembled uncontrollably from head to foot, and then he lost consciousness. Men standing either side of him grabbed hold of Agrippa as his legs gave way, preventing him from hitting the floor.

"Carry him home," commanded Caligula tersely.

So, the king was carried back to his nearby palace on the Palatine and put to bed, still unconscious, and his doctors were summoned.

Caligula was unimpressed. "If Agrippa, who is my dearest and most intimate friend, one bound to me by so many benefits," he complained to staff, "is so completely under the influence of his national customs that he can't bear to hear a word against them, but faints away to such a degree to be close to death, what must one expect of the feelings of others who have no motive or influence in the matter?"

Agrippa lay unconscious all that day and into the evening of the next. Only then did he move, raising his head a little and then opening his eyes. After looking briefly at the friends and staff crowded around his bed, he lapsed back into a deep sleep. After a while, he awoke again. This time, he sat up.

"Where am I?" he asked. "Am I with Gaius? Is my lord himself here?"

When assured that he was in his own palace, alone, Agrippa ordered away fussing doctors and called for plain food and water. After eating sparingly, Agrippa called for writing tablets, saying, "Now I must address myself to Gaius."[228]

The Roman writing tablet was much the same size as the electronic tablet we have today, which takes its name from that Roman original. The wooden Roman tablet was coated with beeswax, and using a stylus, a metal writing instrument that resembled a small knife and which many of Julius Caesar's assassins had reputedly used on the Ides of March, 44 BC, Romans wrote in the wax. If the user wanted to make corrections, he could rub out words using the stylus's blunt end. Once the tablets were filled, they were passed to secretaries who copied what was written on them onto rolls of velum or papyrus using pen and ink, for transmission or filing. The wax could then be wiped clean with a damp cloth for reuse of the tablet, or allowed to harden so the tablet and its contents could be retained for records purposes.

Agrippa penned Caligula a very long letter, begging him to set aside his plan to erect his statue in Jerusalem's temple. He pointed out to the emperor that both his mother's father, Marcus Agrippa, and the emperor Augustus had honored the Temple when they visited Judea, and that Tiberius had shown similar respect for it. Agrippa was aware that Caligula, despite all his venal acts against individuals and his adoption of god status, still observed Roman tradition in many respects.

To bolster his argument that Roman tradition protected the Jews and their Temple, Agrippa attached a copy of a letter from a Roman proconsul repeating a command of Julius Caesar's in which he granted special rights and favors to the Jewish peoples after a Jewish army had helped save him from defeat in Egypt in 47 BC. In summation, Agrippa declared that, for his faith, he was prepared to give up all that Caligula had bestowed on him, and even give up his life.[229]

Once the pen and ink copy of his letter came back to him from a secretary, Agrippa closed it with the addition of his seal, sent it across the Palatine to the emperor, and then waited in trepidation for a response.

Caligula quickly read the letter. Philo said that it made him very angry, but at the same time, the emperor was moved by his friend's courageous appeal. Philo comments, "In some respects he was pleased with Agrippa, and in some he blamed him."[230]

Philo indicates that Caligula soon after responded to Agrippa's letter, but Josephus tells of an event that took place before Caligula made his response. Agrippa, having received no answer to his plea, arranged a sumptuous banquet for the emperor and other members of the court, at his own palace. Josephus tells us that Agrippa went to great lengths to please Caligula by putting on a feast unlike any staged before, spending more than he could afford.[231]

Suetonius, who castigated Caligula for his extravagances, described the emperor at one time "drinking valuable pearls dissolved in vinegar" and holding a dinner party where guests were served "golden bread and golden meat."[232] As Josephus says that not even Caligula was able to equal Agrippa's banquet, it's highly likely that the pearls in vinegar and golden bread and golden meat were served not *by* Caligula but *to* him, at Agrippa's gala. Seneca complains that Caligula "dined one day at a cost of 10 million sesterces," adding that this equaled the tax revenues from three provinces. Seneca doesn't say that Caligula personally spent this amount on the said dinner, and it's possible that this was how much Agrippa splurged on his feast to end all feasts for Caligula.[233]

Agrippa's extravaganza had the desired result. Caligula turned up to his dinner party as guest of honor and was hugely impressed by the extraordinary fare his friend presented. Caligula wasn't a heavy drinker. Not even his greatest critics accused him of being a drunkard. Besides, it took a lot for Romans to become drunk, for, as mentioned earlier, it was their custom to dilute their wine with water. But, says Josephus, Caligula let himself go at Agrippa's party and became merrier than usual. After Agrippa proposed a toast to him, Caligula responded by saying that he knew how much respect his friend had for him, how much kindness he had shown him, and how many perils he'd gone though on account of him. So, he wanted to make amends for everything in which he'd previously been deficient.

"Everything that may contribute to your happiness is yours, as far as I am able," the emperor declared. All Agrippa had to do was name it.

Josephus reckoned that Caligula expected the king to ask for some new country to add to his existing realms, or for the tax revenues from several large cities, which Caligula would have gladly given to restore their friendship to an even keel. Agrippa responded that Caligula had already given him enough. But, as the emperor pressed him, he confessed that he wanted just one thing.

"My request is this," said Agrippa. "That you'll no longer think of dedicating that statue which you have ordered set up in the Jewish temple by Petronius."[234]

Caligula had backed himself into a corner. And perhaps that had been Agrippa's plan in staging the dinner party. With so many witnesses to his offer and Agrippa's request, Caligula had no choice but to grant his wish, which he agreed to do. In the days following this banquet, Caligula wrote to Governor Petronius, instructing him not to allow any alterations or innovations to be made at Jerusalem's Temple, but to punish anyone who hindered the erection of altars, temples, or statues of himself or members of his family in places under his jurisdiction other than Jerusalem.[235]

Then, within days, or perhaps within hours, and without telling Agrippa or Petronius, Caligula issued secret orders for another colossal statue of himself, bigger than the one now nearing completion in Sidon, to be made in Rome, of gilded brass. His cunning plan, said Philo, was to take the new statue with him when he went to the East in the new year, and personally erect it at the Temple at Jerusalem, leaving the other at Sidon so as not to alert the Jews to his intentions.[236] No doubt he had in mind utilizing the giant Egyptian barge sitting idle at Ostia to transport the new statue.

The Jerusalem affair, and his public back down, irritated Caligula beyond description. To put it from his mind, he threw himself into November's Plebeian Games, with three days of chariot racing and several nights of theatrical shows lit by oil lamps. Having clearly forgotten the past exhortations of Macro to always act in a manner becoming an emperor, he proceeded to raise eyebrows by appearing on stage, mute, in various festival plays. Sometimes he was dressed as one or other of his favorite gods, among them Neptune, Hercules, Apollo, and Bacchus—patron god of the theater as well as wine. In other plays he appeared in the roles of the goddesses Venus, Diana, and Juno.

His stage appearances were with great attention to the appropriate props, false beards, wigs, regalia, and dresses. Suetonius says that Caligula had elaborate machinery built to simulate lightning flashes and thunder claps, and some modern authors suggest this was for these stage shows, the production of which he was taking an increasing interest now that Apelles was off the scene.[237]

For some members of the aristocracy, these unbecoming theatrical appearances by the emperor were the last straw. Several men were now arrested for plotting the emperor's removal. Suspects Anicius Cerealis and his son Sextus Papinius were among those put to torture by the Praetorian Guard to extract confessions and the names of fellow conspirators. Cerealis confessed to nothing, but, on the rack, Papinius agreed to name others in exchange for a pardon. When the men named by Papinius were arrested and brought to Caligula in his mother's gardens one night, the emperor had all the named men executed in front of Papinius and then had Papinius himself beheaded.

Another, unrelated suspect, Betilienus Bassus, was arrested. His father, Capito, was also brought to the gardens. Told he must witness the execution of his son, Capito begged permission to close his eyes. Caligula, enraged, ordered both executed, even though Capito had committed no crime. To save himself, Capito then pretended to have been one of the conspirators, promising to name all the rest in return for his life. Capito went on to name members of Caligula's inner circle. He almost got away with it, too, until he named Callistus, Praetorian prefects Clemens and his colleague, and Caligula's loyal wife Caesonia. Caligula, realizing that the man was lying, had Capito executed with his son.

But the seed had been sown in Caligula's paranoid mind. Only wife Caesonia escaped his suspicion as he had growing doubts about his other closest advisers. At one point, he asked Caesonia, "Why are you so devoted to me?" With his characteristic dark, quirky sense of humor, he added, "I should have you tortured to find out."[238]

One day he called in Callistus and the Praetorian prefects, whom he routinely permitted to wear swords in his presence. Unarmed himself, he invited them to kill him on the spot if they considered him a bad ruler. "I'm alone, and there are three of you," he said. "You're armed, and I'm defenseless. If you hate me, and want to kill me, do it now!"[239]

All three men dropped to their knees at his feet and professed their undying loyalty. Apparently satisfied by this reaction, the emperor sent them away. But, after this, Caligula confided only in Caesonia, and he took to personally wearing a sword in the city. When he spoke with Callistus or the Praetorian prefects alone, he would urge each to inform on the other two should they suspect they were plotting against him.

None did inform on the others, but Caligula's change of attitude toward them would have rattled all three; Callistus most of all. Up to this point, says Josephus, Callistus had been extended great trust and power by Caligula, "equal to the power of the tyrant." Believing that he was above suspicion, even as others perished all around him, Callistus had taken full advantage of that power. "All men dreaded him," says Josephus of Callistus. In his opinion, Callistus "was more extravagant in the use of his power in unjust proceedings than any other." Now fearful of losing his wealth, if not his life, Callistus began discreetly ingratiating himself with Caligula's uncle Claudius, as a form of insurance.[240]

Caligula's paranoia was now full-blown. Calling a meeting of the Senate, he informed the senators that he had decided to grant almost all of them amnesty against prosecution for treason. He retained anger, he added, only against a few of them, although he didn't name the exceptions. This made all the senators all the more worried. Who, they wondered, was safe, and who was not?

Caligula's sinister freedman Protogenes was now seen to carry two books around with him. When asked what they were, he replied, "This is my sword, and this my dagger." Later, the two books, *The Sword* and *The Dagger*, would be found to contain the names of men and women under suspicion of disloyalty to Caligula and likely to be the next to be executed.[241]

So often over the last few years, what Caligula perceived as his leniency to some accused men had troubled him like a persistent sore. For months, sometimes years, he would stew over having let people who displeased him survive, only to suddenly pounce on and destroy them. Even though he was secretly planning to erect a new statue of himself in Jerusalem the following year, he'd been stewing over Petronius's attempt to divert him with the claim of famine caused by revolting Jews. The Jews, having learned from Petronius that Caligula had ordered him not to proceed any further with the Sidon statue, had gone back to their cities and farms, and the Judean crisis had been terminated. But, Petronius, the man who had defied his emperor, remained in his post.

That December, Caligula decided to make an example of Petronius. He wrote him a short, sharp letter. First admonishing the governor for siding with the Jews and disobeying him, he then wrote: "I charge you to become your own judge and consider what you must do now you are under my displeasure." He was inviting Petronius to take his own life.[242]

Caligula's freedman Protogenes entered the Senate during a sitting in late AD 40 and was made a fuss of by sycophantic senators who crowded around him. Protogenes's smile faded as he turned to one of their number, Scribonius Proculus, to whom he said, "Do you greet me, too, when you hate the emperor so?"[243]

An old law prevented senators carrying arms into the Senate House, but they were permitted to carry a bag on their belt containing tablet

and stylus for note-taking during sittings. Now a number of senators surrounded Proculus, drew their styluses, and began a stabbing frenzy. They
then had their bloodied, half-alive colleague hauled from the chamber by
Praetorians of the Senate guard, hanged, and finally dragged through the
streets to the Tiber with his innards spilling out into the street. His corpse
was tossed into the river with the trash.

A traumatized Senate subsequently passed motions to placate the
emperor. They voted for festivals dedicated to Caligula. They voted that he
could address them from a high platform, attended by his German Guard.
And they voted that all of his statues from that time forward would have
armed guards. This all pleased Caligula, who felt suddenly generous. His
brother-in-law Quintus Pomponius Secundus, one of Caesonia's half-
brothers, had been arrested and imprisoned, based on a friend's accusation
that he was plotting against Caligula. Pomponius's mistress, a freedwoman,
was tortured to obtain corroborating evidence, but she refused to say a
word against Pomponius. Caligula was so impressed that he had the woman
released, gave her a gift of 800,000 sesterces, and then freed Pomponius.

Some in the Senate praised Caligula for this, "partly through fear and
partly with sincerity," according to Dio, and began to hope that he had
moderated his murderous urges. Others feared that it would only be a
matter of time before he came after them—unless they acted first.[244]

# XXIV

## THE ASSASSINATION PLOT

Three separate plots to kill Caligula emerged in the second half of AD 40. Two, by senators, came to nothing. The third was led by a tribune of the Praetorian Guard, Cassius Chaerea, who had been a young tribune with the legions on the Rhine when Caligula was there as a two-year-old. A career soldier now aged about forty-five, Chaerea was demonstrably no coward, having saved the life of his general, Caecina, during the legion riots on the Rhine back in AD 14. But he had a gentle manner and a soft voice, and when he had to acquire the daily watchword for Rome from the emperor, Caligula frequently teased him by giving embarrassing, effeminate watchwords. Chaerea was also irked by having to collect taxes, usually the onerous task of freedmen. By late AD 40, he'd had enough of Caligula.

Deciding that his emperor had to be removed, Chaerea shared his thinking with another Praetorian tribune, Papinius, who agreed with him. The pair took their grievances to Prefect Clemens, but while Clemens proved to be embarrassed by many of Caligula's deeds and was sympathetic to Chaerea's wish to remove him, he counseled the pair to wait and let events play out. Luckily for Chaerea and Papinius, Clemens kept his mouth shut about their exchange.

Undeterred, Chaerea approached Cornelius Sabinus, commander of the German Guard. Sabinus proved much more interested in eliminating Caligula than Clemens. He also brought one of his tribunes, Julius Lupus, into the conspiracy. Lupus was almost certainly a Batavian-born tribune of a Batavian cohort of the German Guard. Lupus was not a Roman surname; it means "wolf," a common Germanic name. To have the forename Julius, he would have been either a former slave or a foreigner granted citizenship by the imperial family. But it was unknown for a freedman or foreigner to then rise to the rank of military tribune in Rome's citizen units. Like the previously mentioned Gaius Julius Civilis, princely Batavians routinely served as commanders of their nation's auxiliary units.

There was another reason to recruit Lupus into the assassination plot—his sister Julia was married to Prefect Clemens. Chaerea reasoned that the relationship might provide leverage with Clemens should the assassination plot, and Lupus's involvement, be discovered.

Keen to progress the conspiracy, German Guard commander Sabinus put Chaerea in touch with senators whom he knew had previously shelved their own assassination plans. The leader of the first plot had been a Spaniard from Cordoba, capital of Baetica province, whom Josephus identified as Aemilius Regulus. Not only was Regulus never mentioned by any other source, he disappeared from Josephus's account after one reference. Some modern scholars including Anthony Barrett and B. J. Kavanagh have suggested his name may have actually been Aemilius Rectus—Josephus's work suffers from copying errors when it comes to some names. These scholars also suggest that this was the same Rectus executed three days after his friend Canus the philosopher, which would indicate why the man then disappeared from the record.[245]

Chaerea discreetly spoke with the conspiratorial senators pointed out to him by Sabinus and found they were still interested in moving against Caligula. The leader of the second group, Annius Vinicianus, was a nephew of Caligula's brother-in-law Vinicius and had been a close friend of the executed Marcus Lepidus. Josephus says that Vinicianus had a double motive for wanting Caligula dead—vengeance for Lepidus and a fear of being next on the emperor's execution list because of his connection with Lepidus. Chaerea had long held Vinicianus in high regard, and one December day, just after coming off duty as Praetorian tribune of the watch, he sought him out. As he always did when they met, Chaerea yielded the upper hand to Vinicianus as they shook hands.

"What watchword did Gaius give you today?" asked Vinicianus, who knew how Caligula had embarrassed the tribune in the past with demeaning watchwords.

"Do *you* give me the watchword of 'Liberty'?" Chaerea countered.[246]

Chaerea proceeded to fill in Vinicianus on his desire to remove Caligula, and when Vinicianus embraced the idea and discussed the other plot that had come to nothing, Chaerea offered to either follow the senator in the enterprise or to himself take the lead. Considering the difficulties civilian conspirators had experienced previously, Vinicianus encouraged the tribune to take the lead, offering his full backing and encouraging him to recruit more military officers close to the emperor.

Vinicianus's backing extended to putting Chaerea in touch with senators and equites of a like mind. Some came from his group. The others included survivors of the earlier Rectus plot and a group headed by an extremely well-placed freedman—none other than Callistus, Caligula's chief secretary. It seems that Callistus had been involved in a conspiratorial group whose plans had also stagnated for lack of opportunity and a workable plan. One of Callistus's motivations for wanting to remove Caligula was likely to have been jealousy of the increasing influence over the emperor of his new wife, Caesonia.

These groups of plotters now combined under Chaerea, becoming one. As the year came to a close, their scheme gained momentum. The impetus for action was Caligula's announced intention to travel to Egypt early in the new year. According to Josephus, January 25 had been set by the Palatium as the date of the emperor's departure from Rome.[247] As this was two months ahead of the opening of the Mediterranean sailing season, Caligula was apparently planning to make the early legs of the trip to Egypt overland, with half his large entourage to make the trip entirely by land.

Suetonius suggests that rumors of German tribes massing beyond the Rhine and threatening to invade Gaul inspired Caligula's planned trip to Egypt, and his threat to make his capital there.[248] However, the legions on the Rhine and their able commanding generals had that very year shown they were a match for the Germans. Besides, without doubt at the direction of Caligula's Palatium, the two Roman armies on the Rhine were at that moment in a high state of readiness in advance of launching planned major spring offensive campaigns in Germany in March AD 41.

Before the emperor left Rome, he was intending to preside at the Palatine Games on the Palatine Hill in late January. These theatrical games had been founded by Caligula's great-grandmother Livia in memory of her husband, Augustus. An entertaining diversion during January, a month otherwise devoid of shows, the games had been embraced by Caligula, who personally chose the program and the performers, many of whom had come from the provinces at his invitation. There was even talk that Caligula intended making a personal appearance, dancing, on the festival's last night.[249] The festival venue was a temporary wooden drama theater, built annually for the occasion on the Palatine Hill and not far from Caligula's palace.

This event was the plotters' last chance to get within striking distance of the emperor before he left the country, and as the year ended they laid plans to carry out the assassination at the first day of the games in January.

On January 1, AD 41, Caligula sat on a platform of his palace porch at the Temple of Castor and Pollux, as the public heaped gifts of money at his feet. According to Suetonius, Caligula subsequently rolled with glee in the pile of gold and silver coins.[250] He had again appointed himself consul for the year, with Gnaeus Sentius Saturninus as his consular colleague. On January 8, Caligula resigned the consulship, allowing Quintus Pomponius Secundus, previously mentioned as one of Caesonia's half-brothers, to take his place and sit as co-president of the Senate with Saturninus during the emperor's eastern absence.

Caligula was now dealing with business in a totally arbitrary manner. Hearing that Ahenobarbus, the father of his nephew Nero, had died from dropsy (edema) at his country villa, leaving Nero a third of his estate, Caligula erupted. As Nero was the son of his traitorous exiled sister Agrippina, Caligula promptly annulled the will and took all the estate for himself. He left Nero penniless and reliant on his aunt Domitila for survival.

By the night of January 23, tribune Cassius Chaerea was close to tears of frustration. The senators and others in the conspiracy to kill Caligula had lost their courage, and for the first days of the Palatine Games they'd failed to keep their oath to stab the emperor. That evening, Chaerea convened a clandestine meeting of all the conspirators. This flirted with danger, but with just one day of the games remaining, Chaerea was throwing caution to the wind.

At this meeting, Chaerea informed his fellow plotters that he was to command the Praetorian duty cohort the following morning. As a consequence, he would be armed and entitled to be in the emperor's presence. So, he volunteered to strike the first blow and coordinate the actions of Praetorian and German Guard officers sympathetic to the plot, on the condition that the civilian conspirators backed him up and also struck Caligula. When all agreed, Chaerea guided his colleagues in carefully planning where and when the deed would be carried out. As the meeting broke up, Chaerea knew that the removal of Caligula the following day would rely more on Mars than on Minerva—more on courage than on skill.

# XXV

## KILLING CALIGULA

At dawn on January 24, the watch changed throughout the city of Rome. At the numerous city gates, at the civil treasury by the Forum, and at the military treasury up on the Capitoline Mount, men of the Night Watch handed over sentry duties to the fifteen hundred troops of an incoming City Guard cohort and marched back to their barracks. At the fortress-like Praetorian Barracks in the eastern 4th Precinct of the city, the thousand men of the duty cohort of the Praetorian Guard came on duty, mounting guard at the barracks and at the city prison.[251]

On a normal games day, Praetorians would also take up guard duty at the amphitheater or circus. There were to be games today—the emperor's theatrical Palatine Games, up on the Palatine Hill—but the Palatine was the imperial precinct, the domain of the German Guard. On the hill, that guard was also changing, with the Germans who'd stood sentry duty through the night handing over the watch to at least two fresh cohorts of the German Guard who'd crunched across a Tiber bridge in silent formation from their barracks west of the river.

Josephus says that the rank and file of the German Guard were intensely loyal to Caligula, because he paid them exceedingly well. Their loyalty extended, Josephus notes, to being prepared to die for him.[252] The Germans took up their posts at the palaces, as well as inside and outside the temporary open-air theater atop the Palatine that had hosted the previous days of the Palatine Games. The games had just one more day to run. As always, and as dictated by law, all troops on duty that day inside the sacred city boundary were "half-armed," carrying only swords and daggers on their belts. Their shields and spears remained in the barrack arsenals.

Caligula had risen well before dawn to preside at the religious ritual that preceded the day's games. Augustus, in whose memory these games were celebrated, had himself hated early-morning priestly obligations and had evaded them whenever possible. For Caligula, who was securing only three hours, sleep a night, these duties made the hours of darkness go more quickly. He had been up late the previous night, eating a large, rich meal, so he avoided breakfast as he draped his toga over his tunic with the assistance of chamberlain Helicon and his valets.

Meanwhile, the German Guard sentries had opened the theater's single public entrance, which, in most Roman theaters, was left of the stage. The public usually gathered outside Rome's theaters well before dawn to secure the best seats. This day they were out there in their thousands— men, women, and children, free and slave, says Josephus—assuredly wrapped in cloaks against the midwinter chill. As soon as the double doors opened, the crowd flooded in, hurrying to clamber up into the banked seating of the theater's semicircular wooden stands.

Josephus indicates that the theater may have been designed in prefabricated form, for it was "fastened together, as it was every year," with the wooden sections apparently stored in the interim. Apart from the public entrance, the theater had just one other door, which led backstage, and this would be used by the official party. Other than the imperial section, there were no reserved seats, and, says Josephus, the public could sit anywhere, with slaves and senators side-by-side.[253]

Once the theater had quickly filled, Caligula would make his entrance, to witness the morning's religious rituals before the show got under way. Caligula knew from Prefect Clemens that a prisoner from Egypt, a fortune-teller named Apollonius, was awaiting a hearing before the emperor on the charge that in Egypt he'd predicted the time, place, and nature of Caligula's death. Considering this nonsense, Caligula instructed his staff to put off the man's hearing, instead now hurrying to the theater.

As he arrived, the audience rose, and the *Augustales*, priests of the Order of Augustus, waited with the ceremonial implements at an altar in front of the stage. As Caligula watched, an offering was made to Augustus.

Should the sacrificial omens prove bad, the day's proceedings could be canceled. A flamingo was sacrificed; Romans considered that birds offered the best portents, and Caligula only used the most expensive sacrificial victims. Once before, at a similar ceremony, Caligula had presided as one of the priests whose task it was to hit the bird over the head with a mallet, stunning it before another priest slit its throat. Back then, as a joke, Caligula had hit his fellow priest on the head with his mallet.

Today the mallet-wielding priest failed to fully knock the bird unconscious, and the animal flapped its wings as its throat was cut, splattering blood onto Senator Publius Nonius Asprenas's toga. Once the official augur had examined the dead bird's entrails and found them to be without blemish, he pronounced the omens good for the day, and Caligula then led the audience in sitting and preparing for a solid day of song, dance, and drama. Before the day was out, there would be more of the latter than he had bargained for.

The imperial party, made up of senators and equites invited by the emperor to join him, occupied the right side of the theater, which would have been cordoned off. This reserved imperial section covered several levels of wooden seats, near the stage door, which opened from a gallery above the imperial section. In the row immediately in front of Caligula sat one of his brothers-in-law, the current consul Quintus Pomponius Secundus. Another brother-in-law, Vinicius, sat at the emperor's side. Vinicius's nephew Annius Vinicianus, co-leader of the assassination plot, was also seated below the emperor. Caligula's uncle Claudius, who was ignorant of the plot, sat close by together with Asiaticus, the ex-consul whose wife Caligula had once seduced in front of him.

King Herod Agrippa wasn't present. Still in Rome, Agrippa was waiting to return to the Middle East. Perhaps his falling out with Caligula over the Jerusalem Temple issue had left lingering bad feelings. Neither was the empress Caesonia present. Surrounded by maidservants, she would have been preparing for the following day's eastern departure. Once the public had been seated, Chaerea and off-duty tribunes, including co-conspirator

Papinius, took their seats to one side of the theater. Chaerea, as officer of the day, was wearing his armor and sword.

Another of the senators joining the official party, historian Marcus Cluvius Rufus, a member of the murder conspiracy, would later write that he encountered Vatinius the dwarf sitting near the emperor that day.

"What news, Cluvius?" Vatinius whispered to him.

"No news, Vatinius," he replied.

"Know then," said Vatinius, "that the game 'Slaughter of Tyrants' is to be played today."

Cluvius Rufus must have felt a shiver run down his spine, suddenly perceiving that Vatinius, who had Caligula's ear, was aware of the plot. Overcoming his shock, he quickly came back with a caution, using a quote from Homer: "Oh, brave comrade, hold your peace, lest some other of the Achaeans hear your tale."[254]

Josephus says that Caligula surprised all in his party by being in high spirits that morning, in sharp contrast to his dark mood of late, and he proved good company. Two of the plays on the morning's program involved executions and fighting, with the actors using copious amounts of fake blood, which had nervous conspirators raising their eyebrows at each other.

The conspirators knew they had to strike before the change of watch in the early afternoon removed Chaerea from close proximity to the emperor. Their plan was to ambush Caligula when he left the theater for lunch, isolating him beneath the stands. But, after the large banquet of the previous evening, Caligula wasn't hungry; he was in fact feeling queasy. So as the lunch hour arrived, he remained in his seat, laughing as Palatium slaves threw autumnal fruit into the audience from the stage and then released rare birds. The birds went after the fruit, enabling audience members to pounce on them, which resulted in scuffles between audience members. To Caligula, this was all good fun.

As the time passed and still the emperor didn't move, plot leader Vinicianus had to fight down rising panic, fearing that the murder plan was going to fail. Seeing that Chaerea had already left his seat and gone out the stage door, Vinicianus rose to follow suit. At that moment, a particularly bloody scene was playing out on stage.

"Hey, brave man," said Caligula, grabbing Vinicianus's toga as he passed, "where are you going?"[255]

Paling, Vinicianus resumed his seat. A little later, seeing the emperor engrossed in onstage antics, Vinicianus again came to his feet. This time, he was able to slip by and out through the stage door as if going to relieve himself, passing grim-faced German guardsmen stationed at the door. The backstage area was divided by partitions, creating dressing rooms for actors and musicians. Beyond these, a passageway led off to the Palace of Germanicus, where various acts assembled and rehearsed before coming to the theater.

Vinicianus found Chaerea out here, along with Cornelius Sabinus, the ex-gladiator who commanded the German Guard, plus the tribunes Papinius and Lupus and several centurions who'd also been brought into the plot. All were armed with swords. Those men who weren't on duty that chilly day would have been able to smuggle the weapons into the palace under their cloaks. When Vinicianus found Chaerea, the tribune was like a dog straining at the leash; impatiently, he cursed Caligula for taking so long to emerge.

"I've a good mind to go in and fall on him in his seat," Chaerea growled to Vinicianus.[256]

Josephus says that Chaerea hesitated to follow through on that threat only because a public slaying would involve extensive bloodshed among senators and equites. Chaerea must have expected a number to rise to Caligula's defense. Finally the tribune's patience gave way. Calling on the others to accompany him, and with his hand on the hilt of his sword, he strode toward the door to reenter the theater. It was then that word came that Caligula was on his feet and about to make his exit.

It would be learned later that one of the senatorial conspirators, Asprenas, had suggested to Caligula that he take a bath and freshen up, after which he might feel like eating, and Caligula had agreed. Josephus says that, as word spread backstage that the emperor was coming, performers crowded forward, so that Chaerea and the military conspirators had to push them away with the excuse that the emperor would be displeased if they came too close.

The doors opened, and first to emerge from the theater were the tall, limping Claudius, who was probably keen to lunch, accompanied by Vinicius and Asiaticus, all in conversation. The conspirators let that trio pass as they headed toward the Palace of Germanicus. Next through the door were Caligula and an undistinguished fellow by the name of Paullus Arruntius, also in conversation. As soon as that pair had passed, Cornelius Sabinus had centurions close and bar the doors into the theater, shutting out the German guardsmen on sentry duty on the theater side of the door, who had turned from their posts to follow and protect their emperor. Chaerea set off after Caligula.

Claudius and his two companions continued along the main passageway that led into the Palace of Germanicus. The passage was lined with Caligula's waiting servants, including his litter-bearers, and they could hear the angelic voices of a boys choir made up of sons of noble families in Asia, who were nearby rehearsing a hymn dedicated to the emperor. The choir, which was also due to perform a Pyrrhic dance, had not appeared onstage prior to this because their leader had a cold.

Suetonius, who gives several different and conflicting accounts of what happened next, claims that Caligula stopped to talk with these boys. But Josephus, who gives the most detailed account, says that Caligula turned off down a narrow tunnel that led to the imperial bathhouse, *intending* to talk with the boys on his way to the bath.[257]

The choir was either in the tunnel or in a room opening off of it, perhaps the bathhouse's atrium. The very existence of the tunnel was doubted by modern historians until 2008, when it was discovered by archaeologists. A *cryptoporticus*, it was dug into the hillside with one side partly open to the elements. Caligula was on his way down this cryptoporticus when Chaerea called to him from behind, asking for the watchword for the next twenty-four hours. Halting and turning, Caligula saw Chaerea approaching, with Sabinus, tribunes Papinius and Lupus, and several centurions not far behind. At this point, Caligula still suspected nothing.

"Jupiter," Caligula replied, giving the password.

"So be it!" cried Chaerea. Drawing his *gladius*, the Roman short sword, he struck his emperor a slashing blow, fulfilling the warning of Antium's oracle of Fortune that Caligula should beware Cassius.[258] Josephus says that the blade of Chaerea's sword hit Caligula between the shoulder and the neck and cleaved as far as the breastbone, which stopped it. But this wasn't a fatal blow. Chaerea wanted this assassination to be a group execution, not a solo murder. Josephus would rail against Chaerea for this, declaring that he should have killed Caligula and been done with it. As it was, Caligula remained on his feet.[259]

"I'm still alive!" the wounded emperor cried, and, as the choir unwittingly continued to sing in the background, he tried to escape, tottering away down the tunnel.

Sabinus, coming at the run now, easily overtook their victim, and pressing on Caligula's shoulders, forced him to his knees.

"Strike again!" Chaerea yelled to his associates as the others came up.[260]

Not a single senator involved in the plot had put in an appearance. Even Vinicianus had melted away, leaving the dirty work to the military men. So, Papinius, Lupus, and the centurions drew their swords and began to flail Caligula. As the emperor sagged to the stone floor, Sabinus joined in. Josephus says that another thirty wounds were added to Chaerea's initial slash, some to the genitals. The mortal blow, he says, was inflicted by a centurion named Aquila.[261]

The yelling had attracted attention. Two of Caligula's burly litter bearers, sliding their litter poles free, courageously came running from the nearby passageway to defend their emperor, wielding their poles as weapons. At the same time, the German guardsmen who'd been locked out now smashed through the barred door and also came at the run. Sabinus reacted quickly. Sheathing his sword, he led the other officers who'd participated in the assassination toward the guardsmen. Cunningly, he yelled that the emperor had been cut down and his assailants must be apprehended, then led the Germans off on a wild goose chase.

As soldiers and civilians ran in all directions, the bloodied twenty-eight-year-old "ruler of the habitable world," as Philo called him, lay dead and neglected on the tunnel floor. Dio would cynically remark that his body was proof that he was not a god. Josephus, who was three years old and living in Jerusalem at the time, would totally approve of Caligula's murder when he wrote about it three decades later; he would describe it as a "righteous slaughter."[262]

In the chaos that soon overtook Rome, few would have reflected on the similarities between Caligula's assassination and that of Julius Caesar—murdered at Rome, in the environs of a theater, cut to pieces by his own people, just a day or so before he was due to depart for the East, with a soothsayer warning him of his impending doom.

Immediately following the assassination, German Guard commander Sabinus led, and misdirected, his men in a hunt for the murderers, of which he was one. As men of the German Guard surrounded the theater and sealed its public and palace entrances, others ran riot through all the buildings on the Palatine, the private houses as well as the imperial structures, looking for conspirators and killing anyone suspicious they encountered.

Their first victim was Asprenas, the senator who still had blood on his toga from the morning's sacrifice. Thinking this was their emperor's blood, German soldiers cut down Asprenas without pausing to ask questions. While the cause of Asprenas's death was an error on the part of the German troops, Josephus was in no doubt that he was nonetheless one of the conspirators.

Another victim, an innocent one apparently, was the senator Norbanus Balbus. He grabbed the long broadsword of one of the German guardsmen attacking him and went down fighting as other Germans hacked into him, then sliced off his head.

An otherwise little-known figure by the name of Anteius—apparently Publius Rufus Anteius—was another to fall, paying a fatal price for his curiosity. Hearing reports of the murder, Anteius was coming to see Caligula's body for himself, and to spit upon it. Anteius had good reason to want the emperor dead. His father had served under

Germanicus, being one of the officers in charge of building his thousand-ship fleet for the German offensives. He had later been among the clients of Germanicus to desert Agrippina, paying for that desertion by being exiled and then executed by Caligula. Too late, Anteius realized the folly of wanting to view the corpse; as he went to flee, German steel turned *him* into a corpse.

The show in the packed theater had come to an abrupt end. With angry men of the German Guard standing facing them with drawn swords, the shocked audience members remained in their seats, recoiling in horror as more Germans marched in toting the bloody and dripping heads of Asprenas and the other men cut down and decapitated in the passageways and palace halls, displaying them gruesomely on the theater's altar as trophies of their assassin hunt.

As rumors swirled around the theater about the emperor's fate, trapped and terrified men, women, and children begged for their lives, and senators among them fearfully kept their seats and tried to show neither joy nor sorrow lest they stood out. Most of these people were in disbelief, with some no doubt asking how mere mortals could kill a god.

A city crier, Euaristus Arruntius, arrived at the theater in mourning clothes and formally announced that the emperor was dead. Then, escorted by armed tribunes, he went around the colonnades surrounding the vast courtyard at the center of the palace of Tiberius and Caligula calling on German guardsmen to put away their swords and terminate the bloodshed, for the emperor was truly dead. With all doubt erased, the Germans knew they no longer had an employer and were out of a job. Only now were the people in the theater allowed to go free.

The Palace of Germanicus included a room called the Hermaeum, dedicated to the god Hermes, Greek equivalent of Roman god Mercury, the messenger. In the process of the German Guard's room-to-room search of all the palaces on the Palatine, a mature German with a fond memory of Caligula's father, Germanicus, entered the Hermaeum. The soldier's name, says Josephus, was Gratus, which means variously "gratitude," "indulgence," and "beauty."

Spotting feet below a thick curtain drawn over a balcony doorway, Gratus, sword in his right hand, strode to the curtain and drew it back with his left, discovering Caligula's terrified uncle Claudius hiding there on the small balcony.[263] The stressed Claudius, pale and thin according to Suetonius, his thick gray hair soon to turn white, had been deserted by the senators Vinicius and Asiaticus.[264] Recognizing Claudius, Gratus the German guardsman called out to colleagues. "Here's a Germanicus! Let's make him our emperor!"

In his terror, fifty-year-old Claudius lost all strength in his legs. Sagging to the floor, he clasped Gratus's knees like a limpet and begged to be spared.

Gratus, sheathing his sword, said with a smile, "My lord, let go of thoughts of saving yourself." Taking Claudius's right hand, he helped him to his feet. "Come on and accept the throne of your ancestors."[265]

Gratus's comrades flooded around and lifted the late emperor's uncle onto their shoulders, intending to take him to the protection of their barracks across the Tiber and secure themselves a new emperor, and thereby, a new job. Finding an abandoned litter—it may have been Caligula's—this band of German soldiers placed Claudius in it and then carried him away from the palace. Josephus says that they hurried down to the Forum.

Turning left, the soldiers bore the still-terrified Claudius along beside the Julian Basilica as confused members of the public crowded around and asked what was happening to Claudius Caesar and where the troops were taking him. The Germans would have been heading for the nearby Pons Aemilius, aiming to cross the Tiber to the 14th Precinct, location of their barracks. Passing the Rostra, they reached the Temple of Saturn, the podium of which contained the state treasury, the Treasury of Saturn.

At this point, the German party met a large detachment of Praetorian soldiers of the new watch sent by Prefect Clemens to restore order, and the edgy Praetorians halted the German guardsmen there outside the Temple of Saturn and demanded to know what they were doing with the late emperor's uncle. With violence seemingly imminent, the members of the public accompanying Claudius scattered in fear.

The Praetorians and German Guard troops proceeded to argue about what to do with Claudius, until they eventually formed a consensus that he should be taken to the larger Praetorian Barracks, home to the then twelve thousand Praetorians, where they would make him their emperor—if he rewarded them. Jointly now, the Praetorians and Germans rushed Claudius to the protection of the Praetorian Barracks, through a growing crowd and with Claudius looking afraid and uncertain as he was bumped along in the litter.

A Greek physician named Alcyon had meanwhile smuggled some civilian conspirators past the German Guard at the theater by claiming they were being sent to fetch bandages for those wounded by the Guard's furious onslaught. Chaerea the tribune had made a point of ordering the centurions of his own cohort to protect Vinicianus, civilian leader of the conspirators, and he was among several senators hustled away from the Palatine Hill by Praetorian centurions, supposedly for questioning by Prefect Clemens across town at their barracks, well away from the bloody chaos on the Palatine.

When Vinicianus and the other senators were brought to Clemens, he declared, "Tyrants do please themselves and look big for a while," before adding that Caligula had brought his death upon himself. Vinicianus and his companions were set free by the prefect, without charge.[266]

The two sitting consuls Sentius and Pomponius had meanwhile called an emergency meeting of the Senate, sending heralds throughout the city to locate senators. Fearing civil unrest, they also ordered the City Guard to carry the contents of the civil treasury up to the Temple of Jupiter on the Capitoline Mount, to add to the military treasury funds kept in that temple's base. Other City Guard troops sealed off the Capitol and Forum. All the while, rumors flew around the city—that Caligula had committed suicide; that he was in fact unharmed and had staged this whole episode to see how the public would react, testing their loyalty; that he was being attended by a doctor in the palace; that, although injured, he was calling on a crowd in the marketplace to seek out and slay his assailants.

As word spread that their emperor was truly dead, angry mobs roamed the city, seeking vengeance. Josephus says that slaves, in particular, were outraged at his murder, because he had given them the right to lodge complaints against their masters for mistreatment. The senator Asiaticus, on his way to the Senate after being released by Prefect Clemens, was bailed up by angry commoners demanding to know who had killed Caligula.

Climbing to an elevated position above the mob, Asiaticus called, "Who killed the emperor? I wish I had been the man!"[267]

Few of the plotters seem to have given to any thought to who, or what, should succeed Caligula. They just wanted the agony and dread of his reign ended. "It was a motive of self-preservation, not a principle of liberty, that animated the conspirators against Caligula," writes Edward Gibbon, author of *Decline and Fall of the Roman Empire*.[268] With Rome in turmoil, hundreds of senators fled the city for their country villas to preserve themselves, and in hopes that somehow the problem of the now-empty throne would resolve itself.

One hundred more courageous, and in several cases more ambitious, members of the Senate remained in the city, among them the murder conspirators. These senators met in emergency session on the Capitoline Mount, supported by an equal number of equestrians. The meeting was protected by the City Guard, which had thrown its weight behind the Senate, apparently at the behest of their commander the senator Quintus Sanquinius Maximus, who had been city prefect since AD 39. Led by the current consuls Sentius and Pomponius, the senators in session issued an edict calling on Praetorian and German Guard troops to return to barracks, and for the citizenry to go home. This edict would largely fall on deaf ears.

That evening, as the senators debated what to do, Chaerea and other officers involved in the assassination met to discuss the fate of Caligula's wife and child. Until this time, no one had thought about Caesonia and baby Julia Livilla. With much of the German Guard still answering to Sabinus and manning all palace exits, barring the empress's departure, she was known to be still in the imperial apartments. Chaerea was all for the abolition of the monarchy, and to achieve that aim he wanted to eliminate members of the imperial family. Not only was Caligula's uncle Claudius in his sights; Chaerea had resolved that even the emperor's wife and daughter posed a risk of allowing the royal line to continue and so must be eliminated.

With some in the Senate and a large portion of the populace inclining against the conspirators during the afternoon, Chaerea also wanted to implicate Praetorian prefect Clemens in the assassination, and in doing so adhere Clemens and the Praetorians to the assassins and their cause. Josephus says that it was with that objective in mind that Chaerea proposed that Clemens's brother-in-law Lupus, the German Guard tribune, kill Caesonia and the child.[269]

Some of the assassins argued that it was too cruel to kill a woman and child, but Chaerea's forceful view prevailed—that both must also be eliminated to wipe all trace of the tyrant from the face of the earth. Alone, a reticent Lupus went looking for Caesonia and found her in a palace room. According to one account, she was lying on the tiled floor by the cold body of Caligula, hugging it and with her clothes smeared with his blood. Apparently, Caligula's loyal litter-bearers had brought his corpse to her. The emperor's eighteen-month-old daughter lay in a crib close by.

At first, Caesonia thought Lupus a friend. "If only he'd listened to me," she wailed, beckoning Lupus closer. Josephus, who tells us of this episode, was to say that Romans would long debate Caesonia's meaning. Did she mean that she had urged Caligula to be less cruel? Or, just the opposite, had she urged him to put to death every man close to him whom he suspected, so that none survived to assassinate him?[270]

As Lupus approached, Caesonia saw that his hand was on his sheathed sword, and it dawned on her why he'd come. Resolved to her fate, and preparing to join Caligula, she pulled herself up onto her knees, jutted out her neck, and told Lupus to strike. Without hesitation, and anxious to get it over and done with, Lupus stood over her with drawn sword, and with a single blow, decapitated the empress. Once Caesonia's head lay on the floor, Lupus lifted Caligula's crying infant daughter from her crib by the ankles, and dashed out her brains against the wall. He then departed, leaving the bodies where they lay.[271]

Some time that night, Caligula's last remaining friend, Herod Agrippa, found the bodies of Caligula, Caesonia, and their daughter in the emperor's apartments. We don't know what happened to the corpses of Caligula's wife and child, but Caligula's body was taken from the Palatine to the Lamnian Gardens outside the city walls. There, the corpse was so hastily cremated that it wasn't completely consumed. The remains were buried in a shallow, unmarked garden grave.

Meanwhile, as the Senate debate dragged on with Chaerea and the other assassins now impatiently watching, it emerged that a number of the senators were for restoring the republic of old and doing away with the whole concept of rule by one unelected leader. Restoration of the republic was an idea endorsed by Chaerea. As the Senate continued to debate what to do, consul Sentius praised Chaerea for killing Caligula.

"In the first place," said Sentius during a lengthy speech, "we should decree the greatest honors we can to those that have removed the tyrant, especially Cassius Chaerea. For this one man, with the assistance of the gods, has by his counsel and his actions been the procurer of our liberty."[272]

Chaerea, assuming command of all troops loyal to the Senate, asked for the night's watchword for the city, and in answer the consuls gave him "liberty," which City Guard tribunes took away to distribute to their men. Senators who were for change and the equestrians who'd joined them were thrilled that, for the first time since the fall of the Roman republic at the hands of Julius Caesar, the consuls had provided the watchword.

The Senate now sent two tribunes of the plebeians, civil officials, to the Praetorian Barracks to urge Claudius to come and talk to the Senate, but he responded that he was restrained from leaving. The Praetorians and those of the German Guard who had joined them were for putting Claudius on the throne and retaining their jobs, and they weren't letting him go anywhere. Claudius, who had apparently been joined in this mob of soldiers by Eutychus the famous charioteer, meanwhile sent for an adviser he trusted and respected, his Jewish friend King Herod Agrippa.

With Claudius refusing to budge, the consuls and leading senators themselves traipsed to the Praetorian Barracks to talk to him, only to be set upon by the troops and forced to withdraw. Agrippa was then escorted from his Palatine residence to Claudius by Praetorian soldiers, and he appears to have advised Claudius to immediately replace Caligula's Praetorian prefects with an equite named Rufrius Pollio. Claudius agreed, and Pollio quickly took up the role, sending a written order to Chaerea, Sabinus, and the other officers involved in Caligula's murder to stay off the streets.

Agrippa also convinced Claudius to offer the Praetorians 2,500 sesterces per man if they hailed him emperor. When Claudius made the offer, it was enthusiastically accepted by the troops. This was despite the fact that Claudius was personally broke. Reports that Caligula had left the state treasury entirely empty were to prove exaggerated. His more recent taxation measures had restored enough liquidity for the consuls to order the contents of the treasury removed to the Capitol.

Claudius, although hailed emperor by part of the military, remained unrecognized by the Senate, so he settled down to spend the night in the safety of the barracks. Through the night hours his support grew, with Night Watch troops, gladiators, and even sailors from the navy stationed in the city swarming to the now crowded barracks to throw their allegiance behind the brother of Germanicus.

Back on the Capitoline Mount, senators Vinicius and Asiaticus both rose to speak to the Senate, each putting a case for himself to be elected the new emperor by their colleagues. With many senators holding out for a return to the republic, the night ended in stalemate.

January 25 dawned as a bitterly cold winter day, and in the chill, the Senate reconvened. As on the previous day, a large crowd gathered outside the temple where the sitting was taking place, with many in the crowd calling for Claudius to be hailed their emperor. Chaerea and the other assassins appeared before the senators and spoke for an end to monarchy, but were shouted down by watching City Guard troops, who demanded a single ruler.

"If you want an emperor," Chaerea angrily retorted, "I'll give you one. If anyone can bring me the Praetorian Camp watchword from Eutychus, I'll bring you the head of Claudius. It's amazing to me that, after the madness of the last regime, you want to commit our government to a fool!"[273]

But still no agreement could be reached. Twice that morning, King Herod Agrippa came to the Senate, the first time with a message from Claudius saying that he would reign moderately and govern with the Senate's advice. The consuls replied that the Senate had an army behind it and would not submit to slavery. A little later, Agrippa returned with a second message from Claudius. This was an ultimatum—either Claudius would return to the Palatium as emperor and meet the senators there, or, Claudius's troops would meet the Senate's troops outside the city, to decide the empire's future with steel and blood.

This rattled the three cohorts of the City Guard guarding the Senate, who were greatly outnumbered—4,500 of them versus 12,000 Praetorians, 1,500 German Guardsmen, and 7,000 Night Watch troops for a total of 20,500 in all. The City Guard now expressed a reluctance to fight fellow Roman soldiers, and, led by one of their officers, they formed up behind their standards and marched to the Palatine to swear fealty to Claudius, leaving the Senate without protectors and with many senators regretting what they'd said and done. Now, Chaerea suggested they all go to Claudius, but Sabinus opposed the idea.

"I would rather kill myself here in the midst of you all," said Sabinus, "than consent to Claudius being made emperor and see slavery returning to Rome." Turning to his partner in crime, he scolded him. "You're too fond of life, Chaerea. How can you, the first to condemn Gaius, think it a good thing to go on living if everything we've done to regain our liberty comes to nothing?"

"I'm fully prepared to take my own life, Sabinus," Chaerea countered. "But before I do, I want to sound out Claudius to learn his intentions."[274]

Begrudgingly, Sabinus joined Chaerea, Papinius, Lupus, Aquila, and the other assassins in going to the palace, having to push their way through the vast, agitated crowd that had gathered outside. Sheepishly, the consuls and senators followed along behind. Claudius had been joined by his friends, who appear to have included, apart from Agrippa, Agrippa's brother Herod—who was almost certainly in Rome at the time—Prefect Pollio, and others such as Alexander the Alabarch and King Antiochus of Commagene, prisoners of Caligula who had been freed on Claudius's orders. Claudius's young wife, Messalina, had almost certainly also joined the group, for her protection. Heavily pregnant, she would give birth just eighteen days after this, in Rome, to their son Britannicus.

In the meeting that followed, Vinicianus strove to exonerate Chaerea by declaring that Caligula had brought his death upon himself, and his view was supported by other senators. Some of Claudius's friends applauded Chaerea for killing Caligula. Others, no doubt led by the more level-headed Agrippa, told Claudius that letting the killers of an emperor escape at the commencement of his reign would not be a good signal. So, the usually timid Claudius, strongly advised by Agrippa and Pollio, ordered Chaerea, Papinius, Lupus, Aquila, and the centurions who also participated in the assassination disarmed and arrested, to be taken away and executed at once.

German Guard commander Sabinus, on the other hand, was spared, even though he'd made no secret of the fact he'd been a leader of Caligula's assassins and had spoken against Claudius taking the throne. Almost certainly, he owed his life to the intercession of Messalina, his lover. Josephus tells us that Claudius not only pardoned Sabinus, he allowed him to resume his military command. In the same breath, Josephus says that Sabinus committed suicide. Only in a later episode does Josephus reveal that Sabinus's suicide was years later. He tells us that Sabinus returned to the arena as a gladiator, and it's likely Claudius sent him there, expecting him to soon die on the sands of the arena after he'd spent three or four years away from gladiatorial combat commanding the German Guard.[275]

Despised by the public, Sabinus would survive in the arena for years to come. In AD 46, in a contest that took place in front of Claudius and wife Messalina, he was bested by an opponent, who subsequently turned to the imperial box for a decision on Sabinus's fate. Although the crowd and

Claudius wanted Sabinus killed, Messalina used her veto to save him. Sabinus would apparently survive to commit suicide after Messalina was executed by Claudius in AD 48. According to Josephus, Sabinus fell on his sword, doing a thorough job—it went in all the way to the hilt.[276]

Cassius Chaerea, meanwhile, was deprived of his sword by the centurion put in charge of his execution party by Prefect Pollio. Even though the assassins knew they were to die shortly, neither Chaerea nor any of his condemned colleagues attempted to save themselves by offering to name the civilians who were a party to their plot, or to implicate Prefect Clemens.

Accompanied by a massive crowd, the tribunes and centurions who had killed Caligula were taken out of the city by a Praetorian detachment, to a wayside execution place. Chaerea bore himself calmly and courageously, but, once the party came to a halt and the prisoners' military cloaks were taken from them, he noticed that Julius Lupus was crying and shaking. Chaerea told him to pull himself together.

"It's the cold," Lupus came back.

"The cold never hurt a wolf," Chaerea retorted, referring to Lupus's name. Then, as Lupus composed himself, Chaerea called to the centurion who was to be his executioner, a man with whom he was unfamiliar and who seemed quite young for the job. "Are you accustomed to this role?" Chaerea asked. "Or, will this be the first time you've used your sword in an execution?"

The man must have replied that he was an inexperienced executioner.

Chaerea then told him, "Go fetch my sword, the one I used to kill Gaius."[277]

Chaerea's sword, which he would have sharpened for days in the lead-up to Caligula's assassination, was brought forth. Pressed to his knees, Chaerea jutted out his neck in preparation for a clean end. His executioner duly cleaved off his head with a single blow of his own sword. When it came Lupus's turn to meet his end, he proved too tense, and his executioner made a mess of his task, having to strike the tribune's neck several times to part his head from his shoulders.

In February, an urgent dispatch from Rome would arrive by sea at Antioch, Syria, for the governor, Petronius. It advised him of Caligula's death and of Claudius's ascension to the throne. Twenty-seven days later, the earlier letter that Caligula had sent to Petronius, requiring him to commit suicide, finally arrived. Its couriers had been delayed by storms, which meant that their journey from Rome to Antioch took three months. Petronius ignored one missive and celebrated the other, and no doubt gave thanks to Borea, Roman god of the north wind and of winter, for speeding one ship and slowing another.

# XXVI

# THE REVENGE OF CALIGULA'S UNCLE

Among Claudius's first imperial acts, even before being officially hailed emperor by the Senate, was an order for the release of men imprisoned by Caligula, although this was not the sort of blanket amnesty with which Caligula had launched his reign. Those imprisoned for legitimate crimes remained incarcerated. Cassius Longinus, Caligula's onetime brother-in-law, was among the many set free along with King Antiochus and Alexander the Alabarch.

Claudius also ordered the return of many exiles, including Caligula's sisters, Agrippina and Livilla, to whom he restored all property and slaves previously sold off by their brother. Despite having been exiled by Caligula, on their return from the Pontian islands the dead emperor's sisters located his remains, cremated them, and then interred them with full burial rites. Until they did, the Lamian Gardens where he was temporarily buried were said to have been haunted by Caligula's ghost.

The new emperor then embarked on a conscious program designed to wipe from Roman memory both the reign of Caligula and the near revolt that had immediately followed it. The official written transcriptions of the debates of the Senate on January 24 and 25 were destroyed on Claudius's orders, so that no record remained of the brief period during which the abolition of the monarchy was discussed at the highest level of state.

Claudius's attack on his nephew's reign, and reminders of it, was broad. He ordered the priesthoods of Caligula and Drusilla abolished, with the overnight removal and destruction of all statues of Caligula in temples and government places. Nonetheless, many members of the public who possessed statues of Caligula in their homes would retain them. Some have survived to this day. Claudius even ordered the execution of the racehorse Incitatus, such was his determination to be rid of memories of Caligula.

Coins bearing Caligula's image were promptly withdrawn from circulation and melted down. His name was removed from all official oaths, and most of Caligula's edicts were cancelled. Notably, Claudius didn't terminate Caligula's highly popular fifth day of the Saturnalia holidays. Even though Claudius adored his brother Germanicus, he removed his name from the ninth month, which again became September, because the original name change had been an initiative of Caligula's. Claudius strove to make up for this by entering a Greek comedy penned by Germanicus in a contest at Neapolis, today's Naples. Germanicus's play won first prize.

Several of Caligula's freedmen were executed on Claudius's orders, Protogenes and Helicon among them. Caligula's chief of staff Callistus survived this Palatium purge by convincing Claudius that he'd several times ignored orders from Caligula to poison his uncle. Historian Josephus found this hard to swallow; he points out that anyone else who disobeyed Caligula once, let alone multiple times, incurred punishment. But Claudius swallowed it, making Callistus one of the most senior and influential members of his cabinet as secretary of petitions. Shifty Callistus would retain imperial favor for another eleven years. Following the Augustan model, as Caligula had done, Claudius also appointed a second Praetorian prefect, Catonius Justus, to partner Pollio.

Claudius seems never to have liked Caligula's gruff brother-in-law Corbulo, for now he overturned the measures that Corbulo had implemented for Caligula when he'd legitimately fined those officials and contractors who'd failed to maintain the roads. Claudius cancelled outstanding fines and refunded all previous fines using the moneys still in the roads fund, requiring Corbulo to repay the balance from his own pocket when the fund was exhausted by refunds.

Caligula's prefect of Egypt was among officials whom Claudius promptly replaced. However, for the sake of continuity and to show he held no grudge against them, Claudius retained Caligula's sitting consuls until the middle of the year. He also kept Petronius, governor of Syria, in his post for another year, no doubt on the recommendation of Agrippa, who soon set off for Judea to take charge of his Middle Eastern territories, basing himself in Jerusalem.

Claudius gave Agrippa additional territory by extending his rule to lands that today cover Israel, Palestine, and Jordan, and giving him the title once enjoyed by his grandfather, Herod the Great, that of King of Judea. At Agrippa's request, his younger brother Herod was given the territory of Chalcis. As proof that Herod was also at Rome at the time of Caligula's assassination, before Agrippa left Rome both he and his brother gave speeches of thanks in the Senate, and Herod issued a coin once he reached Chalcis on which he showed Agrippa and himself jointly crowning Claudius emperor.

Agrippa returned to Judea that spring of AD 41, reuniting with his loyal wife, Cypros, and their children, and was in Jerusalem in late September/early October in time for the annual Feast of the Tabernacles. Having brought the golden chains that Caligula had gifted him four years earlier, he donated them to the Temple. It was tradition that every seven years the Jewish king read passages from Deuteronomy to assembled pilgrims in the Temple courtyard, and Agrippa now revived that tradition, giving the reading to a massive crowd.

It's reported that when he read: "You may not put a foreigner over you who is not your brother," tears formed in his eyes.

"Don't fear, Agrippa; you are our brother," the people called to him. "You are our brother. You are our brother!" This may have referred to Agrippa's mixed heritage, as some have believed, or the fact that a Roman emperor, a friend of Agrippa's, in reality ruled over the Jewish people.[278]

This same year, Philo of Alexandria finally obtained resolution to his embassy to Caligula, and speedily so. Both the Jews and the gentiles of Alexandria had apparently quickly resubmitted their previous arguments to the new emperor, for, by the autumn, Claudius ruled in the matter. He sent a letter instructing the gentiles of Alexandria to allow Egyptian Jews to live and worship in peace, but at the same time admonishing the Jews for previously disrupting Roman religious festivals in Egypt. He also banned more Jews from settling in Alexandria from Upper Egypt or Syria. Claudius also noted, "I specifically order the Jews not to agitate for more privileges." Claudius's decision was transmitted to the Alexandrians by his new prefect of Egypt, Lucius Aemilius Rectus, in an edict dated November 10, AD 41.[279]

Caligula's extension of the Palace of Tiberius and Gaius to the Temple of Castor and Pollux in the Forum below was demolished by Claudius. The massive ships on Lake Remi would be stripped of most of their above-deck features and abandoned, and at some point they disappeared beneath the surface of the lake. Precisely when is unclear. Some historians suggest that Claudius ordered the barges sunk, while others believe that Nero may have used the barges for pleasure purposes at the lake during his later reign and they were still afloat during the reign of Hadrian. Some think they went down in a storm, while others believe they were deliberately scuttled.

With Caligula's repairs to Pompey's Theater nearing completion, Claudius let the work continue and then led the rededication ceremony in late AD 41, placing his name and Tiberius's name on the pedestal as emperors who'd restored the theater but omitting Caligula's name despite his contribution to the work. He demolished Caligula's amphitheater on the Martian Fields and repaired the damaged Virgo aqueduct next door. Today, the Virgo is the only one of the ultimately eleven aqueducts of ancient Rome to still supply Rome. The waters flowing into Rome's famous Trevi Fountain are delivered by the Virgo Aqueduct.

Claudius was to say he'd assumed a mask of stupidity as a protection against Caligula, and, while demonstrably a fool when it came to matters of the heart, Claudius was no fool when it came to practical matters. He continued Caligula's two ambitious and expensive but immensely practical new aqueducts. They would take another nine years to complete and would be opened by Claudius in AD 50 with great ceremony. One was called the New Anio Aqueduct. Claudius put his name to the other, which became the Claudia, or Claudian, with future generations crediting him, not Caligula, with the innovation of the two mighty structures that would dominate Rome's skyline for centuries to come.

In the same spirit of trashing Caligula's reign, the Senate voted Claudius an Ovation for the successful wrapping up of Berber resistance in Mauretania, even though, as Cassius Dio points out, this had been achieved in the dying days of Caligula's reign, with Claudius having no hand in it.[280]

Caligula's port developments at Reggio and on Sicily were only half completed at his death, with moles built out into the sea offering some protection for shipping. There is no historical evidence that Claudius finished these works, or other major building projects initiated by Caligula around the empire. For example, it is known that the work on the temple of Apollo at Didyma was never completed, and everything points to Claudius abandoning all of Caligula's remaining ambitious projects. Instead, Claudius, who proved an excellent financial manager, did spend some treasury money restoring a temple of his own favored deity, Venus, on Mount Eryx in Sicily.

During Claudius's rule, a fire broke out on the Palatine, causing the tunnel in which Caligula had been murdered to partially collapse. While builders' stamps found in the cryptoporticus tell us that Claudius had the tunnel repaired, the new emperor is known to have undertaken only two major public infrastructure projects of his own.

The first was the draining of the unhealthy Fucine Lake in central Italy, breeding ground for malarial mosquitoes. Claudius astutely provided the land for a drainage tunnel, but not the money. That work, which spanned more than eleven years and involved thirty thousand workmen, was funded by businessmen in return for the reclaimed land for development. Claudius's secretary of correspondence, the freedman Narcissus, acted as the Palatium's project manager, and when the Fucine Lake drainage project ultimately offered less than satisfactory results, it was Narcissus who was blamed by Roman writers, not Claudius.

Claudius's other major construction project, a major new port facility at Ostia, proved much more successful. When Claudius asked the project's architects what the cost would be, he was told, "You don't want to do it." He nonetheless pressed on. Caligula's mighty Egyptian barge sitting at Ostia was filled with concrete and sunk to form a mole as part of the new port, with a lighthouse modeled on the Pharos at Alexandria rising from it. While expensive, as Claudius had been warned, the port development proved a major boon to Rome's trade.[281]

Meanwhile, Claudius's spoiled young wife, Messalina, grew jealous of Claudius's beautiful twenty-four-year-old niece, Livilla, Caligula's youngest sister, and in AD 41 Messalina had the girl charged with an illicit affair with the writer Seneca. Modern historians are split on whether Seneca was literally in bed with Livilla, but, for the accusation to be made, Seneca must have spent a considerable amount of the time at Claudius's Palatium and frequently been in the company of Livilla, and, as later events were to indicate, in the company of her sister Agrippina, to whom he also became close.

Both Seneca and Caligula's youngest sister were convicted of the affair and were banished to distant islands. In Seneca's case, the island was Corsica, where he would languish for eight years but write some of his best work. Even after Messalina was later found to have betrayed Claudius, the emperor retained a dislike of Seneca. Eventually Agrippina talked Claudius into pardoning and recalling Seneca, and eventually she would employ him as tutor to her son Lucius, the future emperor Nero.

The exiled beauty Livilla, Caligula's little sister, was not so lucky. By the end of AD 42 she was dead in exile. Livilla's ashes would later be placed in the Mausoleum of Augustus at Rome, along with those of her parents—apparently by sister Agrippina. The rumor swept Rome that Livilla had died from starvation, with Messalina having ordered that food be withheld from her. But Messalina cynically countered that Livilla's husband, Marcus Vinicius, had been responsible for ordering her starvation. This was the same Vinicius who had walked from the theater with Claudius on the day of Caligula's murder. He was a friend of Claudius, but, unlike the empress, Vinicius was in no position to issue orders or bribes to Livilla's Praetorian jailers.

Asiaticus was the other senator who'd walked with Claudius from the theater that fateful day Caligula perished. While Claudius remained close to Vinicius, he came to despise Asiaticus because he'd striven to secure the throne for himself.

Messalina subsequently propositioned Vinicius in AD 46, and when he refused her, she had him poisoned. Oblivious to all of this, Claudius gave Vinicius a state funeral. Messalina also propositioned the handsome Mnester, Caligula's favored actor, and when he refused her, she had the unwitting Claudius instruct Mnester to do whatever the empress asked of him. And so Mnester became her lover, on the emperor's orders.

Caligula's appointees to the German frontier, Galba and Gabinius, both waged successful spring/summer campaigns in Germany within months of Caligula's death, with Galba defeating the Chatti tribe and Gabinius overwhelming the Cauchi and recovering the last missing eagle standard from the Varus Disaster. The Senate awarded Claudius the traditional title *imperator* for these successes, but, with the campaigns initiated by Caligula and led by generals other than Claudius, some senators were unimpressed with his leadership.

Vinicianus, leader of Caligula's assassination, still had his eyes on the throne, and in AD 42 he conspired with Furius Camillus Scribonianus, governor of Pannonia, to overthrow Claudius. Scribonianus ordered his two legions to march on Rome, but within days the legions turned on him. Fleeing to the Adriatic island of Vis, he took his own life. In Rome, Vinicianus also committed suicide, and the rebellion was snuffed out. Even though it had been quickly terminated, this revolt shook Claudius, and he determined to cement the loyalty of Rome's military by giving them an easy victory—via the invasion of Britain.

Caligula's AD 39–40 preparations for the British invasion offered a ready-made operation. As P. A. Holder says, Claudius had "a force prepared for him for the actual invasion" by Caligula.[282] From the Rhine came three experienced legions and their associated auxiliaries. The two new legions raised by Caligula, the 15th *Primigenia* and 22nd *Primigenia*, were posted to bases on the upper and lower Rhine to replace them. A fourth legion destined for the invasion force marched from Pannonia to join the other assigned legions in camp at Gesoriacum, to use the very embarkation port, lighthouse, and fleet that Caligula had prepared.

One of the four legion commanders for the operation was Vespasian, the official once loaded with mud on Caligula's orders. Now commanding the 2nd *Augusta* Legion, one of Germanicus's old units, Vespasian had astutely befriended Claudius's powerful freedman Narcissus. Probably through his influence, Vespasian's elder brother Sabinus commanded another of the invasion force's legions. Unlike Caligula, Claudius didn't journey from Rome to personally lead the invasion, instead putting a subordinate, Aulus Plautius, in charge.

Just as the operation was about to get under way, the invasion force's four legions went on strike, refusing to embark, just as Caligula's invasion force seems to have done three years earlier. Claudius sent his fixit man, Narcissus, hurrying from Rome, and, with the aid of a sizable bribe, Narcissus convinced the troops to undertake the operation. The army of forty thousand legionaries and auxiliaries landed in Kent in three waves in the late summer of AD 43 and, within months, overran British defenders and occupied much of southern Britain, creating the new Roman province of Britannia.

Only once the fighting was over did Claudius go to Britain, leaving the practiced sycophant but nonetheless able consul Lucius Vitellius in charge at Rome. A little northeast of today's London, at Camulodunum, present-day Colchester, the city that became the provincial capital, Claudius formally took the surrender of twenty British kings. He spent a total of sixteen days in Britain before returning home and, in AD 44, celebrated the first Triumph that Rome had seen since that of his brother Germanicus twenty-seven years before.

Behind Claudius's chariot in the triumphal parade rode his wife, Messalina, in a closed carriage, followed by the generals who'd actually won the victory in Britain. Before long, Messalina's influence over soft, malleable Claudius would go to her head and result in her losing it.

# XXVII

## DÉJÀ VU WITH NERO

Claudius's weakness in matters of the heart eventually cost him his life. After impetuous Messalina almost overthrew him in AD 48, she and her co-conspirators, including the hapless Mnester, were put to death. As the Senate debated the subject of a suitable new wife for Claudius, his senior freedmen promoted competing candidates. Callistus pushed Caligula's rich and beautiful ex-wife Lollia. Narcissus advocated for Claudius's former wife, Aelia Paetina, whom Caligula had forced him to divorce to marry Messalina. Pallas, Claudius's secretary of the treasury, plumped for Caligula's sister Agrippina the Younger, with whom Pallas would later be rumored to be having an affair.

Agrippina, flirting with her uncle, won his heart, with their betrothal requiring the Senate to enact a special law to allow uncles to marry their nieces, and Claudius and Agrippina married. Infatuated with Agrippina, Claudius gave her whatever she asked for. And she asked for a lot. Tacitus indicates that Claudius gave her the Gardens of Agrippina at Rome, which Caligula had cherished, as well as Tiberius's Villa of Lucullus at Misenum and Caligula's villa at Antium.[283]

Plus, around AD 50, when the Rhineland city we know as Cologne was granted colony status, Caligula named it Colonia Claudia Ara Agrippinensium, in Agrippina's honor. It was as a result of this that Cologne today claims to be Agrippina's birthplace, but, as previously mentioned, she seems to have been born in Gaul. Still, Agrippina had plenty of connections with the city—her grandfather Marcus Agrippa founded it; her father, Germanicus, was headquartered there; and she herself spent much of the first two years of her life there.

Agrippina was hugely ambitious for her son Lucius, who took the name Nero Claudius Caesar Drusus Germanicus after being adopted by Claudius at her behest. Seeing herself ruling through the boy, she set out to eliminate a rival heir to the throne, Claudius and Messalina's son Britannicus. Agrippina had Britannicus poisoned, making Nero sole heir to Claudius's throne. Then, enlisting the aid of Claudius's new Praetorian prefect Burrus, Agrippina poisoned Claudius. Just short of his eighteenth birthday, Nero was hailed emperor by the Praetorian Guard. When the Senate followed suit, the public rejoiced that a grandson of Germanicus was their new emperor.

For seven years, young Nero ruled well with the guidance of Burrus and chief secretary Seneca—who, through the agency of Agrippina, had made a spectacular rise to power. After Seneca and Burrus kept Agrippina from exerting her influence over her son, and so maintained their own influence, Agrippina tried every trick she knew to win back Nero, reputedly even offering her body to her boy. Nero, driven to despair by his scheming mother, decided to be rid of her, permanently, and with the help of the admiral of the Tyrrhenian Fleet he conceived a fiendish murder plot.

Nero gave his mother a fine new ship as a gift, a ship that fell apart on cue when she was at sea. Agrippina managed to swim to shore, so Nero had to send the admiral with marines to finish the job with their swords. They killed her as she lay on a couch at her Bauli villa. As the daughter of Germanicus, Agrippina was widely popular, so, to excuse her murder, Nero informed the Senate that she'd been planning to overthrow him.

After Praetorian prefect Burrus died from throat cancer, Seneca fell out with Nero, who later forced him to commit suicide after he was implicated in an AD 65 plot against him—a plot led by a member of the same Piso family accused of the murder of his grandfather Germanicus. Nero ruled thereafter without restraint, with his acts increasingly compared to those of his uncle Caligula for their grandiosity, impulsiveness, and wastefulness.

The devastating AD 64 Great Fire of Rome, which broke out in a shop beneath the Circus Maximus, was to kindle accusations that Nero had deliberately set the fire to enable him to rebuild Rome—accusations that modern historians generally dismiss. He certainly didn't fiddle while Rome burned and, on the contrary, led fire-fighting efforts. Nonetheless, over the next few years, support for Nero crumbled at home and abroad. Revolts against his rule broke out across the empire.

On June 9, AD 68, a day before the anniversary of his aunt Drusilla's death, Nero awoke at his lavish new Palatium, the Golden House, to find it devoid of every single guard. The Senate had declared him an enemy of the state and withdrawn the German Guard. In desperation, he fled to the suburban home of one of his freedmen, only for the Praetorian cavalry to come trotting up the road to arrest him. Putting a knife to his throat, Nero took his own life, perishing at the age of just thirty after a reign of thirteen years. He was the last member of the Caesar family to rule Rome. With this death of Caligula's nephew, the ruling line established by the dictator Julius Caesar came to a bloody end, and Rome was thrown into civil war.

The following tumultuous year, AD 69, became infamous as the Year of the Four Emperors. Three of these emperors, apart from Otho, who'd only been eight years old at the time of Caligula's assassination, had strong links to Caligula. The first emperor after Nero was Caligula's loyal general Galba, who, like his former lord and master, was assassinated. Caligula's close friend Aulus Vitellius, the limping son of Lucius Vitellius, also reigned briefly, before, like Galba, dying violently. And finally Vespasian, Caligula's muddy aedile of the alleys, returned stability to the empire and launched a new imperial dynasty, the Flavians.

And so ends the story of Caligula, his fatal family, and his often ill-fated friends.

# XXVIII

## WAS CALIGULA TRULY MAD?

Today, pundits and psychiatrists furiously debate the definition of "madness." Where do narcissism, self-delusion, and an apparent inability to conceive of consequences of actions cross the boundary between childishness and mental derangement? The story of Caligula offers some enlightening insights into the issue, and into the modern political debate.

Third-century historian Cassius Dio was convinced that Caligula was deranged and "continued to act the madman in every way."[284] What else could explain his deadly rages and cruel whims? Seneca, who knew and crossed rhetorical swords with Caligula and survived to tell the tale, did write of Caligula's "insane" acts. Equally, as German scholar Aloys Winterling points out, Seneca also accused Alexander the Great of acting insanely at times, just as he accused Roman women of the "insanity" of wearing too much jewelry. In fact, Seneca was of the opinion that Caligula was merely wicked. "I think nature produced (him) as an example of the effect of supreme wickedness in a supreme position," Seneca told his mother.[285]

Wicked, many of Caligula's acts were, but ancient Roman biographer Suetonius was convinced that Caligula suffered from mental illness. More recent scholars have been split on the question of Caligula's sanity. In the eighteenth and nineteenth century, says twentieth-century Caligula biographer Anthony Barrett, the prevailing scholarly view was that Caligula was "a totally deranged madman."[286] Edward Gibbon typified this view. Gibbon felt that both Caligula and Rome's eleventh emperor, Domitian, were quite mad, and he repeatedly expressed this view in his monumental *Decline and Fall of the Roman Empire*, a work that educated and influenced Britons and Americans for well over a century. By the 1930s, the pendulum had swung the other way, with the likes of J.P.V.D. Balsdon and Chester Starr offering reasoned, rational explanations for some of Caligula's seemingly irrational acts.

In 2003, Aloys Winterling went as far as criticizing other historians for "inventing the mad emperor." Winterling felt that Caligula was bad, not mad, and made the point that Tacitus wrote, at the commencement of his *Annals*, that historians of his day deliberately and maliciously distorted their accounts of Tiberius, Caligula, Claudius, and Nero. Among other things, Winterling noted that, when senators spoke in the Senate immediately following Caligula's assassination, they condemned him for tyranny, but they never once accused him of insanity.[287]

Barrett expressed the view that Caligula was not clinically insane. He rated him more "a conceited, ill-mannered and rather irresponsible young ruler" who succumbed to the dark side of his power. Barrett pointed out that Caligula was able "to act sensibly in every phase of his reign" and at times make wise, pragmatic decisions, despite sometimes apparently senseless acts. On the other hand, another past biographer of Caligula, Arther Ferrill, wrote in 1991 that the young emperor was irretrievably mad, and "was in fact a monster," expressing the view that "academic efforts to revise this estimate of him are misguided."[288]

So, was Caligula truly mad? Madness takes many forms. People suffering from dementia were once considered mad, as were manic depressives. Winston Churchill was a manic depressive. It's worth looking at the conditions that modern medical authorities have variously ascribed to Caligula's often erratic, sometimes monstrous, and inescapably paranoid behavior—temporal lobe epilepsy, hyperthyroidism, Wilson's disease, schizophrenia, and bipolar disorder/manic depression.

Firstly, temporal lobe epilepsy. We know that Julius Caesar suffered from epilepsy in adulthood and had an attack just as one of his crucial civil war battles was opening, at Thapsus in North Africa. According to Suetonius, Caligula suffered from epilepsy as a child. Childhood epilepsy often spontaneously clears up once the sufferer reaches adulthood. But it can be followed by the onset of an adult form such as temporal lobe epilepsy, which generates hallucinations, memory disorders, and repetitive movements, with the sufferer often later totally unaware of an attack. Memory problems or repetitive movements don't figure in descriptions of Caligula's behavior. While Caligula did several times claim to be speaking with the gods, the one time he claimed that a god, the moon goddess, was actually beside him, this seems to have been a crafty test of Lucius Vitellius rather than a genuine hallucination. This all suggests that Caligula did not suffer from temporal lobe epilepsy.

Hyperthyroidism results from an overactive thyroid gland, which in turn stems from causes including thyroid tumors and Graves' disease. If left untreated, hyperthyroidism can lead to chronic depression and isolated psychotic episodes where the sufferer acts completely out of character. Other general symptoms include rapid heartbeat, sweating, loss of weight, and intolerance of heat, with Graves' disease sufferers also presenting with a swollen neck and bulging eyes. Caligula displayed none of these symptoms, so, hyperthyroidism can reasonably be ruled out in his case.

Wilson's disease is caused by an inborn defect in copper metabolism in the body. It can affect the brain, causing mental retardation and symptoms akin to Parkinson's disease, none of which Caligula displayed. A key indicator of Wilson's disease is a brown ring in the cornea of the eye. No classical authority has suggested that Caligula possessed such an obvious abnormality, so, Wilson's disease should be crossed off the list too.

Schizophrenia has also been suggested in Caligula's case. A genetically inherited, so-called "split personality" disorder, schizophrenia sees sufferers often going from seemingly normal one moment to severely afflicted the next. During attacks, sufferers cannot think clearly and rationally, lose contact with reality, suffer hallucinations and delusions, hear voices, and believe their actions are dictated by or shared with others. They often withdraw socially, becoming paranoid and believing that everyone around them is out to get them.

While Caligula certainly became paranoid toward the end of his life, this could be explained by his fraught existence after his father's death, when he had to be constantly on guard to ensure he didn't share the fate of his mother and brothers. It might be said he was conditioned to fear. And, as historians agree today, some of the plots against him during his reign were real, with, of course, the last one taking his life. Ironically, it was his paranoia that drained him of friends and ultimately led to his murder. Yet, there were long periods when he seemed to be able to think clearly enough, and he never claimed his actions were dictated by voices in his head. Schizophrenia, then, can probably also be ruled out.

The more credible and likely cause of Caligula's behavior is bipolar disorder, previously known as manic depression. Sufferers of bipolar disorder experience remissions and relapses, which would explain why Caligula could intersperse seemingly crazy episodes with periods during which he exhibited rational behavior and made sound decisions. Bipolar sufferers experience dramatic mood swings, going from high highs when they display high energy, hyperactivity, overreaching self-confidence, and loss of touch with reality, to low lows where they become sad, depressed, lethargic, withdrawn, and suffer from physical fatigue. Suetonius says, "I'm convinced that his brain-sickness accounted for his two contradictory vices—over-confidence and extreme timorousness." Suetonius didn't know it, but he was describing the opposite ends of the bipolar spectrum.[289]

As can be seen, many of the above-mentioned bipolar symptoms can be attributed to Caligula, as can the following: reduced need for sleep, impulsivity, anger and aggression, anxiety, apathy, euphoria, irritability, prone to risk-taking, increased need for sex, restlessness, delusions, paranoia. Bipolar sufferers can also have a false feeling of superiority, which Caligula displayed with his overblown belief in his own abilities as a writer, orator, and legal advocate.

Bipolar sufferers at their most manic speak rapidly, sometimes frenziedly, which describes Caligula's recorded public speaking style. "Until the mania gets out of control," says Harvard Medical School of bipolar sufferers, "he/she can be extremely productive and wonderful company." Again, this describes Caligula.[290] At the low end of the manic scale, bipolar sufferers can at times find it difficult to concentrate on the matter at hand, a quality that Caligula exhibited, for example, when he met with Philo and the delegates from Alexandria at Rome.

Bipolar disorder tends to show itself in sufferers between the ages of fifteen and twenty-four. Caligula was just into his twenty-fifth year when Suetonius says he came down with his "brain-sickness." It may have in fact surfaced earlier, only to become more pronounced once he recovered from the physical illness that almost took his life. According to Harvard Medical School, too, "Troubled family relationships may aggravate the disorder." Few people had more troubled family relationships than Caligula.[291]

I am not a medical professional. Even if I were, for a reliable diagnosis the patient would need to be seen in the flesh. So, all I can do is point out that the known symptoms of bipolar disorder match very closely aspects of the recorded behavior of Caligula two thousand years ago. Historical records contain many more examples of his manic "up" periods than of his withdrawn "down" periods, but we do know that he would periodically lock himself away at his mother's gardens and also regularly retreat to one villa or another, so these can be seen as examples of antisocial, depressed behavior.

Today, bipolar, which is thought to affect two percent of the global population, can be controlled by medically prescribed drugs and electroconvulsive treatment. In Caligula's day the disorder was not known to the medical community. So, unlike epilepsy, there was no treatment available at the time, and those around Caligula could only ponder on how to assuage their emperor and literally keep their heads.

Of course, the Roman public was unaware of the extent of Caligula's odd behavior. In those days, no paparazzi, reporters, or cameras poked into every aspect of a celebrity's life. The plebs may have grumbled at Caligula's new taxes, but they also saw all the activity of his building projects, they enjoyed his Ovation parade, and they would have marveled at his crossing of the Bay of Puteoli. They also applauded the doubling of the number of races at the circus and the extra day he added to the Saturnalia Festival.

Caligula's core support from the common people seems to have remained strong through much of his reign. As archeological finds have shown, Romans were to retain Caligula's busts and statues even after Claudius's Palatium ordered their destruction. Dio says that Caligula's licentious behavior was actually admired by the commoners, and his measures to deprive the rich of their wealth would also have been popular. Ultimately, it was a conspiracy of the elite that brought him down, not a revolt of the commoners.[292]

Some modern-day writers have claimed that Caligula actively courted the lower classes and was a populist at heart. This goes against the historical evidence. We have, for example, Caligula's comment about wishing all Rome had but one neck. According to Seneca, who lived through those times, Caligula died "still feeling upset—if the dead have feelings—because he saw that the Roman people were still surviving."[293] Modern attempts to resurrect Caligula's reputation by painting him as a ruler trying to end the world of privilege enjoyed by the Roman elite ignore the many people of all classes who died or were ruined through his cruel, capricious orders.

Caligula began his reign with a determination to be an innovator, the creator, in his own words, of "great enterprises." By the end of his life, Caligula projected no coherent policy agenda, was driven by self-gratification and paranoia, and ruled on impulse. Caligula was changeable, unpredictable, contradictory. He was sometimes cowardly and unable to own up to a mistake. He considered himself a scholar and master manipulator of words; there can be no doubt that had Twitter existed two thousand years ago, Caligula would probably have been an avid user.

So, was Caligula born bad, or did he turn bad? According to an ancient Roman proverb, no one becomes a villain in an instant. And so it was with Caligula. While Suetonius blamed the illness that laid Caligula low early into his reign for his subsequent mental instability and hateful behavior, it's probable that Caligula harbored a dark, resentful side from the beginning of his reign. While subject to Praetorian Guard prefect Macro's control, the young emperor merely "played possum."

As evidence of this, we only have to hark back to the beginning of his reign when Caligula burned written evidence against his mother and brothers, supposedly destroying the names of informants, an act for which he was universally praised at the time. As we know, he quite deliberately kept copies of those incriminating documents, later bringing them out to expose and punish those who'd informed against his family. Clearly, in keeping copies, he'd planned this deadly deception from the outset.

Suetonius believed that, in making his will and leaving everything to his sister Drusilla during his illness, Caligula was convinced he was going to die. Caligula's recovery may well have triggered a decision to live for today, throwing off all shackles and giving rein to his passion for and pursuit of innovations and amusements. His first steps were to remove obstacles to unfettered power, by eliminating his potential rival Gemellus and the manipulating Macro, by sidelining his grandmother Antonia, and by sending his best friend and most trusted confidant Herod Agrippa to the East. With all restraint removed, it was time for revenge, for fun, for mayhem.

# XXIX

## DRAWING PRESENT-DAY LESSONS: IS DONALD TRUMP THE MODERN CALIGULA?

Is it fair and reasonable to compare the unpredictable, ultimately chaotic reign and questionable mental state of Caligula to the administration and personality of the forty-fifth president of the United States? Do comparisons between Caligula and Donald Trump stand up to scrutiny?

As it happens, comparing two historical figures from different times and places is not a new thing in biography. Early in the second century, Greco-Roman writer Plutarch produced a lively set of pocket biographies, *The Lives of the Noble Grecians and Romans*, which included a number of summarizing chapters comparing the lives of leading men of widely different eras: *Romulus and Theseus Compared*, *Cicero and Demosthenes Compared*, and *Antony and Demetrius Compared* among them.

Even before Donald Trump was elected president of the United States in November 2016, he was being compared to Caligula by historians and political pundits. British historian and author Tom Holland, speaking at the Hay Festival in the United Kingdom in May 2016, said, "Donald Trump has fascinating parallels with Caligula."[294]

Few in the media thought that Trump would be elected, but once he beat out Hillary Clinton for the presidency in November 2016 and took office in January 2017 the comparisons with Caligula came thick and fast, in the United States and around the world.

"Trump makes Caligula look pretty good," wrote political commentator Paul Krugman in *The New York Times*. Continuing the analogy, Krugman went on to remind readers that Caligula was "the cruel, depraved Roman emperor who delighted in humiliating others."[295]

In Dublin's *Irish Times*, columnist Laura Kennedy asked, "Trump: Guardian of democratic values or the new Caligula?"[296]

"Donald Trump, Caligula, Michael Wolff, Suetonius, Infamia, and the Fake News Wars," was the title of an article in *Forbes* magazine by political columnist Ralph Benko.[297]

In *The Spectator*, journalist, broadcaster, and former university classics lecturer Peter Jones wrote, "If Trump looks bad, remember Caligula."[298]

"Donald Trump is half Caligula, half the toddler-in-chief," wrote Helen Lewis, deputy editor of the *New Statesman*.[299]

Bob Woodward, veteran American investigative reporter and author, says that former and existing Trump aides told him that, from their experience, President Trump was an "emotionally overwrought, mercurial and unpredictable leader." One White House official told Woodward, "There is literally no telling whether he might change his mind from one minute to the next."[300] The same can certainly be said of Caligula during the last three years of his reign, with Tacitus, you'll remember, describing him as "changeable as a weathercock."

So, just how accurate and legitimate are broad comparisons between Trump and Caligula? Well, to begin with, both rule/ruled the largest military and economic powers of their age. During Caligula's brief reign, he reputedly emptied the treasury with his extravagances. Trump presides over a ballooning U.S. national debt. Neither man had previously served in the military they ended up commanding. And neither of them had any experience in government, at any level, prior to landing the job of head of their government.

Both had few friends growing up. Both had multiple wives—Trump has had three; Caligula married for the fourth time when he was just twenty-six. Both men had successful, wealthy fathers. The parents of both Caligula and Trump all died before their son rose to the highest office in the land. Once in power, both men rid themselves of senior advisers who restrained them or wouldn't do what they wanted. Both were/are sports lovers, building their own sporting facilities in furtherance of their passions. In Caligula's case it was chariot racing and hippodromes. For Trump it's been golf and golf courses.

The role of president of the United States combines the role of head of state and head of government, as Caligula's position did. Few present-day nations apart from mostly Third World countries and dictatorships follow America's example of combining the two roles. Even North Korea technically divides them. After replacing the king of England and his prime minister with a single president in 1776, America's founding fathers gave the country's sole chief executive broad powers that King George III did not possess and that no present-day king or queen possesses. In fact, in giving the president of the United States the powers of veto, pardon, and rule by decree via executive order, the American Constitution makes Donald Trump almost as powerful as Caligula, and potentially as scary.

Then there are the obvious differences. Caligula was twenty-four years of age when he came to power. Trump was seventy when he took the top job. Caligula had absolute power with no specified end date, while Trump can only hanker for such power. Caligula was well-read and an accomplished public speaker with a lively if often barbed wit. Trump's wit can be similarly stinging. But he is an inarticulate man who doesn't read and exhibits a limited vocabulary and an obvious discomfort with formal speeches, to the point that he produces a nervous sniff when out of his comfort zone.

Caligula and Trump developed very different speaking styles. By modern standards, Roman speeches could be long, flowery, and melodramatic—a performance. In contrast, the speeches of modern political leaders have been influenced by the need to create slogans and short grabs that gain attention and airtime. Donald Trump's speaking style in his election campaign and during his presidency has shown another influence—the effect of catchphrases and catchwords.

Early radio stars had their catchphrases. Movies of the 1930s traded on them, with the likes of Laurel and Hardy's "That's another nice mess you've got me into," (often misquoted as "fine mess"). Television then introduced us to catchphrases such as Johnny Carson's *Tonight Show* introduction "Here's Johnny!" and *Get Smart*'s "Would you believe?" In more recent times, Arnold Schwarzenegger became an international movie star with film catchphrases that lodged in the public consciousness, such as "I'll be back" and "Hasta la vista, baby."

It was inevitable that politicians would come to draw on the power of catchwords and catchphrases. In 1932, "Happy Days Are Here Again" became the powerful, but accidental and unofficial, political campaign theme of Democrat presidential candidate Franklin D. Roosevelt after the catchy song of that title was played after his speech at the year's Democratic Convention.

Donald Trump has long known the power of the catchphrase, with his signature "You're fired" from his reality TV show *The Apprentice* entering the popular lexicon. Following attempted pipe bomb attacks on leading Democratic Party figures and CNN's New York City bureau in October 2018, CNN Worldwide president Jeff Zucker declared, "The president, and especially the White House press secretary, should understand their words matter. Thus far, they have shown no comprehension of that." He was referring to a Trump catchphrase that the media was "the enemy of the people," which Zucker contended led to the attack on CNN.[301]

Zucker was both right and wrong. Words do matter; but Donald Trump clearly knows it. His *Apprentice* days taught him that. Despite sometimes being inarticulate whilst ad-libbing, when Trump launches a prepared assault on adversaries he has obviously chosen his words for maximum effect, on both friend and foe.

When Trump made his 2016 presidential run he was using a limited vocabulary, in contrast to a decade and a half earlier, when, according to one former Trump aide, he'd used a broad vocabulary.[302] Whether it was Trump, or an adviser, who pruned his vocabulary to inject catchwords and catchphrases and use them in calculated repetition, we don't know. The strategy began with the unoriginal campaign slogan, "Make America Great Again," a direct borrow from Ronald Reagan's 1980 presidential campaign slogan, "Let's Make America Great Again."

During his campaign and first year in office, Trump continually peppered his speeches and off-the-cuff remarks with simplistic superlatives such as "amazing," "incredible," and "great"—the last being a catchword he shared with Caligula. While perpetuating the "fake news" catchphrase, Trump also regularly bolstered his assertions with "believe me" and "trust me." By 2018 he'd retreated from many of these. While retaining "fake news," he added "tremendous," "disgrace," and "witch-hunt," in habitual repetition.

Trump has made numerous outrageous claims. Some of these are obviously mischievous, some, malicious. Others appear to be the result of ignorance. Caligula made just one outrageous claim—that he and his sister Drusilla were gods. Donald Trump has made no such claim, although, says one Washington political commentator, "Millions of Americans believe God made Donald Trump president."[303]

Earlier, I mentioned the importance of the handshake to Romans, and the likelihood that Caligula yielded the upper hand to best friend Marcus Agrippa. It's instructive to look at Donald Trump's handshake. At his first public meeting as president with Russia's president Vladimir Putin at the 2017 G20 summit in Germany, Trump offered his hand first, and, palm up, yielded the upper hand to Putin. He did the same when meeting France's president Emanuel Macron that same year. In contrast, Trump offered female leaders Germany's chancellor Angela Merkel and Britain's prime minister Theresa May a straight up and down handshake.

By 2018, Trump had seemingly gained more confidence in the company of both Putin and Macron, using an up-and-down handshake when meeting both. Although, Trump still offered his hand first when seen in public with Putin at Helsinki for the first time. Putin later offered his hand first following the infamous press conference where Trump exonerated Russia of meddling in the 2016 U.S. general election—perhaps by way of congratulation, some might say—but straight up and down.

Through late 2018, Trump was photographed yielding the upper hand to Japan's prime minister Shinzo Abe and Australia's prime minister Scott Morrison. And, that October, he did the same with America's then ambassador to the United Nations, Nikki Haley. This occurred during an Oval Office press gathering called to announce that Haley would leave her UN post at the end of that year, an occasion when Haley praised the president. In March, 2019, President Trump yielded the upper hand to another foreign leader, this time in an Oval Office meeting with Irish prime minister Leo Varadker. Does Mr. Trump yield the upper hand through respect, or diffidence? Does he like the other party, or is he daunted by them? Only he can answer that.

In terms of policy, Trump and Caligula are poles apart. Some of Caligula's policies, particularly in the area of public infrastructure, were ambitiously innovative and progressive, if expensive, and in some cases would serve Rome for hundreds of years. While Trump has always painted himself as entrepreneurial and progressive, his policies have invariably been regressive, in the form of a blanket program of retreat. Retreat from the Paris Climate Agreement. Retreat from the Affordable Care Act, or "Obamacare." Retreat from free trade. Retreat from existing and mooted multilateral trade agreements. Retreat from government regulatory control of the economy and the environment. Retreat from international treaties such as the Iran nuclear deal. Retreat from cooperation with allies. Retreat from military boots on the ground in Syria and Afghanistan. And a retreat from civil discourse. With what effect? In January 2019, President Trump's secretary of state Mike Pompeo couldn't have put it better when he said, "When America retreats, chaos often follows."[304]

On a personal level, Caligula and Trump could be said to share narcissistic qualities such as a need for admiration and a lack of empathy. But narcissists also have exaggerated feelings of self-importance, and with both Caligula and Trump being the most powerful men of their time, each had/ have a right to feel important. Neither Caligula nor Trump fall into the category of psychopath, whose defining qualities include a poor socioeconomic background, criminal behavior in childhood, and a suicidal tendency, none of which can be attributed to either man.

They do share sociopathic qualities. One Trump aide has characterized his boss as "impetuous, adversarial, petty," and that certainly could describe a sociopath, and Caligula.[305] Sociopaths also exhibit an apparent lack of shame or guilt for things they've said and done. Neither Caligula nor Trump seemed/seem remorseful about their peccadilloes, joking about their bad behavior. Trump excused his foul language as locker room talk and claimed he could shoot someone on Fifth Avenue and get away with it.

Aldous Huxley, author of *Brave New World*, once said, when speaking of remorse, "Rolling in the muck is not the best way of getting clean."[306] Getting clean was never on the agenda for either Caligula or Trump, with both reveling in a macho "no apologies" persona. "Mr. Trump could not be shamed," said one Canadian newspaper commentator, "for he had no shame."[307] Caligula had no shame, either. "The performances of Donald Trump remind me of male chimpanzees and their dominance rituals," anthropologist Jane Goodall is reported as saying.[308] There's no doubting that Caligula's rages, and purges, were all about dominance and projecting a strongman image.

Sociopaths also have a rock-solid belief that they are by far the best at what they do and that nobody else comes close to them: Caligula considered himself the superior writer, orator, and legal advocate of his age, and Trump called himself a "very stable genius." Joked Republican senator Lindsey Graham, "If he doesn't call himself a genius, nobody else will." In fact, as far back as 2015, when Trump put up his hand to enter the GOP presidential race, London's *Economist* was speaking of his "brazen genius." By 2018, the *Financial Times* was declaring that Trump has a legitimate claim to three kinds of genius: "Political genius, instinctive genius, and evil genius."[309]

So, what other personal characteristics do these men share? Both can be seen to have exhibited a desire to humiliate adversaries. Caligula's reign was rife with the often vile humiliations he inflicted, while Trump turned to schoolyard name-calling in speeches and on Twitter to humiliate adversaries and former allies alike with examples such as "Crooked Hillary" Clinton, "Sloppy Steve" Bannon, Elizabeth "Pocahontas" Warren, "Little Marco" Rubio, "Little Adam Schitt" (Schiff), and "Little Rocket Man" Kim Jun-Un among them.

Anthony Barrett says that Caligula was "indifferent to the consequences of his actions."[310] Meanwhile, it has been said that Trump "sees the virtues of surprise and spontaneity. It's not clear that he understands the risks."[311]

Caligula never forgot a slight, to him or his family, and vindictively enacted vengeance, sometimes years after the event. Similarly, Trump's tweets and off-the-cuff remarks can display a vindictive streak, while British entrepreneur Sir Richard Branson found Trump obsessed with enacting vengeance on men he felt had slighted him.[312] Neither Trump nor Caligula display outward signs of a conscience, personal or social. Nor do they seem to possess the ability to admit they were wrong or made a mistake—apart from Trump's famous Helsinki "I misspoke" moment in 2018.

Can both Caligula and Trump be considered mad? As demonstrated, the evidence for Caligula's mental instability is extensive and compelling. What then of the sanity of President Trump? In 2018 his then White House chief of staff General John Kelly allegedly said, "He's gone off the rails. We're in Crazytown!"[313] But does that mean Trump is crazy or just inept and out of his league? Alternatively, was this an overreaction from a militarist to a nonconformist?

Can Trump's always-unconventional, sometimes-unorthodox, often-irregular approach to government add up to mental instability or a personality disorder? Alternatively, can his frequently simplistic black-and-white responses to complex issues of state and his sometimes detachment from reality be explained by puerile naivety, a lack of worldliness, and lack of experience in government?

Can Mr. Trump's apparent forgetfulness and carelessness with the truth be explained by the onset of senile dementia? One former Trump aide has claimed that, over fourteen years, she saw his mental faculties decline so far that he went from super sharp in 2003 to forgetting in the afternoon what he'd said in the morning by late 2017. Could that be explained by creeping dementia, or merely by the stress of the top job in a tough week.[314]

From the available evidence, it seems Caligula really did suffer from a mental illness. As for Trump, is he mentally ill, a willful child out of his depth, or suffering from senility? Or, is he much more tactically astute, deliberate, and craftily streetwise than many people give him credit for that? Could it be like Caligula's uncle Claudius, Trump is "smart at playing dumb" as one political commentator suggests?[315] This is all, in the words of an ancient Roman saying, still before the judge. Time will tell. Or, in Trumpspeak, "We'll see."

In the end, it was not external foes who brought about Caligula's downfall. What finally brought Caligula down was clawing fear among the Roman leadership as he eliminated many around him, a dread of who would be next. Loyalty and friendship were no guarantee of survival in Caligula's Rome. Similarly, it's been said of Donald Trump by leading conservative commentator David Brooks that "he turns on a dime" when it comes to his friends.[316]

The result in Caligula's case was that, when it was a matter of personal survival, even the most loyal became the most lethal. Already, we've seen one anonymous, well-placed Trump White House official claim that he/she and others have, in effect, become a Callistus and a Petronius and have worked toward frustrating and disempowering their leader at times. Petronius the general put his own life on the line to prevent a Middle East war, while chief of staff Callistus ultimately joined the plot to bring down Caligula. Where will the anonymous White House essayist stand when the chips are down, if indeed he/she is still at the White House?

When Caligula's reign was terminated in Rome at the point of swords wielded by assassins in his own guard, it had lasted around four years, the equivalent of a U.S. presidential term. Perhaps it will take that long for the proverbial knives to come out among the Republican old guard in Washington, DC, today. As was the case in AD 41, it will probably not be a pretty sight.

I suspect that, as with Gaius Julius Caesar Germanicus Augustus, in the long run history will not treat President Donald John Trump kindly. Perhaps his "shakeup" of Washington politics will ultimately be seen as akin to steering the *Titanic* toward the iceberg, not away from it, the same way that Caligula's shakeup of Rome set her on course for the obliteration of the Caesar family, and civil war. Then again, perhaps Mr. Trump will be hailed as the savior of the *Titanic*. With the benefit of time, long after both Donald Trump and I have passed on, future historians will make the final judgment.

# NOTES

## INTRODUCTION

1. Seneca, *On Firmness.*

## I  NURSLING OF THE LEGIONS

2. Seneca, *On Firmness.*
3. Suetonius.
4. Ibid.
5. The 1st Legion then had no title. Previously, it'd been awarded the title 1st *Augusta* by Augustus for valorous service in the Cantabrian War, only to be stripped of it by Marcus Agrippa in 19 BC for cowardice.
6. Tacitus, *Annals.*
7. Ibid.
8. Ibid.
9. Ibid.
10. Suetonius.
11. Tacitus, *Annals.*
12. Ibid.

## II  CALIGULA AT THE BRIDGE

13. Robert Graves, *I, Claudius.*
14. Stephen Dando-Collins, *Legions of Rome.*
15. Tacitus, *Annals.*
16. Ibid.
17. Ibid.
18. Ibid.

### III    SHARING HIS FATHER'S TRIUMPH

19. Suetonius.

### IV    HIS FATHER'S VIOLENT DEATH

20. Tacitus, *Annals*.
21. Harrison, *Paul & the Imperial Authorities at Thessalonica*.
22. Tacitus, *Annals*; Pliny the Elder, *Natural History*.
23. Tacitus, *Annals*.
24. Hunt & Edgar, *Selected Papyri II*.
25. Tacitus, *Annals*.
26. Ibid.
27. Ibid.
28. Suetonius.
29. Ibid.
30. Josephus, *Jewish Antiquities*.
31. Dio, *Roman History*; Suetonius, *Lives of the Caesars*; Tacitus, *Annals*.

### V    A MURDER TRIAL

32. Tacitus, *Annals*.
33. Ibid.
34. Macinnis, *Poisons*; Mellan, *Dictionary of Poisons*; Thompson, *Poisons and Poisoners*.
35. Dio.
36. Tacitus, *Annals*.
37. Ibid.
38. Ibid.
39. Ibid.
40. Ibid.
41. Ibid.

### VI    NURSING A VIPER

42. Tacitus, *Annals*.

43. Ibid.

44. Graves.

45. Philo, *On the Embassy to Gaius.*

46. Suetonius.

47. A. Barrett, *Caligula: The Corruption of Power.*

48. A. Winterling, *Caligula: A Biography.*

49. Suetonius; and Tacitus, *Annals.*

50. Josephus.

51. Suetonius.

52. Ibid.

## VII  CALIGULA'S GRANDMOTHER BRINGS DOWN SEJANUS

53. Dio.

54. Seneca, *Consolation to Marcia.*

55. Tacitus, *Annals.*

56. Suetonius.

57. Suetonius names her Ennia Naeva. Dio gives Ennia Thrasylla.

58. A. Ferrill, *Caligula: Emperor of Rome.*

59. Suetonius.

## VIII  YIELDING THE UPPER HAND

60. Capito's career is detailed on an AD 32 inscription at Chieti, Italy. See Braud, *Augustus to Nero.* Because Capito was a civilian employee of the emperor, past historians have puzzled over how he could send troops after Agrippa, but Capito's dual role as a part-time prefect of Evocati reservists explains this.

61. Josephus.

62. For Tiberius's appearance by this point, see Tacitus, *Annals.*

63. Josephus.

64. Ibid.

65. Ibid.

66. Suetonius.

## IX    FIRST THROUGH THE DOOR IS EMPEROR

67. Philo, *On the Embassy to Gaius.*

68. Dio.

69. Tacitus, *Annals.*

70. Philo, *On the Embassy to Gaius.*

71. Tacitus, *Annals.*

72. Philo, *On the Embassy to Gaius.*

73. Dio includes Tiberius's words verbatim in a speech Caligula gave to the Senate in AD 39.

## X    HAIL, CAESAR CALIGULA!

74. Suetonius.

75. Harrison.

76. Ibid.

77. Suetonius.

78. Dio.

79. Josephus.

80. Suetonius.

81. Ibid.

82. Josephus.

83. Seneca, *Epistles.*

84. Pliny the Elder.

85. Obulus's name was the subject of various spellings by ancient authors. The spelling here was provided by Philo, who met and had dealings with the man.

86. Philo, *On the Embassy to Gaius.*

87. Ibid.

88. Josephus.

89. Ibid.

90. Suetonius; and Kerr, "The Role & Character of the Praetorian Guard."

91. The other authors allowed by Caligula to be republished were Titus Labienus and Cassius Severus.

92. Philo, *On the Embassy to Gaius.*

93. Ibid.

94. Leonardo da Vinci got it wrong in his *Last Supper* painting in the original Greek'; the Christian gospels several times speak of Christ reclining at the dinner table, and of Christ and his apostles, being free men living in a Roman province, reclining, not sitting, at the Last Supper. The Gospel of John, also speaks of the apostle "whom Jesus loved," reclining "on Jesus' bosom." This refers to the person lying in the honored position to the host's right on the central couch during reclined dining.

95. Philo, *On the Embassy to Gaius.*

96. Suetonius.

97. Ibid.

98. Ibid.

99. Martin, *Concise Medical Dictionary.*

100. Philo, *On the Embassy to Gaius.*

101. Dio.

102. Ibid.

103. Suetonius.

## XI    ENTER THE MONSTER

104. Philo: *On the Embassy to Gaius.*

105. Suetonius.

106. Dio.

107. Suetonius.

108. Philo: *On the Embassy to Gaius.*

109. Suetonius gives her name as Livia Orestilla, which most historians accept. Dio gives Cornelia Orestina.

110. Seneca, *On Firmness.*

111. Philo, *On the Embassy to Gaius.*

112. Some writers claim that Clemens's father and son had the exact same name. There is no firm evidence of this. It is likely that Vespasian cultivated the patronage, friendship, and protection of Clemens senior during the reign of Caligula, while Clemens was Praetorian prefect. Not only would Vespasian later make Clemens's son his Praetorian prefect, he would marry his eldest son Titus to a daughter of Clemens.

113. Suetonius; and Josephus.

114. Frontinus, *The Aqueducts of Rome.*

115. Josephus

116. Pliny the Elder.

117. Suetonius.

118. Suetonius; and Barrett, *Caligula.*

## XII　THE DEATH OF DRUSILLA

119. Woods, "Caligula's Seashells."

120. Seneca, *Epistles.*

121. Suetonius.

122. Ibid.

123. Pliny the Elder.

124. Harrison.

## XIII　NEVER MIND THE EXPENSE

125. Suetonius.

126. Dio.

127. Winterling.

128. Suetonius.

## XIV　CALIGULA'S NEW BRIDE

129. Suetonius.

130. Ibid.

## XV　CALIGULA'S INVASION

131. Barrett, confusingly, places this Mevania visit on Caligula's later transit to Gaul for the German campaign. Mevania is not on the direct route from Rome to Gaul, which followed Italy's west coast, but on the Via Flaminia, the highway to Rimini on Italy's east coast. Moreover, Suetonius tells us that Caligula only came by the idea for the German campaign at Mevania, and it would subsequently take many months for campaign preparations, which Barrett himself describes as massive.

Plus, Caligula almost certainly traveled to Gaul by sea; ancient sources tell much of what took place during his passage through Gallic cities but make no mention of visits to cities in Italy or the Alps en route to Gaul proper.

132. Lee Fratantuono, *Caligula: An Unexpected General.*

133. Tacitus, *Agricola.*

134. Ferrill.

135. J.P.V.D. Balsdon, *The Emperor Gaius (Caligula).*

136. Suetonius.

137. Barrett.

138. Suetonius.

139. www.museonaviromane.it.

## XVI   CALIGULA WALKS ON WATER

140. Winterling places the bridge episode in AD 40, after Caligula's return from Gaul, considering it a pseudo Triumph for Caligula. However, Suetonius gives as one reason for the bridge's creation a desire by Caligula to daunt the Germans and Britons *before* he went north, while Dio places the event firmly in AD 39. Most modern historians, and related events, support the AD 39 dating.

141. Dio.

142. Ibid.

143. Suetonius.

144. Ibid.

145. Dio.

146. Ibid.

147. Suetonius; and Dio.

148. Dio.

149. Ibid.

150. Dio; and Suetonius.

151. Josephus.

152. Eusebius, *Ecclesiastical History.*

153. Virgil, *Ecologues.*

## XVII    THE POWER OF WORDS

154. Suetonius.

155. Suetonius.

156. Ibid.

157. Seneca, *On Tranquility of the Mind.*

158. This female associate was possibly Seneca's aunt, his mother's stepsister, whose name is uncertain. Famously shy, she had nonetheless publicly supported Seneca's run for quaestor and may have also gone to Caligula on his behalf. Seneca had lived in Egypt with his aunt and uncle for twelve years, enjoying the warm, dry climate after being diagnosed with tuberculosis and possibly also asthma. So, Seneca's aunt had an intimate knowledge of the state of her nephew's health.

159. Suetonius.

160. Dio.

161. Ibid.

## XVIII    PREPARING FOR WAR

162. Dio.

163. Barrett.

164. Suetonius.

165. Dio.

166. Suetonius.

167. Ibid.

168. Dio.

## XIX    SHOCKS IN GAUL

169. Josephus.

170. Tacitus, *Annals.*

171. Dio.

172. Suetonius.

173. According to the tenth century's Agapius of Hierapolis, Pilate's enforced death at Vienne came during the first year of Caligula's reign, not during the emperor's progress through Gaul. His source for this assertion is unknown.

174. Suetonius.

175. Barrett.

176. Dio.

177. Suetonius.

178. Ibid.

179. Suetonius; and Dio.

180. Dio.

181. Seneca, *Consolation to Helvia.*

182. Suetonius.

183. Philo, *Flaccus.*

184. Ibid.

185. Seneca, *On Firmness.*

186. Suetonius.

187. Barrett.

188. Petronius, *The Satyricon.*

189. Suetonius.

## XX  CALIGULA GOES TO WAR

190. Suetonius.

191. Ibid.

192. Philo, *On the Embassy to Gaius.*

193. Tacitus, *Agricola.*

194. Tacitus, *Germania.*

195. Starr, *The Roman Imperial Navy.*

196. Tacitus, *Annals.*

197. Dio.

198. Suetonius.

199. Starr.

200. Dio.

201. Barrett.

202. Suetonius.

203. Ibid.

204. Ibid.

205. Ibid.

206. Seneca, *On Anger.*

207. Suetonius.

## XXI    CALIGULA'S TRIUMPH

208. Philo, *On the Embassy to Gaius;* and Hunt & Edgar, *Selected Papyri II.*

209. Seneca, *Letters.*

210. Philo, *On the Embassy to Gaius.*

211. Ibid.

212. Josephus.

213. Suetonius.

214. www.museonaviromane.it

215. Suetonius.

216. Dio.

## XXII    THE VICTIMS MOUNT

217. Philo, *On the Embassy to Gaius.*

218. Suetonius.

219. Josephus.

220. Seneca, *On Firmness.*

221. Dio.

222. Pliny the Elder.

223. Dio wrote that the oracle "came to him," i.e., to Caligula. But oracles didn't leave their sanctuaries. Even Nero, when emperor, had to go to Delphi in Greece to receive a prediction from the oracle of Delphi. The oracle of Fortuna's statues at Antium were wheeled out to receive the supplicant's questions, so in that sense the oracle did come to Caligula.

224. Suetonius reports the predictions of soothsayer Sulla and the oracle of Fortuna.

225. Some scholars have suggested that Petronius arrived at Ptolemais as early as May, but Josephus placed his arrival toward the end of the year, and events support that dating. Besides, Philo makes clear that Petronius put his troops into *winter* camp at Ptolemais, not summer camp, which

would have been the case with a spring arrival. Winter camps were established by Rome's legions only from October 19 onward.

226. Philo, *On the Embassy to Gaius.*

## XXIII   RUNNING OUT OF FRIENDS

227. Philo: *On the Embassy to Gaius.*

228. Ibid.

229. Philo quotes this letter in its entirety in *On the Embassy to Gaius*, making it likely he saw a copy, or knew someone who had, such as his brother Alexander.

230. Ibid.

231. Josephus.

232. Suetonius.

233. Seneca, *Consolation to Helvia.*

234. Josephus.

235. Josephus wrote that Agrippa's dinner party took place before Petronius's letters arrived, meaning that Agrippa twice asked Caligula to stop erection of the statue at Jerusalem—at the banquet and then in the letter following his collapse—and that Caligula acceded to his requests *twice*, which is highly unlikely. Philo says that Agrippa went to see Caligula immediately upon his return to Rome, that Caligula had already received Petronius's letters and that their contents subsequently triggered Agrippa's collapse, and that the banquet followed his recovery. This all makes much more sense.

236. Philo, *On the Embassy to Gaius.*

237. Suetonius.

238. Ibid.

239. Dio.

240. Josephus.

241. Suetonius.

242. Josephus.

243. Dio.

244. Ibid.

## XXIV   THE ASSASSINATION PLOT

245. Barrett; and Kavanagh, "The Conspirator Aemilius Regulus and Seneca's Aunt's Family."

246. Josephus.

247. Ibid.

248. Suetonius.

249. Ibid.

250. Ibid.

## XXV   KILLING CALIGULA

251. Some historians question Suetonius's date of January 24. But if Josephus is correct and Caligula was planning to depart Rome on January 25, then January 24 was the last possible date for his assassination.

252. Josephus.

253. Ibid.

254. Ibid.

255. Ibid.

256. Ibid.

257. Suetonius; and Josephus.

258. Suetonius.

259. Josephus.

260. Suetonius.

261. Josephus.

262. Philo, *On the Embassy to Gaius*; Dio; Josephus.

263. Later accounts would offer variations on Gratus's name. One claimed he was a centurion from Epirus; another said that his name was Epirius Gratus; neither survives scrutiny.

264. Suetonius.

265. Josephus.

266. Ibid.

267. Ibid.

268. Gibbon.

269. Josephus.

270. Ibid.

271. Josephus is emphatic that this occurred in the evening. Barrett felt that Chaerea would have acted much earlier; but chaos, uncertainty, and indecision had prevailed through the afternoon, only to give way to pragmatism once the dust had settled and the tide was clearly turning against the conspirators, spurring Chaerea to eliminate mother and child while he still had the chance.

272. Josephus.

273. Ibid.

274. Ibid.

275. Ibid.

276. Ibid.

277. Ibid.

## XXVI  THE REVENGE OF CALIGULA'S UNCLE

278. Josephus.

279. Hunt and Edgar.

280. Dio.

281. Ibid.

282. Holder, *The Roman Army in Britain.*

## XXVII  DÉJÀ VU WITH NERO

283. Tacitus, *Annals.*

## XXVIII  WAS CALIGULA TRULY MAD?

284. Dio.

285. Winterling; and Seneca, *Consolation to Helvia.*

286. Barrett.

287. Winterling.

288. Barrett; and Ferrill.

289. Suetonius.

290. www.health.harvard.edu/mental-health/bipolar-disorder.

291. Ibid.

292. Dio.

293. Seneca, *On the Shortness of Life.*

## XXIX    DRAWING PRESENT-DAY LESSONS:
## IS DONALD TRUMP THE MODERN CALIGULA?

294. Mark Brown, *The Guardian*, June 1, 2016.

295. August 18, 2017.

296. November 24, 2016.

297. January 15, 2018.

298. January 13, 2018.

299. January 11, 2018.

300. Bob Woodward, *Fear: Trump in the White House.*

301. *Chicago Tribune*, October 24, 2018.

302. Omarosa Manigault Newman, PBS *Newshour*, August 13, 2018.

303. Amy Sullivan, *Politico Magazine*, January 27, 2018.

304. Pompeo was speaking in Cairo, Egypt. PBS *Newshour* January 10, 2019.

305. Anonymous Op Ed, *New York Times*, September 5, 2018.

306. Huxley, 1946 Foreword to *Brave New World.*

307. Sarah Kendzior, *Globe and Mail*, January 7, 2018.

308. James Fallows, *The Atlantic*, October 4, 2016.

309. *Wall Street Journal*, January 6, 2018; *Time*, January 8, 2018; *Economist*, July 23, 2015; Gideon Rachman, *Financial Times*, January 22, 2018.

310. Barrett.

311. James Fallows, *The Atlantic*, January 7, 2018.

312. Richard Branson, "Meeting Donald Trump," *Virgin Unite*, October 21, 2016.

313. Woodward. Kelly denies saying it, but Woodward has stuck by his assertion.

314. Omarosa Manigault Newman, PBS *Newshour*, August 13, 2018.

315. Sarah Kendzior, *Globe and Mail*, January 7, 2018.

316. PBS *Newshour*, August 24, 2018.

# BIBLIOGRAPHY

## BOOKS

Balsdon, J. P. V. D. *The Emperor Gaius (Caligula)*. Oxford: Oxford University Press, 1934.

Barrett. A. A. *Caligula: The Corruption of Power*. New York: Simon & Schuster, 1989.

Blair, G. *The Trumps: Three Generations That Built an Empire*. New York: Simon & Schuster, 2000.

Braud, D. *From Augustus to Nero: A Sourcebook on Roman History 31 BC–AD 68*. London: Routledge, 1985.

Caesar, J., T. Rice Holmes (transl.), *The Gallic War & the Civil War*. London: Loeb, 1955.

Carcopino, J. *Daily Life in Ancient Rome*. Harmondsworth: Penguin, 1954.

Dando-Collins, S. *Blood of the Caesars: How the Murder of Germanicus Led to the Fall of Rome*. Hoboken, NJ: Wiley, 2008.

————. *Caesars Legion: The Epic Saga of Julius Caesar's Elite Tenth Legion and the Armies of Rome*. New York: Wiley, 2002.

————. *Cleopatra's Kidnappers: How Caesar's Sixth Legion Gave Egypt to Rome and Rome to Caesar*. Hoboken, NJ: Wiley, 2006.

————. *The Great Fire of Rome: The Fall of the Emperor Nero and his City*. Cambridge, MA: Da Capo, 2010.

————. *The Ides: Caesar's Murder and the War for Rome*. Hoboken, NJ: Wiley, 2010.

————. *Legions of Rome: The Definitive History of Every Imperial Roman Legion*. London: Quercus, 2010.

————. *Mark Antony's Heroes: How the Third Gallica Legion Saved an Apostle and Created an Emperor*. Hoboken: Wiley, 2007.

————. *Nero's Killing Machine: The True Story of Rome's Remarkable Fourteenth Legion*. New York: Wiley, 2005.

Dio, C. *Dio's Roman History, Book LVI*. Cambridge, MA: Harvard University Press, 1924.

Eusebius Pamphilius. *Church History*. Cambridge, UK: Hayes, 1683.

Fratantuono, L. *Caligula: An Unexpected General*. South Yorkshire: Pen & Sword, 2018.

Frontinus. *The Stratagems* and *The Aqueducts of Rome*. Cambridge, MA: Harvard University Press, 1925.

Gibbon, E. *Decline and Fall of the Roman Empire, Book I*. Chicago: Encyclopedia Britannica, 1952.

Grant, M. *Gladiators*. London: Penguin, 1967.

————. *Roman History from Coins*. New York, Barnes & Noble, 1995.

Graves, R. *I, Claudius*. London: Marshall Cavendish, 1988.

Harrison, J. R. *Paul & the Imperial Authorities at Thessalonica & Rome: A Study in the Conflict of Ideology*. Tubingen: Mohr Siebeck, 2011.

Holder, P. A. *The Roman Army in Britain*. London: Batsford, 1982.

Hunt, A. S., and G.C. Edgar (editors). *Selected Papyri II*, London: Loeb Classical Library, 1934.

Huxley, A. *Brave New World*. St. Albans, UK: Panther, 1977.

Josephus. *The Complete Works of Josephus* (W. Whiston transl.). Grand Rapids, MI: Kregel, 1999.

Macinnis, P. *Poisons: From Hemlock to Botox and the Killer Bean of Calabar*. New York: Little Brown, 2005.

Martin, E. A. (editor). *Concise Medical Dictionary*. Oxford: Oxford University Press, 1994.

Mattingly, H. *Roman Coins from the Earliest Times to the Fall of the Western Empire*. London: Methuen, 1927.

Mellan, I., and E. Mellan. *Dictionary of Poisons*. London: Owen, 1958.

Mermet, T. *Histoire de la Ville de Vienne Durant L'Epoque Gauloise*. Bangkok: Nabu, 2012.

Paterculus, V. *Compendium of Roman History* (F. W. Shipley transl.). Cambridge, MA: Loeb, 1924.

Pelletier, A. *Histoire de Lyon: de la Capital des Gaules a la Metropole Europeenne*. Lyon: Editions Lyonaises, 2004.

Petronius Arbiter. *The Satyricon* (W.C. Firebaugh transl.). New York: Boni & Liveright, 1922.

Philo Judaeus. *The Works of Philo* (C.D. Yonge transl.). Peabody, MA: Hendrickson, 1993.

Pliny the Elder. *Natural History* (H. Rackman transl.). London: Loeb, 1913.

Pliny the Younger. *Letters* (W. Melmoth transl.). London: Loeb, 1915.

Plutarch, *The Lives of the Noble Grecians and Romans (the Dryden Translation).* Chicago: Encyclopedia Britannica, 1952.

Seager, R. *Tiberius.* London: Eyre Methuen, 1972.

Seneca, L. A. *Dialogues and Letters* (C.D.N. Costa transl.). London: Penguin, 1967.

———. *Letters from a Stoic* (R. Campbell transl.). London: Penguin, 1969.

———. *Minor Dialogues* (A. Stuart transl.). London: Bohn's Classical Library, 1900.

Smallwood, E. M. *Documents Illustrating the Principates of Gaius, Claudius and Nero.* London: Cambridge University Press, 1967.

Starr, C. G. *The Roman Imperial Navy 31 BC–AD 324.* Cambridge, UK: Heffer & Son, 1960.

Stevenson, S. W., C. R. Smith, & F. W. Madden (eds.). *Dictionary of Roman Coins, Republican and Imperial.* London: Bell, 1889.

Suetonius, G. S. *The Twelve Caesars* (R. Graves transl.). London: Penguin, 1989.

Syme, R. *The Augustan Autocracy.* Oxford: Clarendon Press, 1986.

Tacitus, P. C. *The Agricola* and *The Germania* (H. Mattingly transl.). London: Penguin, 1948.

———. *The Histories* and *The Annals* (A.J. Church and W.J. Brodribb transl.). Chicago: Encyclopedia Britannica, 1952.

Thompson, C. J. S. *Poisons and Poisoners: With Historical Accounts of Some Famous Mysteries in Ancient and Modern Times.* New York: Barnes & Noble, 1993.

Trump, D. J., and T. Schwartz. *Trump, The Art of the Deal.* London: Century, 1988.

Virgil. *The Poems of Virgil* (J. Rhaodes transl.). Chicago: Encyclopedia Britannica, 1952.

Wallace, L. *Ben-Hur, a Tale of the Christ.* London: Ward Lock, 1902.

Webster, G. *The Imperial Roman Army of the First and Second Centuries.* London: Black, 1979.

Webster, G., and D. R. Dudley. *The Conquest of Britain.* London: Pan, 1962.

Winterling, A. *Caligula: A Biography.* Berkeley: University of California Press, 2011.

Woodward, B. *Fear: Trump in the White House.* New York: Simon & Schuster, 2018.

## SCHOLARLY ARTICLES AND PAPERS

Kavanagh, B. J. "The Conspirator Aemilius Regulus and Seneca's Aunt's Family." *Historia,* Bd 50, H.3, 2001.

Kerr, J. L. "The Role & Character of the Praetorian Guard & the Praetorian Prefecture Until the Accession of Vespasian." PhD thesis, University of Glasgow, 1991. www.theses.gla.ac.uk/875/.

Woods, D. "Caligula's Seashells," *Greece & Rome*, Vol. 47, No. 1. April 2000.

## NEWSPAPERS AND MAGAZINES

*Atlantic*, Washington DC, 2018

*Chicago Tribune*, 2018

*Economist*, London, 2015

*Forbes*, Jersey City, 2018

*Globe and Mail*, Toronto, 2018

*Guardian*, London, 2016, 2018

*Irish Times*, Dublin, 2016

*New Statesman*, London, 2018

*New York Times*, 2017–2018

*Politico Magazine*, Arlington, 2018

*Spectator*, London, 2018

*Time*, New York, 2018

*Wall Street Journal*, New York, 2018

## OTHER

Harvard Health Publishing, Harvard Medical School: www.health.harvard.edu/mental-health/bipolar-disorder, 2019

Museo delle Navi Romane, Nemi, Italy. www.museonaviromane.it, 2019

PBS Newshour, 2018–2019

*Virgin Unite*, www.virgin.com/company/virgin-unite, 2016

# INDEX

CPSIA information can be obtained
at www.ICGtesting.com
Printed in the USA
LVHW091524130819
627496LV00009B/184/P